Gender and Text
in Modern Hebrew
and Yiddish
Literature

Gender and Text in Modern Hebrew and Yiddish Literature

edited by
Naomi B. Sokoloff,
Anne Lapidus Lerner,
and Anita Norich

THE JEWISH THEOLOGICAL SEMINARY
OF AMERICA
NEW YORK AND JERUSALEM

DISTRIBUTED BY HARVARD UNIVERSITY PRESS
CAMBRIDGE, MASSACHUSETTS AND LONDON

Library of Congress Cataloging-in-Publication Data

Gender and text in modern Hebrew and Yiddish literature / edited by
   Naomi B. Sokoloff, Anne Lapidus Lerner, Anita Norich.
         p.   cm.
      Includes bibliograohical references and index.
      ISBN 0-674-34198-8
      l. Hebrew literature, Modern--history and criticism--Congresses.
   2. Women in literature--Congresses. 3. Women and literature-
   Congresses. 4. Feminist literary criticism--Congresses.
   5. Yiddish literature--History and criticism--Congresses.
   I. Sokoloff, Naomi B. II. Lerner, Anne Lapidus. III. Norich,
   Anita, 1952-
   PJ5013.W66G46   1993
   892.4'609352042--dc20   92-33134
                                                               CIP

❧ CONTENTS ❧

ᮠ PREFACE ᮠ

This volume arises out of a confluence of interests in feminist criticism and in Hebrew and Yiddish literature. While world literature has, for some time, benefited from the insights of feminist thinking, the impact of gender studies on the fields of modern Yiddish and Hebrew literature was not perceptible until the mid-1980s. *Gender and Text* brings together a range of important work in this area and points to work yet to be done. The diversity of approaches, perspectives, and themes encompassed in this collection is augmented by the annotated bibliographies of other work to provide the reader, academic or casual, *entrée* into the field. It is our hope that this volume will provide impetus for widening the critical debate and enhancing the study of both modern Hebrew and Yiddish writing.

Clearly, the volume has multiple foci, as it addresses several audiences. The essays collected here attempt to speak at once to those interested in Jewish literature, feminism, or comparative studies.

No doubt, many of our readers will be concerned with the exploration of Yiddish and/or Hebrew texts. Feminist thinking has a great deal to contribute here. In many ways Jewish culture is strongly patriarchal, emerging as it has out of a literary culture that had been male-dominated for thousands of years. In addition, Jewish life as it developed in Europe was marked by an internal bilingualism, with its languages presenting contrasting and gendered faces to the world. Hebrew, *leshon hakodesh*— the holy tongue—was the traditional language of Jewish learning and prayer and was for centuries largely inaccessible to women. Yiddish, known as the *mameloshn*—the mother tongue—was the language of daily life for both men and women, and a cultural vehicle as well. In this century, Jewish bilingual culture produced two different literatures that raised distinctive questions about gender and writing.

Part of the reason feminist criticism holds so much promise and potential for exploring these literatures is the fact that it has developed varied modes for dealing with literary texts. It is far from a monolithic movement or a narrowly ideological set of prescriptions for reading. Among the major accomplishments of feminist criticism is its success in expanding the domain of thematic inquiry. While documenting stereotypes, omissions, and misperceptions of women in a wide variety of texts, it also has called attention to depictions of women and women's roles previously neglected by critical studies. Insights from fields outside of literature have enriched a range of such thematic studies. Feminist revisions of psychoanalytic theory, in particular, have proved indispensable for rereadings of many texts and for understanding ways in which culture constructs gender. Important contributions have come also from feminist revisions of history, religion, and sociolinguistics. Other feminist critical approaches have focused on women writers; on styles and genres prevalent in writing by women; on the psychodynamics of female creativity; on female literary traditions; and on issues of canonicity and authoritative readings.

All of these matters are applicable to the reading of Hebrew and Yiddish literature and so may help to illuminate a variety of texts. At the same time, this anthology is designed to introduce the fields and problematics of modern Yiddish and Hebrew literature to those interested in feminist theory and criticism. The place of this Jewish writing in the context of Western literature is often neglected. Jewish literature is sometimes considered religious or provincial, too far from the mainstreams of European literary creativity to warrant inclusion. Jewish literature itself, however, may profitably be regarded as a fertile field of comparative study. It is a substantial and rich area in its own terms and a useful complement to the study of other literatures. Because of the closeness of Yiddish and Hebrew, and because of the considerable differences between them as well, these literatures provide a significant basis for cross-cultural comparison. We hope that the essays in this volume will facilitate the testing of a variety of theories about gender and writing.

We hope, too, that this book will provoke the interest of the general reader. Our aim has been to provide the translations and clarity of language which will ease our communication with an audience reaching far

beyond professional literary scholars. Anyone interested in Jewish literature or feminism will find productive material in these essays.
Transcription of Yiddish follows standard YIVO orthography except in a
few cases where it reflects the original sources from which a particular
poem was taken.

Gender and Text opens with an introduction by Anita Norich that maps
out the structure of the volume and places it in the context of ongoing
feminist critical debate. As it engages the distinctive gender issues posed
by Hebrew and Yiddish literature, this first essay considers the kinds of
approaches that appear at the intersection of feminist thinking and
Jewish literary studies and poses challenges for future work in this area.
In doing so, it provides both a contextual and a theoretical framework
within which to read the essays that follow.

* * *

All but three of the essays included in this book emerged from a conference entitled "Gender and Text: Feminist Criticism and Modern
Jewish Literature," which was held at The Jewish Theological Seminary
of America on 10-12 June 1990. We are grateful to The Jewish Theological
Seminary and its chancellor, Ismar Schorsch, as well as to its Board of
Directors, for the Seminary's major role in funding the conference, and to
the Jewish Studies Program and the Department of Near Eastern
Languages and Civilization at the University of Washington for addi-
tional financial support. We would like to acknowledge here the work of
the Conference committee: Anne Lapidus Lerner and Naomi Sokoloff,
co-directors; Anne Golomb Hoffman, David Roskies, John Ruskay, Renee
Guttman, and Janet Ozur. Many others contributed to the success of the
conference through their participation as presenters or moderators: Yael
Feldman, Nurith Geertz, Nili Gold, Zilla Goodman, Paula Hyman,
Francine Klagsbrun and the Friends of the Library at the Seminary, Alan
Mintz, Elisa New, Avram Novershtern, and Norma Fain Pratt. Sonia
Grober provided much appreciated assistance in making arrangements
from Israel. Eitan Even, producer of *Aviah's Summer*, graciously helped
arrange for us to screen this film at the conference. Each of us who partic-
ipated in the conference was informed by the questions and comments of
the large and diverse group in attendance, as well as by those who
presented papers.

We are grateful to The Lucius N. Littauer Foundation for a generous
publication grant. We thank our publications consultant, Jean Highland,
who has skillfully shepherded this manuscript to book form, and our

copy editor, Sarah Brzowski. The jacket design, taken from the conference logo, is a paper-cut by Deborah Ugoretz.

We would also like to express formally and publicly what the three co-editors have been joyfully saying to one another privately: how exciting it has been for us to work together and how delighted we are at our realization of a successful model of cooperation. We have communicated in person, on the phone, via *bitnet,* and by mail. We rejoice in the smooth workings of this complicated relationship and in the friendships it has supported.

Each of us, too, has gained from the inspiration and support of other individuals. Our list of acknowledgments would be egregiously incomplete without mention of these names: Doug Berry, Rachel Berry, Michelle Berry, Stephen C. Lerner, David Gavriel Lerner, Rahel Adina Lapidus Lerner, and Lillian Lapidus.

N.B.S.
A.L.L.
A.N.
July 1991

Jewish Literatures and Feminist Criticism: An Introduction To Gender and Text

This volume offers a range of views exploring some of the ways in which the reading of texts written in Jewish languages may be enriched by the trends in feminist literary criticism and theory that have arisen in the latter decades of this century. At the same time, the editors wish to suggest that including the often unexamined body of Hebrew and Yiddish literatures into the broader feminist discourse may not only enlarge the corpus of works it encompasses, but also offer provocative challenges to the ongoing conversation on gender and text.[1]

The methodological approaches articulated here represent a range of feminist scholarship. They reflect the dynamics of Jewish literary and political history which, we have come to understand, tends to follow general movements belatedly but in a more compressed and accelerated fashion. The infiltration of Enlightenment ideas and texts is a familiar example of this process: the impact of the Enlightenment was felt later in Eastern Europe than in Western Europe, and later still among Jews. Similarly, such diverse cultural or political developments as the use of the vernacular, the rise of the novel, or the emergence of nationalist ideology took several generations in the Christian West before they erupted among Hebrew and Yiddish writers.[2] Jewish feminist criticism is following a similar pattern determined by the synchronic influences, political moment, and training critics share with their contemporaries in the wider academic and cultural world, but also by a sense of the particularities of the Jewish dynamic.

This is an especially auspicious time in feminist literary analysis for
the confluence of interests represented in this volume. Critics have peri-
odically sought to reassess developments in the field since the publication of Kate Millett's *Sexual Politics* in 1970. Toril Moi's apt rewriting of
that resonant title, rendering it as *Sexual/Textual Politics* (1985), underscored the significance and varieties of feminist theory and practice as
they had evolved through the parallel development of Anglo-American
and French criticism. Indeed, the differences between Anglophile and
Francophile critics have formed the contours of feminist thought until
recent years. What can be succinctly if schematically cast as a debate
between Elaine Showalter's gynocritics and Alice Jardine's gynesis[3]
reflects a wider tension between Anglo-American and French criticism.
Gynocriticism asks what is specific to the condition of women (as authors
or characters) in literature; gynesis focuses on questions of repression,
exploring the symbolic space the feminine inhabits in culture, even when
that space is understood as a gap or lacuna, as something not consciously
represented.

In the feminist battle of the books, which has been more productive
than divisive, the Anglo-American approach seems to be most commonly represented by Sandra Gilbert and Susan Gubar's influential
study, *The Madwoman in the Attic* (1979), the French approach by Julia
Kristeva's "*La Femme, ce n'est jamais ça*" (1974) or Luce Irigaray's *Ce Sexe
qui n'en est pas un* (1977). Anglophile critics engage, for the most part, in a
quest to uncover women's texts, to explore the conditions of their production and what they reveal about women in specific social terms; they
comment both on what the text reveals about a particular moment and
how it is determined by that moment. Francophile critics focus instead
on questions of representation and the textual implications of gender;
they are concerned, for the most part, not with women as either social
subjects or as authors but rather with that which is symbolically
constructed as feminine in culture and thereby excluded or relegated to
the status of the other, the unconscious, the unarticulated.[4] While both
approaches are informed by psychoanalytic and Marxist readings, the
French generally have been considered to be more influenced by the
former and the English by the latter.[5]

Moving beyond this dichotomy, feminist critics have increasingly
engaged in questions about specific identities and how differences in
race, ethnicity, class, or sexuality may determine the construction of
gender. In at least that regard, Jewish feminist criticism suggests a check
on essentialist models of the female self and of the conditions that

determine female literary production. As this criticism enters into broader feminist discussions, it seems, at the present moment, to be practicing the kind of critical eclecticism that Annette Kolodny advocated more than a decade ago (1980). A primary concern with the ways in which Jewish women are represented or present themselves may be discerned in many of the essays in this collection. If, as the editors believe, these essays are representative of the field, then it seems clear that Jewish feminist criticism is echoing the kind of feminist critique that was familiar in the 1970s: one that examined "images of women" presented by male and female authors. We also encounter in this volume an insistence on equal rights—to the canon, the curriculum, the Jewish symbolic universe. At the same time, we may perceive both a focus on woman as other, and an alternative position that celebrates the otherness, makes of it not an absence, but a presence to be discerned. Whether reading texts by women in order to uncover their voices or texts by men in order to uncover—in some cases, deconstruct—images of women, the essays in this volume are concerned with the ways in which the feminine as a social construct is rendered into the female as an articulating presence.

Jewish feminist criticism may also offer a more synthetic idiom for the broader study of Jewish literatures. No critic of Hebrew and Yiddish can avoid confronting the history of modern Jewish culture. Although responsive—as many of the essays in this volume are—to current challenges to the realist and humanist traditions, critics of Jewish literature nonetheless invariably seem firmly to ground their studies historically and socially. Running like a refrain through these pages is a recognition of the familiar tensions between the public or collective focus in Jewish life and letters and the private or individual voice as it seeks to express itself.

Twentieth-century Jewish history has, paradoxically, brought us back to the tensions between the individual and society that writers of the previous century might have thought they had resolved. Eastern European mass emigration, the Zionist revolution, devastating wars and radical political and social movements sent Hebrew and Yiddish literatures along different trajectories despite the parallel paths they had followed until at least the turn of the century. Not only had many authors written in both languages, but the argument has been made that Jewish literature must be regarded as entirely bilingual and cannot be meaningfully separated into its two component languages.[6] Affected by Enlightenment ideas, Hebrew and Yiddish writers could claim a legitimate place for the individual Jew, no longer responsive solely to religious ideals or messianic hopes. For almost all of the writers discussed in this volume, that claim would be severely challenged if not rendered insignificant by more recent Jewish history. Most obviously after World War II, Hebrew and Yiddish literature respond in similar ways, although motivated by different cultural realities. Each literature confronts Jewish history, but in each the primary points of reference are quite distinct. In reading any Yiddish writer, we discover how difficult it is to claim a place for the individual in a post-Holocaust universe. And Israeli writers reflect the ongoing dialectic between the individual's claim for precedence and the collective mandate in a newly emerging state.

There are other significant distinctions between the two languages and literatures as developed in this volume. Primary among these is the implicit understanding of Yiddish as the mother tongue—as matrilineal, matronymic—and of Hebrew as the father tongue—patrilineal, patronymic, a language in which the influence of tradition is paramount. The relative status of Hebrew and Yiddish as literary languages changed so radically as to be nearly reversed in the twentieth century—as have the anxieties female writers have experienced as they inscribe themselves into a culture that can hardly be said to have embraced them. Although Yiddish continually reminds us that language is not only patriarchal, it should not be construed as the "women's language" some French critics seek. Contained, controlled, set apart in Jewish culture within its domestic, feminine images, Yiddish was nonetheless the common language accessible to the masses of Eastern European Jews. Once the vernacular, the language of the home and the street, Yiddish now has become domesticated in a different way as the sign of both mourning and memory. As its speaking population diminishes, it assumes the kind of scholarly, textual, perhaps even sacred role once reserved for Hebrew. That father tongue becomes, at the same time, the language of the new state and its streets.

In the critical consideration of both literatures, there is an ongoing, if problematic, search for what may be considered authentic texts: those that present a truthful, recognizable reproduction of some world that we can understand as having once existed. Adhering primarily to the Anglo-American school, critics continue to seek those texts that reflect writers'—in this case, female writers'—experiences within some social framework. Following traditional Enlightenment endeavors, we may expect arguments in this volume pointing to the need for the individual to adopt a unified, integrated self-identity that can be expressed within that context. But, informed by such critics as Michel Foucault and Hélène

Cixous, the notion of the unified, integrated self is under considerable attack in contemporary theory and that, too, is reflected here. Even further, following Jacques Derrida and Julia Kristeva, an understanding of the limitations of male-female dichotomies may be discerned in the following pages. The movement away from binary concepts, whether viewed as social or "natural" biological constructs, once again challenges the humanistic notion of identity with which most readers are familiar.

The search for authenticity and for the society within the text in Hebrew and Yiddish criticism is complicated by the largely unexplored but nonetheless persistent tendency to read women's texts as confessional or unself-consciously autobiographical, as somehow unmediated. To read such texts in order to ferret out something that will reveal to us the writer and her world is to adopt a realist bias whose implications should be made explicit. Perpetuating a tension between male and female creativity, the confessional mode of reading suggests that women's writing is naturally closer to personal experience than is men's, that it reveals the unconscious in ways men's texts may not. In effect, then, the female writer becomes less the writing subject than the object being written. Reading the writer and not the text means seeing the text as a reflection: it is either a version of Irigaray's speculum[7] mirroring woman, or of a strict verisimilitude mirroring a real world that, invariably in Jewish and Western thought, is masculine. As the French have taught us to recognize, such a perspective also leads us to privilege "voice" over "writing."

In Hebrew literature, the tendency to see texts as revealing the author within a realistic social structure emerges with the demands of creating a new culture and the urge to give it expression. Israeli culture constructs itself in opposition to the Diaspora experience but nonetheless quite literally emerges from it. There is an attenuation within modern Hebrew letters of the dialectic between the collective and the individual, generally in favor of the former. Similarly, there is a tension between poetics and accessible thematics in a literature whose social function in an embattled society is considered inescapable. But this tendency to favor the collective and to examine the function of literary texts is equally pronounced in Yiddish despite its lack of a homeland. In that regard, designating Yiddish as the mother tongue takes on yet another symbolic meaning. It puts any Yiddish text in the position of the female, reflecting something other than itself. Viewed as a reflection of a dispersed and destroyed culture, Yiddish texts come to be regarded as completely sepa-

rate and framed entities no longer developing or inviting analysis, but
rather simply objects at which we gaze in awe or discomfort.

Another troubling question for scholars of Hebrew and Yiddish literature is the ongoing debate about the canon raised by contemporary criticism. Canonicity appears as a quintessentially Jewish concept, dependent
as it is on the existence of authoritative texts and a hermeneutical tradition. But the parameters of the canon—clearly defined in the Jewish religious context—are not at all clear in either the modern Hebrew or
Yiddish contexts. As much of the academy has been growing weary of
the unresolved canon debates, scholars of Jewish literature—once again
following the belated dynamics of Jewish cultural time—are still concerned with establishing a literary canon distinct from though informed
by the canon that religious authority and exegetical procedures have
sanctioned. This synchronic dissonance may actually constitute a unique
cultural moment during which feminist and Jewish critical concerns
intersect: instead of asking *how* we can expand the canon, we may now
be inspired to examine *why* we are seeking such an expansion and
whether it is useful to continue the quest. What, for example, does it
mean to argue for a more inclusive canon that allows Hebrew and
Yiddish into the discussion of Western literatures while simultaneously
struggling to allow women into the consideration of Hebrew and
Yiddish? Particularly in the case of Yiddish, this is a highly problematic
quest, since it is not at all clear that we agree in the first place on what the
canon has been. And, at the same time, whatever we take it to have been,
it is unlikely to acquire new texts. The Hebrew canon, in contrast, is
understood to have the kind of consequential, dynamic role in the
cultural life of a nation which Yiddish cannot assume.

Still: insisting on the place of women within the Hebrew and Yiddish
canon—however conceived—expands the borders of the concept without
challenging it at its roots in ways feminist scholars have urged. Canon
seems necessarily to imply hierarchy and tradition—even "new traditions," to borrow an oxymoron used in contemporary canon debates. It
should be possible to argue for an expansion of the canon even as we
question its construction. Can we, for example, imagine or theorize literary study as a noncanonical quest, one that tries to find ways not to
expand the privilege to certain texts or to choose among them, but rather
one that is structured around the interplay between varied texts and various readers? Perhaps it is time for us to relinquish the search for canons
and for the literary models to be found in our "mothers' gardens"[8] and to
turn (return?) instead to a symbolic vocabulary that is at once more

individual and more inclusive, one that allows many different voices to enter the discourse without canonizing them. Such an enterprise would ask us to explore the relationship between text and reader, or interpretive strategies informed by equal attention to historical and textual considerations.

A related concern asks how "tradition" and intertextuality, which mean quite different things in Hebrew and Yiddish, function. Hebrew is the father tongue in that it has been more centrally influenced by tradition—even in its appropriation and subversion of tradition. And tradition, we have come to recognize, signals the patriarchal domain. In order to rebel, to appropriate and subvert, in order to rewrite you have to have access to the already written and that, surely, has been a male domain in Hebrew. If tradition is the sign of the father, why should we women rush to write ourselves into it? Implicit in this volume is the question of how we may conceptualize texts by women that construct themselves as neither part of a traditional *goldene keyt* [golden chain] nor simply as representative of a clichéd break with the past.

Another question emerging from these discussions concerns the role of the creative artist. If, as both the Romantics and the Modernists have suggested, the author occupies, on the secular plane, the place of the Creator, if *he* assumes transcendent divine powers, then what room does that leave for female creativity in the Jewish context in which the Creator is invariably the ultimate patriarchal figure? The feminine aspects of God and the imaging of God as immanence and presence rather than pure transcendence is also part of Jewish tradition, but these are not the dominant images through which creative urges and powers are figured. The Romantic anthropomorphic iconography is disturbing in a Jewish context, approaching as it does the language of idolatry. Jewish feminist criticism may contribute new ways of distancing readers from such constructions of literary creativity by challenging the cult of the artist figure.

Finally, we need to consider what we mean by a Jewish language. Hebrew and Yiddish are quite different in this regard, too, and the Hebrew canon will never be fixed as the Yiddish canon can be; the former continues to develop as the latter reaches its foreseeable end. Boundaries of audience are also entirely different for the two languages as the status of each changes, the Yiddish readership declines, and Hebrew literacy increases. But more to the point is not why modern Hebrew and Yiddish are combined in this volume, but whether English, the important body of American Jewish literature, and other literatures (in particular, Latin American, French, and German) should have been included as well. Undoubtedly, English is becoming or already is a competing language, not a Jewish language in the strict sense, but increasingly an international, public language for Jews as for the rest of the world. Still, it remains distinct from those languages that develop in response to the kinds of cultural influences we have explored in these essays. Here, we reenter the familiar debates within Jewish scholarship between literatures written in Jewish languages and those written in *la^caz* (a Hebrew acronym for "a language of a strange people")—vernaculars used by Jews but deriving from non-Jewish languages and thus not considered the repositories of Jewish history and consciousness.[9]

The essays in this volume could have been structured in a number of equally sensible ways. They could have been divided by genre, by language, by distinctions between critics and imaginative writers. Readers will notice that only one male critic is included here and may speculate, along with the editors, about the significance of such an observation. It is at least clear that feminist studies of Jewish literature have rarely examined the kinds of controversial questions about gendered readings raised by Jonathan Culler's "Reading As A Woman" (1982) or Robert Scholes' "Reading Like A Man" (1987).[10]

The first five essays in this volume are primarily concerned with women's voices or their appropriation, and the last three offer the views of contemporary women writing fiction; in the middle are three essays considering male writers. Alternatively, one may see this volume as structured in two parts: the first six essays primarily concerned with poetry and the remaining five essays with prose. The volume concludes with bibliographies annotating research on feminist approaches or women-related issues in modern Yiddish and Hebrew literature. Taken as a whole, the analyses of well-known and already forgotten writers found in these pages should challenge prevailing assumptions about feminist inquiry, Jewish culture, and literary production.

Anne Lapidus Lerner begins this volume by analyzing a major Hebrew writer, Esther Raab, pointing to the anomalies of the poet's themes and style when compared to others of her generation. Here, we encounter a female poet profoundly influenced by the literary and religious traditions of her forefathers but with no inclination to become part of that male tradition. Ilana Pardes examines the poetry of Yocheved Bat-Miriam and its attempt to reconstruct a noncanonical but nonetheless powerful matrilinear tradition. The punishment meted out to women who, like the biblical Miriam, seek a place and a voice in the canon, is explored in this essay. Dan Miron illuminates the Yiddish as well as the Hebrew context in his consideration of the beginnings of women's poetry in Hebrew. Resisting simple outcries of misogyny and double standards, Miron (referring to Esther Raab and Yocheved Bat-Miriam among others) explains why no significant women poets could appear in Hebrew at a time that was rather more receptive to female voices in Yiddish. Miron discusses the appropriation by the Hebrew writer Uri Nisan Gnessin of a Yiddish poem by Celia Dropkin as an illustration of the complex relationships among Hebrew, Yiddish, the male tradition, and female writers.

Celia Dropkin emerges in this volume as a powerful if previously underrepresented figure. In addition to being the subject of the next essay by Janet Hadda, Dropkin appears, as well, in the essay by Kathryn Hellerstein, and is referred to yet again (as the Yiddish Sylvia Plath) by Chava Rosenfarb. Dropkin's work will no doubt have to be reexamined in light of this evidence of renewed interest. Hadda's essay develops a psychoanalytic theory of the intersubjective relations among writer, text, and reader. She comments on Dropkin's erotic themes and emphasizes the connections between the poet's autobiographical and poetic "I." Hellerstein takes a different approach in her essay, insisting on the crucial difference between the poetic "I" and the autobiographical "self" in Yiddish women's poetry, and focusing on the former. Combining new translations and analyses of several important poets (Yehudis, Anna Margolin, Miriam Ulinover, Dropkin, Malka Heifetz Tussman), Hellerstein traces a deliberate resistance to confession and self-revelation in women's Yiddish poetry.

Hamutal Bar Yosef's analysis of Hayyim Nahman Bialik—the most influential Hebrew poet of this century—also enters into the controversy concerning psychoanalytic readings. She shows the effects of Decadence and Symbolism on Bialik's poetics and on his conceptualization of femininity. Like Miron, who argues that Bialik's influence was a major factor in excluding women from Hebrew poetry before 1920, Bar Yosef urges readers not to categorize and dismiss Bialik as a misogynist but rather to consider his work in terms of the cultural conventions and stereotypes to which he responded.

Turning to Hebrew prose, Naomi Sokoloff and Anne Golomb Hoffman expand the analysis of the cultural construction of gender. Sokoloff's reading of Ahron Appelfeld's *Tzili* asks why the author chose a girl as the protagonist of a story that so closely resembles his own autobiographical experiences as a survivor of the Holocaust. Parallels between the struggles of women and of survivors to find a voice are central to Sokoloff's consideration of Appelfeld's story. Similarly, the parallel position of the female and of the Jew in society, and the poetics of interiority are examined by Sokoloff. Anne Hoffman's essay concerns a different process of feminization—this time of another eponymous figure, the male protagonist in A. B. Yehoshua's *Molkho* (Five Seasons) . Undoing both gendered dichotomies and the Oedipal plot, Hoffman sees *Molkho* as disrupting the assumptions about public and private in Israeli fiction through its interrogation of a complex relation to the body.

The essays that follow these critical approaches offer the extraordinarily compelling voices of three contemporary writers. The Yiddish novelist, essayist, and playwright, Chava Rosenfarb, describes her relationship to feminist thought. Claiming an interest in it even as she explains why it has not been more central to her thinking, she suggests that the successful work is one in which the writer achieves a presence that transcends the boundaries of gender. For a Yiddish writer who has survived the Holocaust and writes knowing that her readership has not, the problem of women's place within the culture cannot claim precedence over the problem of the survival of the culture as a whole. Ruth Almog, the Hebrew novelist and short story writer, makes a curiously similar claim about the modern Israeli experience. Coming of age as a writer in the shadows of the 1967 Arab-Israeli war, she is compelled to ask what place can be found for the inner life of women who confront such overwhelming communal realities. At the end of the next essay, Amalia Kahana-Carmon, the Hebrew prose writer and outspoken feminist, announces the hope for a new era in Israeli literature, one considerably more receptive to women's literary voices. But until that time, she suggests, our gaze remains fixed on the collective to which women's perspectives are rarely admitted. Adjusting the form and content debate in criticism to the Hebrew context, Kahana-Carmon argues against the prevalent mode of reading which sees meaningful content as inhering in male texts and form as the provenance of women.

In at least one major sense, the creative writers included here are *not* representative of the corpus of Jewish literature. They are all novelists and, as several of these essays indicate, there is an inescapable preponderance of poets among women writing in Yiddish or Hebrew. Jewish literature calls into question any generalized view of the novel—domestic, romantic, self-referential as it may be—as a form particularly appropriate to women. In fact, a vexing question raised by several of these essays and familiar to all readers of Yiddish and Hebrew concerns the ongoing gender and genre discussion. What is it that encourages women to write poetry in these Jewish languages, or what hinders many of them, until more recently, from producing novels? Certainly, there is nothing intrinsically feminine in the one genre nor masculine in the other. A similar phenomenon is not evident in European literatures, nor in Jewish American literature written by women. Is there something peculiar to Hebrew and Yiddish about this preference for one genre over the other?

Several responses emerge. The most common one suggests that neither immigrant nor Eastern European life allowed women to write novels. In a culture in which a woman's life was so busy, where there was neither a room of her own in which to write, nor the time or resources to publish, novel-writing was simply too vast an undertaking. The image that comes to mind is of a woman with little bits of paper coming out of her apron pockets, jotting down another short line of poetry between the soup and the *tsimes*. Surely no poet, however, would proffer the argument that poetry takes less time or concentration than prose. One may recall the old and by now bankrupt notions about female creativity to which such writers as Emily Dickinson were once subject; such criticisms suggested that the fragmented reality of women's lives leads to the more compact form of the poem. As Dickinson has been redeemed from such criticism, so should we be able to redeem female Jewish poets.

Another view holds that Jewish women could not, for the most part, write novels because the expansive social worldview implicit in that genre was inaccessible to them. This, of course, does not account for the extent to which Eastern European women and not men were wage earners, in contact with the wider economic world. It is, however, certainly true that the literary world was not open to them in the same way. Storytelling suggests, in ways poetry need not, a grounding in the social structure within which or against which the tale is told. It implies, in other words, a kind of rootedness in culture which, for Jews in general and still more recently for Israelis, has been remarkably different for men and women.

It may be helpful to recall the diachronic and synchronic tensions invoked earlier, which female writers reproduce in a somewhat different way. That is, it is a truth at least widely (if not universally) acknowledged that poetry precedes prose in literary history. And so we might have expected that when Jewish women as a group finally turned to writing, they would recapitulate this process and turn to poetry first—as

indeed they did. There are, of course, exceptions to this pattern, particularly in the case of modern Hebrew writers, among whose early ranks we
do find women. Nonetheless, even here the majority of female writers
were poets and, as a group, women writers in both languages have been
associated with achievements in poetry rather than prose. It is also true
that women entered the Jewish literary world when Hebrew and Yiddish
literatures were under the sway of modernist literary movements, which
both primarily entered through poetry. The turning to poetry by women
may thus have been doubly determined.

In short, to understand why Jewish women have written more poetry
than fiction in Hebrew and Yiddish, scholars will need to look more
closely at the valence of each genre within Jewish letters rather than at
the economic or social conditions of women at a particular historical
moment. We will want to ask if in Hebrew or Yiddish, with their connections to a Jewish story-telling tradition in Bible, Aggadah and
Midrash—traditions denied women for the most part—prose may
indeed appear more characteristically as a masculine genre in ways that
are not true of other cultures.

Jewish literature lends a significantly different perspective to what is
naively held to be another universal truth about the oral tradition. We
need only recall the accepted wisdom about the writings of Black women
or Southern women in America to recognize that women are generally
considered to be the bearers of the oral story-telling tradition. Within the
Jewish context—certainly within the Hebrew context—that is simply not
true given the significance and status of the oral tradition and its inscription into the culture. Here, emphasis must be placed as strongly on tradition as on orality. The connections between Jewish oral and written law
as they relate to modern story-telling have yet to be adequately explored
from a feminist perspective. In this exploration, it will be helpful to keep
in mind two ostensibly contradictory expressions. One (following Chava
Rosenfarb) reminds us that women are said to have *nayn mos reyd* (nine
measures of talk). While this implies that women have a wonderful
capacity for articulation, it is also understood as suggesting that women
have more speech than sense. The second expression reminds us of those
stories told *tsvishn minkhe un mayrev* (between afternoon and evening
prayers), as it were, from which women were excluded. The status of
both kinds of story-telling—those attributed to women in the kitchen and
to men in the synagogue—forms an important part of the story told in
this volume.

But it is not the complete story, since it obscures the extent to which Jewish culture has offered deeply nourishing soil for modern writers. Lamenting the plight of women or castigating patriarchal culture are easy tasks which, we are repeatedly reminded in this volume, do not, in themselves, produce the kinds of compelling poetry or prose discussed here. The connections between a traditional, religious culture and a modern and increasingly secular one are of paramount significance, and repeatedly we encounter texts sustained by their pursuit of a delicate balance between the two. In the traditional Jewish world, women's written creativity took quite particular forms; work on *tkhines* (petitionary prayers) has revealed one of the ways in which women adopted traditional forms.[11] But modern Hebrew and Yiddish literature emerge from a complex relationship to tradition, which eventually opened the cultural world to women but which, paradoxically, may have initially left them with less of a footing in a coherent cultural universe than they had previously been able to claim. In the apocalyptic moments of twentieth-century Jewish history, the problem of listening to women's voices rarely appeared on anyone's agenda.

It appears quite frequently now. In this volume and elsewhere, the exploration of writing by and about women produces provocative views not only of women's voices but more generally of Jewish literary culture. Questions about tradition, canon, genre, gender, and culture can only be addressed fully when they are addressed simultaneously. Feminist and Jewish literary critics speak most productively to one another when they allow the confluence of interests outlined here both to expand the range of questions they ask and to enlarge the cultural perspectives they examine.

NOTES

1. For their generosity in reading and commenting on various drafts of this essay, I am indebted to Arlene Agus, Sidra Ezrahi, Anne Herrmann, June Howard, Avram Novershtern, Adela Pinch, and Athena Vrettos.

2. Dan Miron's *A Traveler Disguised* (1973), especially chapter 1, remains the most comprehensive analysis of this process, particularly as it applies to the development of the Yiddish novel.

3. As discussed in Showalter (1984, "Women's Time, Women's Space").

4. For a fuller view of this debate and an overview of the development of feminist criticism, see, especially, Moi (1985); Showalter, ed. (1985, *The New Feminist Criticism*) and her 1984 essay; Rita Felski (1989); Elizabeth Meese (1990); and June Howard (1988).

5. Another provocative schematization of feminist criticism is in Felski's *Beyond Feminist Aesthetics*. Following Showalter, Felski suggests that English feminist criticism has been understood to stress oppression, French repression, and American expression (20).

6. For a fuller development of this argument see Benjamin Harshav (1990), especially, chapter 5.

7. Irigary (1974), *Speculum de l'autre femme*.

8. This quest has been most provocatively—and positively—undertaken by black feminist critics seeking a tradition into which to inscribe themselves. (See, especially, Alice Walker [1983].) More recently, it has been developed by lesbian and Chicana critics. But such concepts are necessarily different for Jewish writers already steeped in a strong (male) literary tradition and for whom female archetypes are not rare.

9. See, for example, Max Weinreich (1980).

10. For an interesting analysis of the issues raised by these critics, see Diana Fuss (1989). Also, a response to *Men in Feminism* by Joseph Allen Boone (1989), and Moi's response to Boone in the same volume.

11. See Chava Weissler (1987).

WORKS CITED

Boone, Joseph Allen. 1989. "Of Me(n) and Feminism: Who(se) is the Sex that Writes?" In *Gender and Theory*, ed. Linda Kauffman, 158-180. Oxford: Basil Blackwell.

Culler, Jonathan. 1983. *On Deconstruction: Theory and Criticism After Structuralism*. Ithaca, N.Y.: Cornell Univ. Press.

Felski, Rita. 1989. *Beyond Feminist Aesthetics*. Cambridge, Mass.: Harvard Univ. Press.

Fuss, Diana. 1989. *Essentially Speaking: Feminism, Nature and Difference*. New York: Routledge.

Gilbert, Sandra M. and Susan Gubar. 1979. *The Madwoman in the Attic: The Woman Writer and the Nineteenth-Century Literary Imagination*. New Haven: Yale Univ. Press.

Harshav, Benjamin. 1990. *The Meaning of Yiddish*. Berkeley: Univ. of California Press.

Howard, June. 1988. "Feminist Differings: Recent Surveys of Feminist Literary Theory and Criticism." *Feminist Studies* 14, 1 (Spring): 167-109.

Irigaray, Luce. 1974. *Speculum de l'autre femme*. Paris: Editions de Minuit.

——, 1977. *Ce Sexe qui n'en est pas un*. Paris: Editions de Minuit.

Kolodny, Annette. 1980. "Dancing Through the Minefield." *Feminist Studies* 6; reprinted in Showalter, *The New Feminist Criticism*, 144-167.

Kristeva, Julia. 1974. "*La Femme, ce n'est jamais ça*," *Tel Quel* 57-58: 19-25.

Meese, Elizabeth. 1990. *(Ex)Tensions: Refiguring Feminist Criticism*. Urbana: Univ. of Illinois Press.

Millett, Kate. 1970. *Sexual Politics*. New York: Doubleday.

Miron, Dan. 1973. *A Traveler Disguised: A Study in the Rise of Modern Yiddish Fiction in the Nineteenth Century* . New York: Schocken Books.

Moi, Toril 1985. *Sexual/Textual Politics: Feminist Literary Theory*. London: Routledge.

———, 1989. "Men Against Patriarchy." In *Gender and Theory*, ed. Linda Kauffman, 181-188. Oxford: Basil Blackwell.

Scholes, Robert. 1987. "Reading Like a Man." In *Men in Feminism*, ed. Alice Jardine and Paul Smith, 204-218. New York and London: Methuen.

Showalter, Elaine. 1984. "Women's Time, Women's Space." *Tulsa Studies in Women's Literature* 3, 1-2: 29-44.

———, ed. 1985. *The New Feminist Criticism*. New York: Pantheon.

Walker, Alice. 1983. *In Search of Our Mothers' Gardens: Womanist Prose*. San Diego: Harcourt Brace Jovanovich.

Weinrich, Max. 1980. *History of the Yiddish Language*. Chicago: Univ. of Chicago Press.

Weissler, Chava. 1987. "The Traditional Piety of Ashkenazic Women." In *Jewish Spirituality: From the Sixteenth Century Revival to the Present*, ed. Arthur Green, 245-275. New York: Crossroad.

"A Woman's Song":
The Poetry of Esther Raab

స్త ANNE LAPIDUS LERNER స్త

In memory of my beloved father
יוסף בן ירחמיאל ומלכה, *Joseph Lapidus*

The development of modern Hebrew poetry gave rise to a burgeoning of poetic activity among women. Rahel, Yocheved Bat-Miriam, Esther Raab, and Elisheva were the most prominent of a cluster of women who started writing and publishing Hebrew poetry in the early 1920s after a puzzling total absence of women Hebrew poets from 1890 to 1920.[1]

Among these poets, Esther Raab (1894-1981) is distinguished both by her poetry and by her biography. She is the only one of the group who was not part of the Russian poetic tradition. Harold Schimmel suggests that Raab, like Emily Dickinson, stands outside the poetic mainstream (9-10).

Her birth in 1894 in Petah Tikvah gives Raab the distinction of being the first woman born in the Land of Israel to become a Hebrew poet. This accident of birth distinguishes her poetry from that of her contemporaries. Actually, it is not really fair to refer to this as an accident of birth, because her father, Judah Raab, who made *aliyah* in 1876 and married Esther's mother in 1878, intended to re-establish his family's European agricultural heritage in the Land of Israel.[2] His childhood had been formed by his experiences living on an agricultural estate in Hungary; his children were, he hoped, destined to be Jewish farmers who experienced no conflict of homeland or landscape.

Thus, Esther Raab—unlike Leah Goldberg, for example—had no deep European forests, no church spires flashing through her consciousness. Unlike Hayyim Nahman Bialik, the greatest Hebrew poet of the previous generation, Raab was not the poet "of the hills, woods and streams of Volhynia" (Aberbach, 1988, 50). At a point when her contemporaries were, in a sense, a *dor midbar*—a wilderness or transition generation who relished the opportunity to settle in Israel but still hankered after their childhood or early adult experiences in Europe—Raab wrote through her primal contact with the land. Raab herself was aware of the importance of these influences (1989b).

Her birth in Petah Tikvah also affected her language. For most Hebrew writers of Raab's generation, Hebrew was not the first language. Spoken Hebrew was not even an early language. While Raab clearly knew Yiddish (originally in a Hungarian form; later, influenced by a wave of settlers from Lithuania who came to Petah Tikvah, in its classic, Lithuanian form), she had an early, natural connection with the Hebrew language.[3] Of course, at the turn of the century, modern Hebrew was in the process of developing the vocabulary and syntax that would allow it to become a flexible medium of expression. Raab later described that process: "Every Hebrew word was new and shining with a wealth of colors like a bird's wings. . . . And I caught it as one catches a bird; I loved to pronounce it" (Be'er, 11 March 1988, 11). It was not an acquired language for her, but an innate vehicle of expression which grew and developed as she did.

The nature of her connection with the land, unique in her generation, may have contributed to Raab's fate as a poet who has been undeservedly overlooked in the study of modern Hebrew poetry.[4] In his lengthy introduction to the 1982 *Yahdav* selection of her poetry, Reuven Shoham offers a number of explanations for this oversight (52). It may have been because her corpus was not large to begin with and that less than half of it was published in a collected volume during her lifetime. In addition, Raab never really belonged to the generation of writers who were her contemporaries; she was somehow too independent—a loner out of sync with the zeitgeist, the spirit and experience of her generation of poets. Finally, Shoham suggests, Raab's language, in its concreteness, set her apart from the norm. Miron's emphasis on Raab's unwillingness to adapt her poetic voice to that of a "submissive" woman provides yet another tantalizing explanation.[5]

Taste and the establishment of the canon are issues which are most complex. None of the explanations Shoham puts forth can be easily dismissed or readily accepted. True, Raab's corpus is small, and she underwent a long period of silence from 1935 to 1947.[6] Yet, it is far from the smallest corpus of the period and, with Bialik's protracted silence before us, we can scarcely say that a poet whose muse is sometimes absent is always dismissed. And, while Raab was in many ways unique, she describes herself as having been in touch with many of the great writers of her time.[7] If there is one salient difference between Raab and others of her generation, it is precisely that she does not seem to belong to that generation in terms of theme or style. As Shimon Ginzburg wrote of her poetry in 1936: "she captures the look of the landscape of the Land of Israel in a manner different from that of most of our poets who come from the foreign countries, in a natural and true presentation, unadorned, without the falseness of sentimentality" (279). Raab's style is clearly different, for she accepts as a given the Land of Israel, its flora and fauna, and uses them throughout her poetry.

Raab's poetry deals with issues that arise from her unique situation, as well as those connected with her ties to Jewish religious tradition—questions that pervade modern Hebrew literature. To illustrate, I will focus on one of her later poems, which serves well as a lens through which can be refracted a number of issues relevant to the broader corpus of her work.

I have selected "Shirat ishah " or "Woman's Song" (1969), because in both title and themes it is a complex and multivalent poem. In its rich layers of meaning, the poem incorporates three major themes: womanhood, religion, and poetry.[8] Its very autobiographical ambiguity—disclosing and veiling self—is part of its fascination. A poem as rich as this one affords a challenge to those who would presume to analyze it, for, in so doing, one must necessarily unravel the seamless nature of the work. I will first examine each of the three strands, and then consider nature, the thread which is dominant in much of Raab's work but missing here.

שִׁירַת אִשָּׁה

בָּרוּךְ שֶׁעָשַׂנִי אִשָּׁה—
שֶׁאֲנִי אֲדָמָה וְאָדָם,
וְצֵלָע רַכָּה;
בָּרוּךְ שֶׁעֲשִׂיתַנִי
עִגּוּלִים עִגּוּלִים—   5
כְּגַלְגַּלֵּי מַזָּלוֹת
וּכְעִגּוּלֵי פֵּרוֹת—
שֶׁנָּתַתָּ לִי בָּשָׂר חַי

פּוֹרֵחַ,
10 וַעֲשִׂיתַנִי כְּצֶמַח הַשָּׂדֶה—
נוֹשֵׂא פְּרִי;
שֶׁקִּרְעֵי עֲנָנֶיךָ,
מַחֲלִיקִים כְּמֶשִׁי
עַל פָּנַי וִירֵכַי;
15 וַאֲנִי גְדוֹלָה
וּמְבַקֶּשֶׁת לִהְיוֹת יַלְדָּה,
בּוֹכִיָּה מִצַּעַר,
וְצוֹחֶקֶת, וְשָׁרָה בְּקוֹל,
דַּק מִן הַדַּק—
20 כְּצִרְצַר זָעִיר
בְּמַקְהֵלַת כְּרוּבֶיךָ
הַנַּעֲלָה—
קְטַנָּה שֶׁבַּקְּטַנּוֹת—
אֲנִי מְשַׂחֶקֶת
25 לְרַגְלֶיךָ—
בּוֹרְאִי!

Woman's Song	*A Woman's Song*
Blessed He who made	Blessed be He who made
me a woman—	me a woman,
that I'm earth* and Adam,	That I am earth and man
and a tender rib;	And tender rib;
Blessed who made me	Blessed be You who made me
5 circles upon circles—	5 All in circles–
like wheels of planets	Like heavenly spheres
and like circles of fruit—	And circles of fruits–
who gave me living flesh	That You gave me
which blossoms,	Blossoming, live flesh,
10 and made me like	10 And You made me Like
plant of the field—	a plant of the field
that bears fruit;	Bearing fruit;
so that Your cloud-tatters,	That Your ripped clouds
slide like silk	Caress like silk
on my face and thighs;	My face and hips;
15 and I am big	15 And I am grown
and want to be a girl,	And want to be a girl
weeping from sorrow,	Crying of sorrow
and laughing, and singing	And I laugh and sing
with a voice, thinner than thin—	With the faintest voice

20 like a wee cricket
     in the chorus of your lofty
     cherubs—
     smallest of the small—I play
25 at Your feet
     my Creator![9]
	20 Like a small cricket
	     In the lofty chorus
	     Of your cherubs–
	     The smallest of small–
	25 I play at your feet,
	     My Creator![10]

* "earth", in Hebrew *adamah*, from
whence Adam's name

First published in 1972, in the collection of Raab's poems entitled *Tefilah aharonah* [A Final Prayer], "*Shirat ishah*" is a relatively short poem—although of about average length for Raab—in which the poet expresses her personal attitudes toward being a woman.[11] It is a poem of joy, of reveling in womanhood. The unequivocally positive mood which pervades the poem does not always strike a welcome note in the minds of contemporary feminist readers, because they often feel that the poem minimizes the power of women.[12]

The title "Woman's Song" does not tell us anything about the connection between the subject of the poem and the narrator.[13] Where we might expect some first person signifier in the title—perhaps something along the lines of Bialik's "*Shirati,* " [My Song]—we find instead a title that is telling in its very spareness. As defined by the title, this is a poem of more than personal significance. Although the poem itself is boldly first person, Raab is, through the title, telling us that her song can be the song of any woman. Her experience, to the extent that it is herein reflected, is not special, singled-out, unique. Yet, she simultaneously indicates—with a modicum of hubris—that her poem also is the quintessential poem of a woman. In so doing, Raab opens, particularly for her women readers, the issue of their identification with what is expressed in her "Woman's Song" or their rejection of it.[14]

Raab's opening sentence, in both its form and its substance, addresses gender issues. She plays with the words *adamah* (earth) and *adam* (man), while engaging the accepted notion of the earth-mother. When Raab's first-person narrator states "*ani adamah*," (I am earth) the reader hears a simple statement of this metaphor. When the narrator adds, "*veʾadam*" (and man), the reader recognizes that this is a multivalent line. On the one hand, Raab is telling the reader that the land is both feminine and masculine. After all, if there were a need to create the masculine form of *adamah*, it would necessarily be *adam*. This takes the reader back to the second Creation story, in which God formed "man from the dust of the earth" (haʾadam afar min haʾadamah) (Gen. 2:7). It is significant in this context that, in other poems, Raab sometimes reverses the trite earth-mother, male-fructifier image to give the female the penetrating role.[15] Yet there is another reversal inherent in this line. The feminine form of adam would be adamah. Hebrew's lack of nongendered language often leaves us using adam to mean person, for wont of a less gendered word.[16] Through the use of this juxtaposition, Raab is saying, "I am both mother-earth and father-earth; I am both the male and the female first human."

The imagery from the Creation story continues as Raab lists the third component in her makeup as "tselaʿ rakah" (a soft rib), alluding to the formation of Eve from Adam's rib described in the second chapter of Genesis. This is an oxymoron, for ribs are bony and not soft. Clearly, in these two lines, Raab is composing a midrash on Genesis, introducing a distinction between male and female, perhaps even addressing the question of the appropriateness of fashioning a woman out of a man's bone. From her positive opening we may reasonably deduce that the softness she attributes to the rib is a positive characteristic, appropriate to the somewhat androgynous creature whose Creator she praises.

The intimate, second-person God is praised for having created the narrator in circles—first plain circles, then the circles of the planets or spheres, and finally circles of fruits.[17] Beyond the rolling g.l. (gimel-lamed) onomatopeia of the circular words Raab uses, what do mazalot (planets) and peirot (fruits) signify? In addition to their being largely circular or rounded in shape themselves, fruits and the heavenly spheres are often found in orbits or arranged in circles, like the ʿigulei deveilah (round cakes of pressed figs) mentioned in rabbinic literature.[18] They are thus circles of circles. The fruits are the symbols of female fertility and sexuality; the planets represent Raab's reach beyond Earth to the cosmic. The planets are of the heavens; the fruit, of the earth; and the "blooming, living flesh" that is the woman represents an intermediate plane.[19] It is on this intermediate plane that the poem focuses. At the same time, all of these circles, particularly the cosmic ones, are also cycles and remind us of the cyclical nature of a premenopausal woman's life.[20]

Female fecundity is further underscored by Raab's use of the words "ketsemah hasadeh" from one of Ezekiel's visions. God dictates to Ezekiel the following: "When I passed by you and saw you wallowing in your blood, I said to you: 'Live in spite of your blood.' Yea, I said to you: 'Live in spite of your blood.' I let you grow like the plants of the field [ketsemah hasadeh]; and you continued to grow up until you attained to womanhood, until your breasts became firm and your hair sprouted. You were still naked and bare" (Ezek. 16:6-7).

The appropriateness of the verse—which also appears as part of the midrashic section in the Passover *Haggadah*—to Raab's context can be seen both in the ending of the verse, which she does not quote, and in the way the verse is used in other midrashic contexts (Goldschmidt, 1960,120).[21] The "growth of the field" is, for Ezekiel, part of a metaphor comparing the people of Israel to a woman who is unclothed, unkempt, uncivilized. Rabbinic interpretation expanded this negative statement, suggesting that the Children of Israel were "naked" of God's command-ments, or *mitsvot*. But for Raab, it is a positive metaphor: the salient characteristic of this woman is that she is "bearing fruit"; the covert characteristic is her rounded and mature sexuality, her firm breasts.

Even in Raab's simple statement that a woman, like the plants of the field, bears fruit, there is a biblical reference which emphasizes her par-ticular vision. The first Creation story in Genesis informs the reader that on the third day God had the earth bring forth "trees of every kind bearing fruit" (Gen. 1:11). While the biblical translator has chosen to use the term "bearing fruit," the Hebrew has "ʿoseh peri," better translated as "making fruit." Raab compares her woman to a plant "bearing fruit" (*nosʾe prei*). In echoing, but not repeating, the language of Genesis, she underscores the woman's role. While a woman cannot "make" fruit without a man, she "bears" the fruit alone.

From the covert sexual imagery of the growth of the field metaphor, Raab moves to a fairly explicit description of physical pleasure. The sensual experience of being caressed by torn clouds which feel like silk on the narrator's face and thighs is barely a touch, but enough for the reader to imagine the narrator seen large and tall across the landscape. Clouds are common in Raab's poetry and prose, but torn clouds, imply-ing perhaps a struggle, or at least an imperfection, are not.[22] The feel of the silk, its rarity, and its connection to the boudoir introduce a new element into the poem.[23]

The second half of the poem, opening with a contrastive *vav*, focuses not on the creation of the narrator, but on her feelings.[24] She expresses her ambivalence about whether she wants to be grown-up or "a girl".[25] While Raab tellingly does not enumerate any of the advantages of being grown-up, she does describe for us the things about childhood that she misses. Essentially, she characterizes childhood as a period in which one is free to express oneself in pain, in joy, or in song. She has not forgotten the pain. In fact, she mentions it first; but it is followed by the joy of her laughing and singing aloud.

Her ambiguity about her stature is also reflected in the many examples of alternating heavenly and earthly metaphors to be found in the poem. The round metaphors of the planets and the fruit, the contrast between the field and the clouds, and the sounds of the cricket and the cherubs allow the reader to sense the ambivalence that underlies the image of the poem's narrator. One is reminded of the Hasidic tale which suggests that a person always carry in one pocket a note saying, "I am but a little lower than the angels," and in the other a note saying, "I am but dust and ashes."

The comparison Raab draws between the narrator and a cricket is particularly striking. One expects to find crickets fairly close to the ground. The cricket described by the narrating persona in Bialik's "*Shirati*," for example, is in the cold hearth. It sings, as pointed out by Ziva Shamir (1986), in response to the Sabbath songs sung by the narrator's family and by the Sabbath angels (71). Raab, in describing the voice of her first-person narrator as that of a cricket, moves rapidly from earth to heaven, for her cricket situates itself in God's exalted cherubic choir. One experiences again the ambivalent mix of hubris and modesty. While she hears her voice as that of the lowly cricket, it is only so in relation to the heavenly chorus; while she sees herself as the smallest of the small, it is only in relation to the feet of God the Creator.[26]

The question of relative size or, perhaps, of relative importance, raises a central feminist issue. In her article about Israeli women poets, Lilly Ratok discusses this issue in the context of the conflict between feminine and literary values among women writers. She maintains that the primacy of female values would, perhaps even unconsciously, influence a woman writer to forgo vying for excellence or for a central position in the field of literature (1988, 58-59).

Raab here emphasizes the significance of the insignificant. Her self-portrayal as small, a cricket, a voice in the chorus, raises the hackles of those who maintain that women, like men, must see themselves as persons of considerable magnitude.[27] Yet it is a vision of self which, while not exclusive, appears elsewhere in Raab's work, as well. In anticipating her own death, for example, she said: "I believe that the spirit is not lost. I leave a little, something, one point within eternity, some drop in the sea" (Be'er, 1 April 1988,15).

Clearly, for some, the male model of dominance is not the only one. In this poem, Raab seems to be suggesting that her different voice is also important. Her integration of another standard, her emphasis on being at one with nature, precludes her viewing a hierarchical male standard as the only one.[28] She is more comfortable recognizing the consequence of the quotidian.

In sum, "Woman's Song" presents us with a version of what being a woman means to Raab. It involves a sensual joy in being female, a reveling in the roundness of female physiology and fertility, and a being at one with the cosmos. But from the preceding analysis of the poem, I have deliberately eliminated the other salient themes. "Woman's Song" is not just a woman's poem, it is also a poem in which Raab attempts to come to terms with God and Judaism, as well as a vehicle for expressing some of her feeling about the craft of poetry.

Writing in Hebrew, one is forced to heed the echoes of traditional texts and attitudes which pervade the language. A Hebrew writer is hard-pressed to avoid the encounter with tradition. For Raab, "Woman's Song" represents an attempt to articulate both her reconstruction of parts of traditional Judaism and her relationship with God.

The opening line represents her direct challenge to the Jewish tradition of her childhood. In the observant community of Petah Tikvah where she was raised, Esther Raab's education was interrupted when David Hayyun, the new principal in the local school, decided that young men and women would study together in co-educational classes. This met with the opposition of her own beloved and admired father, who decided that his daughter could not continue her studies in mixed classes.[29] She must often have bristled at the denigration of women implicit in having men praise God daily for not having created them women. While she may have known that it was the requirement that males perform more *mitsvot* than females and not rampant misogyny which gave rise to this wording, she dealt directly with the issue in the opening line of this poem by simply omitting the negative from the blessing traditionally said by men. It is a modest protest, one couched in omission, but one which is also quite effective, for it echoes the liturgy while reversing its sense. At the same time, to the female reader whose ear may be better attuned to the female version of the blessing, Raab confirms the divine plan. While men say the words previously mentioned as part of the liturgy, women positively bless God for having made them according to his will.[30] By conflating the texts, a woman hears that God made her a woman, which is according to the divine will. She retains the rest of the blessing, having turned its sense on its head, and continues, for example, to refer to God in the third person, as does the fixed form of traditional blessing.

The previously discussed criticism of the Creation story in Genesis, implicit both in Raab's use of *adam* and *adamah* and in her conversion of the bony rib into a soft one, is a further example of her quiet but firm challenge to accepted texts and approaches. One wonders whether Raab was familiar with the possibility raised in the Talmud that the language used in that version of the Creation story points to the woman's having "more understanding than the man."[31]

After the description of her creation, Raab's first-person narrator returns to the blessing formula with which she had opened. This time she introduces another, more subtle modification. *Berakhot*, or blessings, traditionally shift from the second person to the third. While opening with "*Barukh atah* " (Praised are You), they proceed to acknowledge God as ruler of the universe in an apostrophe and then shift to third person language. The fourth line of the poem starts as essentially a reprise of the first, except for the person of "*ʿasitani*" (You made me), an archaic and formal form of the verb, which has now been changed to the second person.

This seemingly minor grammatical shift establishes the intimate I-Thou relationship between the speaker and God which suffuses the poem.[32] Yet it is only in the final line and word of the poem that the speaker, who had been addressing God as You throughout, actually uses one of God's epithets.[33] The name she uses is "*Borʾi*," (my Creator), which brings the reader full circle to the Creation motif of the opening lines. By framing her poem in the context of Creation, Raab repeats the ambivalent message of the poem. On the one hand, this is the poem of Everywoman, or, perhaps, Eve-rywoman; on the other, this is the poem of a unique woman—strong and significant.

There are also additional instances in which Raab's speaker grapples with Jewish tradition. The word she uses for aloud, "*bekol*," takes us directly back to the familiar rabbinic dictum "*kol beʾishah ʿervah*" (a woman's voice constitutes lewdness) (*Berakhot* 24a). Once more, Raab is taking on traditional Judaism in a straightforward, but mild-mannered way. She does not criticize the tradition, but simply states that she sings "aloud," or "in a voice."[34]

The metaphor that has the narrator playing at God's feet is yet another implied critique of the traditional image of woman's role. One well-known version of the World to Come has men sitting and studying Torah, while women sit at their feet. Raab has twisted that tradition by accepting what is a subservient role, but she sits not at the feet not of a man but of God, Whom she here characterizes as *"Borʾi,"* (my Creator).

In closing her poem with that single word *"Borʾi,"* Raab does more than return to the Creation with which the poem opened. Replacing the impersonal "Woman's Song" of the title is the strongly possessive "my Creator" at the closing. On the one hand, Raab is writing of total subservience to God and God's will; on the other, she is defining God in terms of the narrating woman whom God has created. The way in which God, as the subject of the opening word *barukh* and the referent of *Borʾi* at its close, frames the poem is striking. The effect of the frame is further underscored by the repetition of the *"b.r."* sound at the beginning of the opening and closing words of the poem. Although its title is "Woman's Song," the poem itself is a Romantic expression of an intimate relationship with God expressed in natural terms (Zach, 1964, 87).

Submission to God's will is a sentiment which Raab expressed quite vividly in her *The Notebook of Hell*, a collection of vignettes and brief reflections dating some time from 1970 to 1977. In one passage she wrote: "I have not betrayed the form in which God created me—if it was not as perfect, perhaps, as that of others—it was mine, and I fulfilled the intention which was entrusted to it by my Creator (*Yotsri*)—whether good or bad."

While the theme of the craft of poetry does not vie with Judaism or womanhood for dominant rank in this poem, it is clearly significant. By titling what is obviously a poem or song (the terms being identical in Hebrew) *"Shirat ishah,"* Raab leads us to consider poetry per se.

Her use of the weighty, feminine noun *shirah* instead of the less formidable, masculine *shir* tells us that her poem is significant. When we consider the word *"shirah,"* we realize that at the same time that Raab is avoiding pomp, she is taking on circumstance. *"Shirah"* immediately evokes *Shirat hayam*, the majestic poem sung by Moses after the Israelites crossed the Reed Sea as they left Egypt (Exod. 15:1-18) and *Shirat Devorah*, the poem with which Deborah, one of Raab's models, celebrated her victory over Sisera (Judges 5).[35] An ordinary poem is a *shir*; an extraordinary one may be classified as a *shirah*. Indeed, despite twelve poems with the word *shir* in their titles, eleven poems or groups of poems with the word *shirei*, and five with *shirim*, this is Raab's only use of the word *shirah* in a title of a poem.

Raab's choice of title is also dictated by an implicit comparison with Hayyim Nahman Bialik, generally considered the "master" of modern Hebrew poetry, a judgment with which Raab concurred.[36] Bialik's

"*Shirati*," previously mentioned, describes the twin sources of his poetry: his father's poverty and his mother's sadness. It is a poem which is quite explicitly autobiographical, alluding to Bialik's own family situation. In contrast, Raab's poem is not specific and does not embody any truly autobiographical element other than the references to poetry.

Bialik's influence is also perceived in the voice of Raab's narrator, particularly in the thin voice of the small cricket.[37] Beyond the ono-matopoetic effect of the word *tseratsar* (cricket) lurks another deep inter-textual connection with "*Shirati.*" Bialik is the master against whom all modern Hebrew poets must be measured, whose influence they must confront.[38] On the surface, nothing could be farther from Bialik's poetry than Raab's. Her poems do not follow his traditional rhymes and meters; her stanzas and his are totally dissimilar. His rich weave of biblical and rabbinic allusion is absent from her poetry, and her intimate contact with the Land of Israel does not pervade his. Yet, as though validating Harold Bloom's dictum that no poet "speaks a language free of the one wrought by his predecessors"(1973, 25), Raab must have had "*Shirati*" in her consciousness.

The recognition of the connection with "*Shirati*" gives us an insight into Raab's message. Her poem is a counterpoint to Bialik's. While the most apparent distinction between them may be that Raab discusses her experiences in the Land of Israel while Bialik writes about his in the Diaspora, it is not to this distinction that Raab relates. She sees her poem as a woman's poem and must, perforce, see his as that of a man. For this reason, it is most telling that Bialik divides his poem into two halves, devoted respectively to a description of his father's contribution to his poetry and to his mother's. Raab borrows only the cricket in which Bialik, calling it the "poet of poverty," embodies his father's voice. She does not attempt to capture his mother's tear. How revealing that is of the father's impact on Raab's consciousness and artistic formation and of the absence of the mother.[39]

The thin voice that Raab describes, for all its crickety chirping, is also Raab's poetic voice.[40] Like Rahel, Emily Dickinson, and other poets, par-ticularly women, Raab does not see her work as something grand; as something, to borrow a phrase from Horace, *aere perennius*.[41] In its form, "*Shirat ishah*" incorporates Raab's view of poetry, a view which she has, consciously or unconsciously, embedded in the poem by describing one of the three components of woman narrator as *tsela*ᶜ *rakah*. While the pri-mary meaning of *tsela*ᶜ is, as previously indicated, rib, it also came to be used in medieval Hebrew poetry as a term for a half-verse of poetry.[42] In writing about her rejection of fixed poetic meter, Raab uses the same word *tsela* in a somewhat idiosyncratic way, to mean a fixed form, a strait-jacket. "Sometimes I used to write in rhymes, and that is a *tsela*, and did not find favor in my eyes" (Shoham, 1977, 84). In that context, she clearly intended to refer to something hard and not soft. One may therefore conclude that one of the features of the woman narrating this poem is a "soft," perhaps flexible, verse.

"*Shirat ishah*" is a spare poem of twenty-six short lines, only one of which has as many as four words and two of those monosyllables. More than half the lines have but two words; none has more than three accented syllables. The anapest does dominate the poem, but in no fixed pattern. Shoham, in his article entitled "Free Rhythms in Esther Raab's Poetry," asserts that none of her poems uses either tonic/syllabic accents or end-rhyme. This poem is certainly true to form—or more precisely, to non-form. In describing her own use of established forms, Raab states: "I listen only to vague impulses and musical rhythms. Rhyme cuts my wings. At seventeen or eighteen, when I started to write, I immediately wrote in the same free meter, I did not feel that it was daring on my part or that I was influenced by anything" (Shoham, 1977, 84).[43]

Raab's declared independence from literary tradition may be viewed either as a statement of self-reliance and self-worth, or as a reflection of her lack of aspiration to become a link in that chain of literary tradition. Here, again, there is a feminist issue of competing agenda. Are we to heed Patricia Meyer Spacks who takes Anne Sexton to task for not having "generalized and universalized her experience—linked it to traditions outside of itself—to have made it into good poetry?"(4) Or, are we rather to consider Suzanne Juhasz's view that "Sexton's poetry, like that of many women, is different, because it refuses to generalize or universalize its individual experience; because its sources are other than the literary (or religious) traditions of the patriarchal society in which it exists?"(116) Particularly in Jewish culture, where patriarchy is pervasive, is there room for another voice—one which aspires to join not the male chorus but the divine?

In a letter to Shoham, Raab expanded on her view of poetics—a view which is embodied in this poem. She indicated that she tried to write in rhymes but found it too constraining. Once she felt free, she reported: "And then the short lines came, dashes and single words as a line, something like musical notes. . . . One word like an explosion as an ending (finale)" (1977, 84). It is certainly a modest, rather than a grand view of poetry that she presents here.

While some may feel diminished to a degree by the apparent lack of self-assurance and low self-esteem of the poetic persona Raab projects here, others may well perceive that Horace's voice is a male's and that women may have a different, less hierarchical perspective on their place in the grand scheme of things, valuing different kinds of work more equitably.[44]

Having analyzed the themes which Raab *does* explore in this poem, it is appropriate to turn to the one she does not. The lack of specificity in the descriptions of nature here is too striking to overlook. Specific use of flora and fauna is the hallmark of Raab's poetry. Zach opens his essay on Raab with a long catalog of the plants she named and which he does not recognize (86). Shoham lists the words Raab introduced into Hebrew poetry. Schimmel, in the introduction to his unpublished volume of English translations, discusses in some depth the plants she incorporates in her work and their significance (7-8). But in this poem, the only specific term used is the *tseratsar*, or cricket. While Raab knew the cricket from her own experience, she might just as well have borrowed it directly from Bialik. All other terms are quite vague: *adamah*, earth; *peirot*, fruits; *tsemah*, growth; *sadeh*, field; *peri*, fruit; ʿ*ananim*, clouds. It is almost as though in this strongly feminine poem she abandons her loudest note.

In an article entitled "Imagining Women: Notes toward a Feminist Poetic," Mary Carruthers discusses three themes which, in twentieth-century American poetry by women, "are central to the way women imagine their lives: the relationship of mother and daughter, the tradition of romantic love, and the nature of the powerful woman" (1979, 282). Carruthers's thesis is that poetry written in the United States before and after the watershed era of 1968-1970 deals differently with these issues. In looking at the poetry of Esther Raab, I am struck by the extent to which these are *not* her themes. Raab does not dwell on her mother in poetry. She relates to her father in a much more significant way. There is little about romantic love in her poetry—unless one broadens that concept to include an ongoing affair with the Land of Israel; and, although Raab seems to admire her father's heroism, she seems to need to see herself as a woman writ small, and not heroic (Schimmel, 10-11).

This poem presents the reader with a version of what being a woman means to Raab. It is, in Carruthers's terms, one of her attempts at "imagining women." This imagining, counter to Carruthers's view, does not see woman in relation to a man, or even to another woman (283). The primary relationship outlined in this poem is with God, described through nature in terms that are, for Raab, unusually spare. The poem carries no hint of another human being beyond that embodied in the impersonal reference to Adam and his rib.[45]

In its deep sense of acceptance of the divine, this poem echoes the "Prayer" Raab embedded in *The Notebook of Hell*:

> My God, receive my soul which rises to You—You have known it from the time I came forth from my mother, from the time I used to awaken at night and go out to the garden to see Your miracles, to see the eucalyptuses standing in the silence, to see how they move slightly, as though You had blown into them—to see the dewdrops on the lilies—and the moonbeams shattering against them into splinters recoiling from Your spirit which passes over my head, You hovered in space over my head, I felt You with all my being—Remember this for me—Gather me up in Your hand and I will not fear—You to Whom the truth is known—.[46]

In addition to the development of a relationship with God, Raab describes in this poem her positive evaluation of womanhood and, in so doing, subtly points at places where traditional Jewish views merit revision. She repeatedly confronts established concepts and, through her use of language, counters her readers' expectations. She also elaborates her view of the significance of poetry. It is both "Woman's Song" and a poem which gives us rich insight into Raab's poetry.

NOTES

1. An extensive treatment of these four women Hebrew poets, who started publishing between 1920 and 1922, is to be found in Miron's article "Founding Mothers, Stepsisters" (1989, 1 and 1990, 2). A section of that article in translation appears in this volume. Miron addresses a number of factors that contributed both to the absence of women in the earlier period and to their sudden emergence. The contrast between the relatively easy *entrée* afforded women novelists and the obstacles women poets faced is also complicated by the view of poetry as a holy calling and the consequent connection between the priest and the poet. In this connection, see Gilbert and Gubar (1979, xxi). Gilbert and Gubar also point to the expectation that English poets be immersed in classical poetry as a factor which reduces opportunities for women. As Miron indicates, this phenomenon is, of course, paralleled in Hebrew literature.

2. Esther Raab provided many insights into her childhood home life to interviewers. A series of articles by Be'er, from which I quote in this essay, interweaves a number of these. For providing me with them and a great deal other material about Esther Raab, I am deeply grateful to her nephew, Ehud Ben-Ezer.

3. "Only when we were older did we speak Hebrew. . . . Certainly, in school [kindergarten], when it was founded, we spoke Hebrew." The context makes it clear that even at an early age Raab knew more Hebrew than the teacher, for she mocked

the teacher's errors (Dor, 1971). Unless otherwise indicated, translations of texts that are not biblical are mine. Biblical translations are from the Jewish Publication Society translation.

4. It is of note that of the four poets Miron considers together (1989,1:41), Raab was the only one whose works were not published in the influential periodical *Hatekufah*.

5. Miron characterizes the four "founding mothers" as no less the products of revolution than such male counterparts as Avraham Shlonsky and Uri Tsvi Greenberg. He further posits that Rahel and Elisheva constitute the more conservative wing among the four women poets; Raab and Bat-Miriam, the more radical (1: 36, 58; 2: 176-177).

6. Raab's first book, *Thistles*, appeared in 1930; her second, *Poems of Esther Raab*, in 1964. Initially, one reason for the silence may have been the death of her beloved husband, Isaac Green, in 1930, shortly before the publication of *Thistles*. She later wrote of his death: "Ten years was the number of this life of friendship and serenity [their marriage], and suddenly he [Isaac] went and I was as though I were not widowed but orphaned. . . . I felt great loneliness, as though I had been uprooted from fertile land [and transplanted in] to an empty desert of sand—and the situation had a serious impact on me, I did not write, I did not publish for three years, I was frozen (1990)." I suspect that the flawed syntax is a reflection of the emotional toll of writing about her husband's death. But there is no reason given for her more protracted silence.

7. In an interview with Moshe Dor in 1971, Raab mentions that she published her first poem in Glickson's *Haʾarets* and that she also published in Asher Barash's *Heidim*. When the "avant-garde" movement of Avraham Shlonsky, Eliezer Steinman and Yizhak Norman started, she was involved in *Ketuvim* and *Turim*. Writers associated with many of the literary groups active at the time frequented her home in Tel Aviv.

8. The text is from Raab (1988, 176).

9. Translation by Harold Schimmel, from his unpublished manuscript "Poems of Esther Raab."

10. Translation by Elchanan Indelman, published in *Lamishpaḥa*.

11. While this article attempts to draw the classical distinction between poet and poetic persona, it is not always reasonable to do so. In discussing contemporary poetry by women, Alicia Suskin Ostriker pithily challenges the conventional wisdom: "For most of the poems in this book, academic distinctions between the self and what we in the classroom call the 'persona' move to the vanishing point. When a woman poet today says 'I,' she is likely to mean herself, as intensely as her imagination and verbal skills permit, much as Wordsworth or Keats did, or Blake, or Milton, or John Donne of the Holy Sonnets, before Eliot's 'extinction of personality' became the mandatory twentieth-century initiation ritual for young American poets and before the death of the author became a popular critical fiction" (1986, 12).

12. This has been my experience in teaching the poem in both university and adult-education settings.

13. Because there is no indefinite article in Hebrew, either Indelman's translation, "A Woman's Song," or Schimmel's, "Woman's Song," could be correct. My sense is that the latter is more likely. The title of this paper uses "A Woman's Song" because it

is closer to the topic of the paper which deals not with women's poetry in general, but with the poetry of a specific woman.

14 For an instructive discussion of a feminist critic's rejection of a woman's work because she instinctively rejects its views of women's experience, see Juhasz (1977, 119-126).

15. This is the way in which Shoham, (1982, 46) correctly, I believe, understands the relationship between the vine (*gefen*) and the earth (*adamah*) in Raab's poem "Portrait of a Woman."

16. Shoham quotes a sentence in which Raab refers to herself as *adam* (1982, 46).

17. I am indebted to Rebecca Jacobs for having pointed out to me the echo in this line from the prayer "*Asher yatsar.*" This blessing, which praises God for having "formed man [*adam*] in wisdom and having created in him many passages and vessels" (lit., orifices, orifices, hollows, hollows; in Hebrew, *nekavim, nekavim, halulim, halulim*) is particularly apt as a subtext. Like Raab's poem, it uses both the term *adam*, human, and the root *b.r.a.* to create *ex nihilo*, which concludes the poem. Further, *n.k.v.*, the root of the word *nekavim*, used in the prayer to mean orifices, is also the root of *nekeivah* which means female. Standard Hebrew text, here cited with the quoted translation in Hertz (10-11). The literal translation is mine.

18. For example, *Ta'anit* 28a.

19. One might reasonably argue that the same binary opposition with a link between them is embodied in the *adam, adamah,* and *tsela'* nexus of lines 2 and 3.

20. According to *Pirkê de Rabbi Eliezer*, the reward of the Israelite women who refused to cooperate in the building of the Golden Calf is that in the world to come they "are destined to be renewed like the New Moons" (1916, p. 352).

21. R. Nahora'i is quoted in the *Mekhilta* (*Bo*, 12: 41-42) as putting this verse from Ezekiel together with Exod. 1:7 and deducing that the Israelite women in Egypt bore sextuplets (Goldschmidt, 1960, 21-42).

22. The only other reference to torn clouds is in "A Strange City," where Raab writes: "On the roofs/Antenna-forks—/Stirring torn clouds" (1988, 176).

23. While one may argue that silk has many uses in women's fashion, I would maintain that in this context it is a not terribly veiled reference to sexuality. In his article on the women Hebrew poets of the 1920s, Miron says that Raab and Bat-Miriam were the ones who dared introduce female sexuality into Hebrew poetry (2: 162).

24. The letter *vav* added at the beginning of a Hebrew word may have one of a number of meanings. The most common is "and". Note that both Indelman and Schimmel, in their translations, interpret this *vav* as meaning "and." I feel that "but" is preferable.

25. Indelman and Schimmel avoid, in different ways, the ambiguity of the word "*gedolah*" in this context, translating it as "grown" and "big,"respectively.

26. Rabbi Matityah, the son of Heresh, said, "Be rather a tail to lions than a head to foxes." (*Ethics of the Fathers*, 4:20; Hertz, 677). Raab here locates her poetic persona in accordance with that counsel; she enjoys the small.

27. Having taught this poem in various contexts over the past two or three years, I am struck by the frequency with which adult readers, many of whom are not particularly *au courant* in feminist theory, point to what they consider to be the problem of the small, even diminishing, stature of this poem's narrator.

28. Interestingly, Ratok states, virtually as a given, that one of the goals of the feminist tradition in poetry is "breaking down the lofty image of poetry [*shevirat hatadmit hashemaymit beshirah*]" (62). In a diary entry written in 1910, Raab describes herself as quite depressed, unable to accomplish what she wants to do. Trying to encourage herself to study, she writes: "Yes, you must work, for you were created for great things!" (Hayardenit [Raab], 1981, 47).

29. The story of her being forced to leave the school because of the coeducational classes instituted by David Hayyun is quoted by Shoham (1982, 52). It is interesting that her father had no problem teaching her the "manly" arts of horseback riding, swimming, and shooting (Raab, 1983, 45). This lends credence to the theory of her nephew, Ehud Ben-Ezer (44), that Raab's father (his grandfather) actually pulled her out of school for financial reasons, because of the heavy load of debt he was carrying during that period. As a proud man, he could not concede failure and so used this plausible excuse instead.

30. "Blessed art thou, O Lord our God, King of the universe, who hast not made me a woman" (*Barukh atah Adonai Eloheinu Melekh ha'olam shelo 'asani ishah*) is the blessing recited by men. "Blessed art thou, O Lord our God, King of the universe, who hast made me according to thy [lit., His] will" (*Barukh atah Adonai Eloheinu Melekh ha'olam she'asani kirtsono*) is the blessing recited by women (Hertz, 20).

31. "*And the Lord God built the rib,* which teaches that the Holy One, blessed be He, endowed the woman with more understanding than the man" (*Niddah* 45b, in *Seder Tohorot*; Slotki, 315). The basis for this rabbinic comment is the unusual choice of the word "*vayiven*" (he built) in Genesis. The rabbis connected that root *b.n.h.* with the similar root *b.y.n.*, which means "understand."

32. Unfortunately, neither Schimmel nor Indelman conveys this shift in person in his translations.

33. It is interesting to note that Zelda, a religious poet, often keeps the religious theme of a poem hidden until the very end, when a reference to God comes as a surprise and infuses the poem with new meaning (Bar Yosef, 1988, 136-137).

34. In "Sea Songs," Raab uses a theme similar to that of "Woman's Song," but there the narrator describes herself as "motionless, voiceless" (1988, 160). In an autobiographical story about being confined one night to the cellar as a punishment (1983, 76), Raab describes her voice in loud and penetrating terms as suffusing the whole space.

> "I cried for a long time, I sobbed until my strength was gone and I became silent; and suddenly, without paying any attention to it, my foot struck a barrel and it emitted a soft sound, I touched it again, and I began humming softly, to myself, what a sweet tune rose from within my throat, from within my chest, from my whole being. I took off my sandal and began to bang with it on the barrel, and I sang something unknown, something that I had never heard, that suddenly arose, warm and resonant . . . . As I dared to raise my voice more and more—so I felt that I was approaching the great pardon, that my voice is heard on high, in the upper reaches of the house. The cellar was filled with the sound of strong and loud singing. . . .

35. It is noteworthy that each of these poems is connected with a biblical heroine. The first is followed by Miriam's dance (Exod. 15:20); the second glorifies a victory for which two women, Deborah and Jael, were responsible.

36. When asked in 1971 what writers she enjoyed, Raab answered: "'And of ours [Hebrew]—is it at all possible without Bialik, for there is no Hebrew and no Hebrew literature without him?'" (Dor)

37. Her only other use of the word "thin" (*dak*) in connection with sound is her description of a *semamit*, a spider or a lizard, chirping thinly (1988, 204). Miron points to Raab's sensitivity to small changes in smell, temperature, sounds, air currents, and so on in her early poetry (2: 174).

38. The issue of Bialik's dominance in the poetry of the period from 1890 to 1920 has been treated at length by Miron (2: 133-142, pass.).

39. Reading her volume of autobiographical short stories as well as her poetry, one is struck by the extent to which the father is, for Raab, the dominant parent. For example, in writing of her time in Cairo, living with the aunt who was to become her mother-in-law, Raab explains that she related to her aunt better than she did to her mother "because she was my father's sister, and that family connection was in her as well" (1990). It is also telling that Raab is the only one of the four early women poets who uses her father's name as part of her professional identity.

40. It is noteworthy that Raab refers to the German poet Walther Kalle, whom she acknowledges as having had a slight influence on her as a "*lyrikan dak*" (a slight or spare lyricist), using the same word (Shoham, 1977, 84).

41. In her 1926 poem entitled "*Niv*" [Expression], Rahel writes, "I have known countless words—/Therefore will I remain silent." In "*El artsi*" [To My Land] (1926), Rahel expresses the same idea somewhat differently, claiming that she has not sung paeans of heroism and battles to her land, but has brought it only a small gift-offering (52, 58). Schimmel's introduction to *Poems of Esther Raab* includes an instructive comparison between Raab and Dickinson (9-11). Carolyn Heilbrun offers a valuable contrast between Dickinson and Walt Whitman, comparing her "I'm nobody" with his "I celebrate myself and sing myself/And what I assume, you shall assume" (1990, 204).

42. I am grateful to Professor Avraham Holtz for having pointed out this double entendre.

43. Later, Raab freely admitted that she considered François Mauriac her "*maître*" and had been influenced by Rilke, Hofmannstahl and Walther Kalle. She also indicated that in her childhood she was exposed to a great deal of the poetry of J. L. Gordon and Menahem Mendel Dolitzky (Dor).

44. Miron considers the poetry of Raab's first period to be that of female power and posits that it was precisely her unwillingness to appear to be submissive which gave rise to her ensuing long period of silence (2:162, 173-77). In contrast, this poem, written long after the silence had been broken, clearly does not resonate with female dominance.

45. In "*Rondo*," one of the few poems in which Raab uses the word *ishah*, Raab addresses a group of young girls saying: "Let us go up to the goal,/ the goal: to be a woman [*ishah*], mother, beloved." Clearly, for the narrator of that poem, the girl's emerging identity will be defined in terms of others, including males (1988, 40).

46. This prayer echoes the following part of the daily prayer service, referred to as "*Elohai neshamah*"(Hertz,19):

O my God, the soul which Thou gavest me is pure; thou didst create it, thou didst form it, thou didst breathe it into me. Thou preservest it within me, and Thou wilt take it from me, but will restore it unto me hereafter. So long as the soul is within me, I will give thanks unto thee, O Lord my God and God of my fathers, Sovereign of all works, Lord of all souls! Blessed art thou, O Lord, who restorest souls unto the dead".

WORKS CITED

Aberbach, David. 1988. *Bialik.* London: Grove Press.

Bar Yosef, Hamutal. 1988. *ʿAl shirat Zelda* [On Zelda's Poetry]. Hakibbutz Hameuhad.

Beʾer, Hayyim. 1988a. *"Kayits eḥad shalem shamanu zemirim baʾeukalyptusim bePetaḥ Tikvah."* [One Whole Summer We Heard Nightingales in the Eucalyptuses in Petah-Tikvah]. *Devar hashavuʿa* (11 March): 14-15. Part 1 of a series.

———. 1988b. *"Heḥalutsim heiviyu li et Eiropah letokh Malabas, el bein hagémalim veheʾavak"* [The *Halutzim* Brought Europe into Malabas for Me, Among the Camels and the Dust]. *Devar hashavuʿa* (18 March): 10-11. Part 2 of a series begun on 11 March.

———. 1988c. *"Zeh kemo ʿof, kemo eizeh davar sheba mitaḥat lesaf hahakarah kamuvan."* [It Is Like a Bird, Like Something that Comes into the Unconscious of Course]. *Devar hashavuʿa* (25 March): 10-11. Part 3 of a series begun on 11 March.

———. 1988d. *"Ani bodeidah. Beli shirim hayyiti meitah mizman."* [I am lonely. Without Poems I Would Have Died Long Ago]. *Devar hashavuʿa* (1 April): 14-15. Part.4 of a series begun on 11 March.

Ben-Ezer, Ehud. 1981. *"Yoman néurim shel Esther Raab."* [A Youthful Diary of Esther Raab]. *Moznayim* 54,1 (December): 44-46.

Bloom, Harold. 1973. *The Anxiety of Influence.* Oxford: Oxford Univ. Press.

Carruthers, Mary. 1979. "Imagining Women: Notes Toward a Feminist Poetic." *The Massachusetts Review* 20: 281-307.

Dor, Moshe. 1971. *"'Ani giliti et hanof haʾeretsyisraʾeli.'"* [I Discovered the Landscape of the Land of Israel]. *Maʿariv* (3 October): 14.

Gilbert, Sandra M. and Susan Gubar, eds. 1979. *Shakespeare's Sisters: Feminist Essays on Women Poets.* Bloomington and London: Indiana Univ. Press.

Ginzburg, Shimon. 1945. *Bemasekhet hasifrut.* [Regarding Literature]. New York: Committee for the Publication of the Works of Shimon Ginzburg.

Goldschmidt, Daniel. 1960. *Hagadah shel Pesaḥ vetoldoteha.* [The Passover Hagadah: Its Sources and History]. Jerusalem: Mossad Bialik.

Hayardenit [Raab], Esther. 1981. *"Sefer zikhronot lishnat 5670."* Moznayim 54:1 (December): 46-50.

Heilbrun, Carolyn. 1990. *Hamlet's Mother and Other Women.* New York: Columbia Univ. Press.

Hertz, Joseph H., ed. 1948. *The Authorized Daily Prayer Book.* New York: Bloch Publishing Co.

Indelman, Elhanan, trans. 1982. "A Woman's Song." *Lamishpaḥah* 20, 2 (February): 192.

Juhasz, Suzanne. 1977. "The Critic as Feminist: Reflections on Women's Poetry, Feminism, and the Art of Criticism." *Women's Studies* 5: 113-127.

Mekhilta d'Rabbi Ishmaʾel. 1970. Jerusalem: Bamberger et Wahrman.

Miron, Dan. 1989 and 1990. *"Imahot meyasdot, aḥayot ḥorgot."* [Founding Mothers, Stepsisters]. *Alpayim,* 1(June): 29-58; and 2: 120-177.

Ostriker, Alicia Suskin. 1986. *Stealing the Language: The Emergence of Women's Poetry in America.* Boston: Beacon.

Pirkê de Rabbi Eliezer, trans. Gerald Friedlander. 1916. London: Kegan, Paul, Trench, Trubner and Co.

Raab, Esther. 1964. *Shirei Esther Raab.* [The Poems of Esther Raab]. Ramat Gan: Massadah, s.d.

———. 1983. *Gan sheharav.* [A Garden Destroyed]. Tel Aviv: Tarmil.

———. *Kol hashirim.* 1988. [All the Poems]. Ed. Ehud Ben-Ezer. Tel-Aviv: Zemora.

———. 1989a. *"Maḥberet hagehinnom."* [The Notebook of Hell]. Published from the estate by Ehud Ben-Ezer. *Haʾarets* 29 September: D3.

———. 1989b. *"'Al hanof vehaḥai veʿal tekufot hanof beʾErets Yisraʾel."* [On the Landscape and the Living and on the Periods of Landscape in the Land of Israel]. *Devar hashavuʿa* 20 October.

———. 1990. *"BeKahir"* [In Cairo]. *Haʾarets* 3 October.

Rahel [Blaustein]. 1965. *Shirat Raḥel.* [The Poetry of Rahel]. Tel Aviv: Davar.

Ratok, Lilly. 1988. *"Deyokan haʾishah kimshoreret Yisraʾelit."* [Portrait of a Woman as Israeli Poet]. *Moznayim* 62,2-3 (May-June): 56-62.

Schimmel, Harold, trans. *Poems of Esther Raab.* Tel Aviv: Institute for the Translation of Hebrew Literature, ts. s.d.

Shamir, Ziva. 1986. *Hatseratsar meshorer hagalut: ʿal hayesod haʿamami bitsirat Bialik.* [Poet of Poverty: Folkloristic Elements in Bialik's Works]. Tel Aviv: Papyrus.

Shoham, Reuven. 1977. *"Haritmus heḥofshi beshirat Esther Raab."* [Free Rhythm in Esther Raab's Poetry]. *Hasifrut* 24 (January): 84- 91.

———. 1982. *Esther Raab veshiratah.* [Esther Raab and her Poetry]. In *Yalkut Shirim.* [A Collection of Poems]. Tel-Aviv: Yahdav: 7-52; 155-157.

Slotki, Israel W., trans. 1948. *Seder Tohorot.* [The Talmud]. Isadore Epstein. London: Soncino.

Spacks, Patricia Meyer. 1976. Review of *45 Mercy Street* by Anne Sexton. *New York Times Book Review*, 30 May, 4.

Zach, Natan. 1964. *"Nofah shel meshoreret nof"* [The Landscape of a Landscape Poet]. *Amot* 2,4: 86-91.

Yocheved Bat-Miriam:
The Poetic Strength of a Matronym[1]

✑ ILANA PARDES ✑

"'Bat-Miriam' is surely a pseudonym of a male poet."[2] So claimed Yirmiyah Frankel in a review of Bat-Miriam's first collection of poems, *Merahok*, upon its publication in 1932. Later, when it became evident that the bearer of this name was actually a female poet, he apologetically explained his mistake to Dov Sadan, saying that

דרך השירה, העושה בלשון ובצירופיה בתעוזה מפליאה, הוא
שלחש לי, כי הוא דרך גבר בשירה.

> this poetry's way of mastering language and its idioms with
> an astonishing audacity is that which whispered to me that
> this was the way of a man with poetry.

Sadan's apt rebuke was:

אדרבה התעוזה הזאת שאינה משעבדת עצמה למסורת הלשון גם
אם אינה בת־חורין הימנה, היא המוכחת היפך דעתך.

> On the contrary, this audacity which does not enslave itself to
> the tradition of language even if it is not free of it proves the
> opposite of your claim.

In his final remark on this conversation, Sadan reaffirms his original response as a young critic:

ולפי שבינתיים קניתי לי ידיעה בשירתנו המודרנית, שלא
היתה בי בימי קריאת מחזור "מרחוק", ונאבקתי, על פי
תכונתי והשקפתי, לאמונה באשה וברוחה הגואלת — והכוונה
אינה לסונטית או פוזמק כחול, אלא בפירוש למשוררת — לא
חסרתי ואיני חסר גם עתה ראיות לכך.

- 39 -

> And since in the meantime I have acquired some knowledge of
> our modern poetry, which I did not have when I first read
> *Meraḥok,* and I struggled, in accordance with my character and
> perception, to believe in woman and her redeeming soul - and
> I do not mean savantes or bluestockings but rather a poetess - I
> did not lack then and I do not lack now proof of that.

Let us first examine Frankel's observations. The matronym "Bat-Miriam," literally the daughter of Miriam, is necessarily a pseudonym, and in this respect Frankel is right. It isn't the sort of name that is passed down within a patrilineal naming system. While patronyms with the word *ben* (son) as prefix are common Hebrew surnames, matronyms are rare and nontransferable. The name Miriam Ben-David, for example, is as banal as Mary John*son*, but a name such as David Bat-Miriam, whose English equivalent would be David Miriamdaughter, is unheard of. But how could Frankel have attributed a matro-pseudonym that is preceded by a feminine proper name to a male poet? It is the forcefulness of Bat-Miriam's work which misled him, he claims, implying that feminine writing is normally submissive and gentle.

Sadan's critique, albeit brief, of conventional assumptions concerning writing and sexual difference is wonderful. Mocking Frankel's perception of "the way of a man with poetry" (a phrase with overtones of sexual dominance, echoing Prov. 30:19—the "way of a man with a maid"), he defines the audacity of Bat-Miriam's work as *necessarily* feminine, suggesting that no man would have dared to write in such a manner.

But what is poetic strength, and what makes it feminine? Poetic strength is the unmistakable specialty of Harold Bloom. In *A Map of Misreading*, Bloom argues that "poetic strength comes only from a triumphant wrestling with the greatest of the dead and from an even more triumphant solipsism" (1975, 9). He goes on to explain that a strong poet is one who engages in an Oedipal struggle with a ghostly literary father, for his "deepest desire is to be an influence, rather than to be influenced." But even in the strongest of poets, "the anxiety of having been formed by influence still persists" (12-13). As Sandra Gilbert and Susan Gubar point out in *The Madwoman in the Attic*, Bloom's male-oriented psycholiterary model, with its focus on the father-son dyad, is inapplicable to the experience of the female poet. Having to deal with precursors who are exclusively male and therefore different from her, she experiences an anxiety that is more primary than the Bloomian "anxiety of influence." Gilbert and Gubar (1979, 49) call this anxiety "the anxiety of authorship." The female poet, they suggest, confronts a literary past in which women hardly participate, in which writing is primarily a male prerogative, and thus her anxiety "is a radical fear that she cannot create, that because she can never become a 'precursor' the act of writing will isolate and destroy her" (ibid.). How, then, does a female poet acquire strength?

Through a rereading of Bat-Miriam's matronym, I will argue that unlike the male strong poet who struggles to send his forefather back to hell (or heaven), the strong female poet is one who is capable of raising the dead, or rather of raising a foremother. Virginia Woolf raises Shakespeare's sister, Sylvia Plath resurrects Lady Lazarus out of the ashes; and Bat-Miriam, I would suggest, derives her strength from conjuring up the name of Miriam the prophetess's and reconstructing a matrilineal poetic/prophetic tradition whose beginnings lie in the prophetess's ardent singing of the Song of the Sea (Exod. 15:20). The evocation of the name and song of the biblical Miriam is beautifully depicted in "*Kifsukim hayamim*" [Like Verses, the Days], one of Bat-Miriam's early poems from *Meraḥok*:

"כִּפְסוּקִים הַיָּמִים"

וְנִשְׁמַע לִי: עוֹלֶה וְחוֹזֵר וְנִשְׁנֶה
שְׁמִי שָׁעוֹד רָעַד עַל גַּלֵּי מֵי שָׁחוֹר.
שְׁחוֹרִים הֵם פָּנַי, כְּבוּאָה רְחוֹקָה
נִשְׁתַּיְּרָה מִדּוֹרוֹת חֲרֵדָה בַּיְאוֹר.

וְנִרְמֶה: הִנֵּה אַשְׁלִיכָה אֶת יָדִי
וְאֶקְשֹׁר הַמָּחוֹל בְּעוּגָב וָגִיל,
תִּתְעוֹרֵר, תִּתְלַקַּח וְתַעַן לִקְרָאתִי
שִׁירַת־יָם־קְדוּמִים שֶׁנָּגְזוּ בַּגְּוִיל...

And it harkens to me: my name rises time and again
still shaking upon the waves of black water
black is my face, a distant reflection,
a remnant from way back, tremulous in the Nile.

And it seems: Here I will throw my hands
and launch the dance with pipe and joy
an ancient apocryphal sea song hidden in parchment
will awaken, will flare up and answer me . . .

(1972, 77)

But there is more. When Yocheved Bat-Miriam, née Zhelezniak, chooses to call herself the daughter of Miriam, she not only raises a female precursor but also commemorates her biological mother, who was indeed called Miriam.[3] Bat-Miriam's choice of a name, then, needs to be seen both as a concrete challenge to the patrilineal naming system and as a critique of a culture in which literary tradition, like names, is passed down from father to son.

It would be misleading to suggest that the male poet has no need to discover admirable literary forefathers or that Bloom's model needn't be somewhat modified even with respect to the father-son dyad. (His de-idealization of the so-called Western perception of tradition somewhat misreads Freud's depiction of the ambivalence which marks the son's relation to the father.) In modern Hebrew literature in particular, due to the unusual circumstances of its emergence, the male poet surely has had to raise the dead. The difference has to do with the fact that for the modern Hebrew female poet, formulating tradition, or rather formulating a female literary past, is far more urgent and far more difficult: the dead haven't quite been born yet. Bat-Miriam's poem *"Kifsukim hayamim"* makes this point clear, for it depicts the reflection of the biblical Miriam, which floats upon the black waves of the Nile, as a dim and distant one. Similarly, the work of the prophetess is almost invisible: it is "an ancient apocryphal sea song hidden in parchment" (*shirat yam kedumim sheganzu bagevil*). If Bat-Miriam is a strong poet it is precisely because she manages to "kindle" the remnants of her foremother's work, calling into question the male criteria of the canon.

Let me add that, unlike Bloom, I do not perceive the word "strong" as synonymous with the center of the canon. Although Bat-Miriam received some of the most prestigious Israeli literary prizes, she was a rather marginal member of the Hebrew *Moderna* (or Palestinian Generation). Her lack of popularity may be, in part, attributed to the cryptic and dense character of her symbolist poems. Few critics—with the notable exception of Ruth Kartun-Blum and Dan Miron—have attempted to analyze her idiosyncratic diction, elliptic syntax, and esoteric references.

I would suggest, however, that the patriarchal aesthetic presuppositions made explicit in Frankel's review and held by far too many readers of Hebrew poetry are another crucial factor accounting for the lack of interest in her work. Even Avraham Shlonsky, the revolutionary founder and spokesperson of this literary circle, is not free of such stereotypical assumptions. Under the influence of the Russian revolution, he may provocatively call for the abolition of the traditional sex roles, yet his perception of sexual liberation in a literary context is not as radical as it sounds. In a manifesto against the *melitsah* (high-flown rhetorical style) Shlonsky (1973a, 154) proclaims:

המילה נכנעת, מוחלת על כבודה. המילה אינה רוצה לצאת
לחפשי: אהבתי את אדוני! ולכן רצעו את אזניה במרצע אל
המזוזה... רואה אני: המליצה השחילה חוט אפור בחורי
אזניהן הרצועות של מילים-שפחות... המילה (בשלטון
המליצה של הלשון) – כאשה (בשלטון הפטריארכלי של
החברה) אינה בת-חורין: ברשות בעלה היא תלויה וסמוכה
על שולחנו... מרדנו: "אהבה חופשיה"! "נישואין
אזרחיים"!... – מה לי אבא? מי לי אבא? יש לי משלי
רב...

> The word surrenders, forgoing her honor. The word does not
> want to be free: I love my master! Therefore pierce her ears
> with an awl to the *mezuzah*. . . I see: the *melitsah* put a grey
> thread through the pierced ears of the (female) slave words. . .
> The word (under the rule of the *melitsah*) - like woman (under
> the patriarchal rule of society) is not free: she is dependent on
> her husband. . .We rebelled: "free love!" "civil marriage!"What
> is a father? Who needs a father? I have plenty of my own. . .

Note that in Shlonsky's scenario of literary/sexual liberation, the
word/woman is liberated despite her tendency or need to worship her
master. Lacking the revolutionary drive or consciousness, the
woman/word must be, paradoxically, forced to be free. Consider
another passage from a manifesto entitled *"Ra'ananut"* (Freshness)
(1973b, 155):

הזוכרים אתם את פיגסוב? רצה הלה להוציא פעם מפיה
הקוקטי של האשה את הקול הפשוט, הטבעי, מה עשה? התגנב
מאחורי גבה ובכול עץ – הך על ראשה! וכשפרצה זעקה
גדולה מפי ההמומה והכואבת, ידע: הנה הקול הטבעי!
זהו! יותר מדי מן בחינת נוקבא יש בה בספרות וביחוד
בשירה.

> Do you remember Pigasov? Once he wanted to make the
> coquette's mouth emit a simple voice, the natural one. What
> did he do? He sneaked behind her back and with a block of
> wood—he struck her head! And when a great cry burst out of
> the mouth of the shocked sufferer, he knew: this was the
> natural voice!

> That's it! There is too much of the feminine in literature and in
> poetry in particular. . . .

For Shlonsky, as this striking anecdote makes clear, literary revolu-
tions must involve a victory of masculine writing over the inferior, inau-
thentic feminine use of language. The depiction of the blow to the
woman's head is metaphorical, but it may also express the poet's discon-

tent with the fact that poetry is the preferred genre among women writing in Hebrew. In any case, both quotations ignore the possibility of a different mode of rebellion—a feminine one. Bat-Miriam, I would suggest, could not have been a central figure in a generation whose founder's definition of poetic strength is as male-oriented as Bloom's.[4]

I. Reconstructing Miriam

In what follows, I further examine Bat-Miriam's matronym and poetic strength through a close reading of "Miriam," the one poem Bat-Miriam wholly devotes to her foremother. I regard the poem as a later expansion (it was first published in 1939) of the stanzas quoted above from *"Kifsukim hayamim."* Two questions are of special interest in my reading: How does Bat-Miriam use the biblical portrait of Miriam in reconstructing her foremother? What characterizes this literary mother-daughter relationship?

Before exploring these questions, I would like to stress that my focus on the relation of Bat-Miriam to the biblical Miriam needn't imply that the prophetess is the only female precursor to be raised in Bat-Miriam's work. Much like Rahel Blaustein and Saul Tschernihovsky, Bat-Miriam depicts a variety of biblical figures[5] but has a special relation to the one biblical character whose name she bears. To put it differently, Bat-Miriam's primary identification is with Miriam, but this does not mean that she has no other "substitute mothers," not to mention nontraceable female precursors.[6] As for the unidentified foremothers, I wholly agree with Sadan's (1977, 145) laudatory comment on the occasion of Bat-Miriam's reception of the Hayyim Greenberg Prize:

ומי ישער כמה געגועי דורות, כיסופי נערות ונשים לארשת
לירית, נגאלו בשירה הזאת. ואין צורך לומר, כי מתן
גאולה זה וכזה היא לה זכיה גדולה, אם לא הגדולה
בזכיותיה, ביחוד אם נתן אל לבנו על דבר הפלא, כי מתוך
שירתה דוברות אמהות ואחיות, והיא, המשוררת, אינה
יוצאת מכלל עצמה, ונתונה כל־כולה לעצמה, — היא לשירתה
ושירתה לה.

Who can conceive how many yearnings of generations, longings of maidens and women for lyrical expression, were redeemed in this poetry. Needless to say, conferring a redemption of this sort is her great achievement, if not the greatest, especially if we bear in mind the miracle, that from her poetry mothers and sisters speak, and yet she, the poetess, does not go beyond herself, she remains all enclosed within herself, she for her poetry; her poetry for her .

מִרְיָם

עָמְדָה מוּל הַסּוּף וְהַגֹּמֶא
וְנָשְׁמָה כּוֹכָבִים וּמִדְבָּר.
עֵין אַפִּיס עֲגֻלָה וְרוֹדֶמֶת
הֵצִיפָה כְּחוֹלָהּ הַמֻּזְהָר

עַל הַחוֹל, עַל אָוְשָׁתוֹ הַזּוֹהֶבֶת,
עַל חִיּוּךְ בַּת מְלָכִים הַנִּלְאָט,
עַל שִׂיחַ חַרְטֻמִּים עֲלֵי אֶבֶן
וְזֶמֶר הֵיכָלִים הַמִּצְעָד.

מִנֶּגֶד, בְּדֶשֶׁן הַזֵּכֶר,
כִּשְׁפִיפוֹן בְּתַאֲוַת עוֹלָם,
אֻמְצָה גֹשֶׁן הַנִּדְרֶכֶת
דִּמְיוֹן שְׁבָטִים מְעֻמְעָם.

— אִתָּךְ, אִתָּךְ בַּסְעָר
גוּפֵךְ מִשְׁתַּרְבֵּב כָּתֹף,
אִתָּךְ בִּמְחוֹלֵךְ מוּל לַהַט
רֵיחַ חוֹלוֹת וְאֵין־סוֹף,

— אֲסַפֵּר מְקַנְּאָה וּמְצֹרַעַת,
אֲסַפֵּר מַלִּינָה עַל עַצְמִי.
הִשְׁבַּעְתִּיךְ בִּנְזִירוּתֵךְ לֹא נִכְנַעַת,
בִּבְדִידוּתֵךְ הַזְּהוּרָה נָא חַיִּי!

עָמְדָה מֵהַלַּחַשׁ מְנָדְנֶדֶת
כְּמַלְבֵּן פַּעֲמֵי הַגַּל.
נָחֲנָה עַל הַתִּינוֹק כְּנֶדֶר,
כִּצּוּ,

כִּפְדוּת,

כְּגוֹרָל.

Miriam

(1)   She stood facing the reeds and papyrus
       and breathed in stars and desert.
       The round sleeping eye of Apis
       flooded its glimmered blue

(5)   Upon the sand, on its goldening rustle,
       upon the smile of a princess hidden,
       upon a dialogue of hieroglyphs on stone
       and a marched palace song.

(9)   At a distance, in the fertilizer of memory,
       like a horned viper in everlasting desire,
       trodden Goshen adopted
       a dim tribal imagination.

(13)   —With you, with you in the storm
        your body protruding as a timbrel,
        with you in your dance facing fervor
        smell of dunes and infinity,

(17)   —I shall tell jealous and leprous,
        I shall tell complaining of myself.
        I adjure you in your monasticism not surrendering,
        In your resplendent isolation do live!

(21)   She stood rocked by the spell
        as by the white of the wave's beats.
        She bent over the baby as a vow,
        as decree,

                        as redemption,

                                as fate.
                            (1972, 179-180)

The title of the poem—"Miriam"—serves as an organizing allusion and is immediately accompanied by two markers[7] in the first line—*gomeh* and *suf* (reeds and papyrus). These words invoke the biblical scene in which Miriam stands at a distance, watching over her brother's ark as it lies afloat on the Nile, hidden among reeds (Exod. 2:4). Bat-Miriam's reconstruction of Miriam's first appearance in the Bible is surely different from the canonical one. While in Exod. 2:4 Miriam's name is not mentioned (she is defined as Moses' sister), here Moses is absent, and Miriam becomes the focus of attention. From mere babysitter she is raised to the position of a focalizer, the subject whose perspective the speaker seems to adopt. Through Miriam's eyes, we are taken into a mysterious pagan Egyptian setting which is nonexistent in the biblical account of this scene.

One of the influential participants in this enigmatic setting is Apis, an Egyptian bull deity. Apis was originally a form of the Nile god Hapi and, like other bull deities in Egypt, he was probably at first a fertility god. Later, he became associated with Ptah, the paramount deity of Memphis, as well as with Osiris, the god of the underworld. Interestingly, Apis was renowned for his oracular capacity. His priests drew omens from his behavior. Thus, for example, "when the bull licked the garments of the celebrated Eudoxus of Cnidus, this signified the astronomer's approaching death; a like fate was predicted to Germanicus when it refused to eat at his hand" (Spence, 1915, 286).

Miriam's prophetic work, Bat-Miriam seems to suggest, is not as monotheistic as one would assume from the little that is said about it in the Bible. The prophetess's gazing at the magical "round sleeping eye of

Apis" (line 3) makes her analogous to the pagan priests of Memphis who followed the bull's movements with great care. This is by no means an attempt to ridicule Miriam's capacity. On the contrary, for a symbolist such as Bat-Miriam, magic, or the quest for a dreamy reality that transcends the phenomenal world, is an essential ingredient of poetry. By linking Miriam to such a deity, Bat-Miriam thus attempts to raise a foremother who could serve as a prototype of a female symbolist.

Apis's sleeping eye is precisely the sort of eye a symbolist must follow. Transcending its confines (note the way the enjambment from line 4 to the second stanza accentuates this overflow), Apis's eye floods "its glimmered blue/ Upon the sand. . . upon the smile of a princess. . .upon a dialogue of hieroglyphs . . . and a marched palace song" (lines 4-8). Furthermore, like a proper symbolist eye, it has the ability to blur the demarcation between past and present, living and dead, animate and inanimate, sights and sounds. Under Apis's ocular spell, the sand acquires a "goldening rustle," carved hieroglyphs can converse, and the whispered/hidden smile of the Egyptian princess (the only biblical element in this stanza) blends with the objects surrounding it.[8]

But perhaps no bull's eye attracts Miriam's attention. That is, perhaps her gaze never left the Nile and the reeds. Apis's original role as a Nile god and the double meaning of the word ʿayin (it means both eye and spring), may suggest that Miriam derives her prophetic "symbolist" insights from watching the flooding of Apis's spring, or rather from following the actual flooding of the Nile. If, so far, my reading has suggested that the sleeping is literal and the flooding figurative, now I am proposing that the opposite reading, if less apparent, is also possible.

The latter reading reinforces the notion that Bat-Miriam's reconstruction of this scene by the Nile relies on the midrashic depiction of Miriam's miraculous well. According to *Bamidbar Rabbah* I.2, Miriam's well accompanied the Children of Israel in their wanderings in the desert, rolling over mountains and valleys and, most important, producing water upon the people's singing: "Rise up, O well!"[9] Bat-Miriam thus provocatively presents Apis's spring as the pagan model of Miriam's well and, metaphorically, as the source of her work.

The blending of Hebrew and Egyptian traditions becomes the explicit topic of the third stanza. Such cultural intermingling is depicted as a fertility ritual, perhaps an outcome of the flooding of Apis's eye/spring. The feminine element in this ritual is associated with Goshen (a feminine noun in Hebrew)—the fertile region on the eastern delta of the Nile inhabited by the Israelites. The lascivious "horned viper" and the "fertilizer of memory" (*deshen hazekher*)—note that the word "memory" (*zekher*) and the word "male" (*zakhar*) share the same root in Hebrew—represent the masculine element. Just as the agricultural prosperity of Goshen depends on the flooding of the Nile so, Bat-Miriam seems to suggest, on the cultural level, the development of the Hebrew imagination depends on its capacity to adopt stimulating Egyptian traditions.

II. Oh (M)other!

The turning point, which involves a transition from third person to second person, takes place in the fourth stanza. As if unable to remain a mere observer, the female speaker appears and addresses Miriam, her foremother, as she joins her ardent dance. The repetition of *"itakh, itakh"* (with you, with you) accentuates the excitement which this sudden encounter creates. Although Miriam's name isn't mentioned, the presence of a timbrel seems to disclose the identity of the female addressee; that is, it serves as a marker which leads us to the biblical description of Miriam's singing of the Song of the Sea in Exodus 15: "And Miriam the prophetess, the sister of Aaron, took a timbrel in her hand; and all the women went out after her with timbrels and dances. And Miriam sang unto them. . . . "(lines 20-21).[10] Bat-Miriam evokes this scene by means of a simile which is based on a metonymy—"your body protruding as a timbrel." Miriam's body becomes the timbrel she is holding, the timbrel which in modern Hebrew is named after her.[11] The song, the body, and the timbrel become one, just as the speaker and the addressee merge, in this erotic transcendental dance "facing fervor."

Following Exodus, Bat-Miriam thus shapes a feminine ritual in which women *converse* as they sing, dance, and play. In "Miriam," however, the exchange between the speaker and her foremother hovers between external and internal modes of communication; it is a dramatized internal dialogue in which, to return to Sadan's description of such "miraculous" phenomena, "mothers and sisters speak, and yet, she, the poetess, does not go beyond herself." In *A Map of Misreading*, Bloom (19) analyzes a similar dialogue:

> But who, what is the poetic father? The voice of the other, of the *daimon*, is always speaking in one; the voice that cannot die because already it has survived death . . . A poet, I argue in consequence, is not so much a man speaking to men as a man rebelling against being spoken to by a dead man (the precursor) outrageously more alive than himself.

In Bat-Miriam's case, however, we find no rage or frustration vis-à-vis a demonic precursor who has the nerve to be alive and kicking in his descendant's work. On the contrary, the encounter with the (m)other, which involves the oscillation of *both* between the living and the dead, is an inspiring sensual exchange. Instead of struggling with an omnipresent intruder, the speaker attempts to contact a distant unknown relative, beyond reach or, as Bat-Miriam would have it, to smell the infinite (line 16).

Let me propose another reading of the fourth stanza. Bearing in mind that the voices in this dialogue are unidentified and that the boundaries between the (m)other and her descendant (like all boundaries in this poem) are somewhat blurred, this fervid address could be perceived as Miriam's. Perhaps she arises from the dead and discovers, with excitement, that her follower's work is the mirror image of her own. Or perhaps she comes back to life to join her daughter's dance precisely because it is a clear continuation of her own. This alternative reading is compatible with *"Kifsukim hayamim,"* where the speaker tries to revive her foremother's song by singing and playing the way her precursor would: "Here I will throw my hands/ and launch the dance with pipe and joy/ an ancient apocryphal sea song hidden in parchment/ will flare up and answer me . . . "

At this climactic point of the poem it becomes clear that Miriam's polytheistic tendencies may be traced back to the Bible itself. Bat-Miriam seems to suggest that Miriam's dance/song/music/ritual is as pagan as the "marched palace/shrine song" (*zemer heikhalim hamuts°ad*) that Apis's eye flooded.

It is noteworthy that the pagan resonance of the Song of the Sea has indeed been acknowledged by various biblical scholars. Thus Umberto Cassuto (1951, 78) argues that the Song of the Sea bears a resemblance to ancient pagan myths "appertaining to the revolt of the sea against his Creator in the cosmic beginning, to the rebellion of Rahab, the prince of the sea, and his allies the sea monsters."[12]

By reviving the repressed pagan facets in the Song of the Sea, Bat-Miriam thus tries to retrieve the uncensored ancient "sea song" of her foremother, kindling Miriam's mitigated challenge to the predominant patriarchal-monotheistic discourse of the Bible. While in Exodus we find only traces of paganism—Miriam's singing is, after all, yoked to national and monotheistic interests (God's victory over the Egyptians)—in Bat-Miriam's reconstruction of her foremother's work, the Father's rule is more fully called into question. If the Song of the Sea celebrates the birth

of a nation and the successful deliverance of the Hebrews, the poem
"Miriam" leads us back to the fleshpot, to Egypt and its pagan idols. The
monotheistic revolution of Miriam's brother is undermined. The limits
God set to the sea in Genesis and Exodus collapse.

III. "I Shall Tell Jealous And Leprous"

Moving from the singing in Exodus, Bat-Miriam goes on to capture
Miriam's explicit criticism of Moses in Numbers. To get a better understanding of Bat-Miriam's allusion to this rather unknown incident in line
17 (the markers being "jealous" and "leprous"), it is worthwhile to
analyze Numbers 12 in detail.

12:1 וַתְּדַבֵּר מִרְיָם וְאַהֲרֹן בְּמֹשֶׁה עַל־אֹדוֹת הָאִשָּׁה הַכֻּשִׁית אֲשֶׁר לָקָח
כִּי־אִשָּׁה כֻשִׁית לָקָח:
2 וַיֹּאמְרוּ הֲרַק אַךְ־בְּמֹשֶׁה דִּבֶּר יְהוָה הֲלֹא גַּם־בָּנוּ דִבֵּר וַיִּשְׁמַע יְהוָה:
3 וְהָאִישׁ מֹשֶׁה עָנָו מְאֹד מִכֹּל הָאָדָם אֲשֶׁר עַל־פְּנֵי הָאֲדָמָה:
4 וַיֹּאמֶר יְהוָה פִּתְאֹם אֶל־מֹשֶׁה וְאֶל־אַהֲרֹן וְאֶל־מִרְיָם צְאוּ שְׁלָשְׁתְּכֶם
אֶל־אֹהֶל מוֹעֵד וַיֵּצְאוּ שְׁלָשְׁתָּם:
5 וַיֵּרֶד יְהוָה בְּעַמּוּד עָנָן וַיַּעֲמֹד פֶּתַח הָאֹהֶל וַיִּקְרָא אַהֲרֹן וּמִרְיָם
וַיֵּצְאוּ שְׁנֵיהֶם:
6 וַיֹּאמֶר שִׁמְעוּ־נָא דְבָרָי אִם־יִהְיֶה נְבִיאֲכֶם יְהוָה בַּמַּרְאָה אֵלָיו
אֶתְוַדָּע בַּחֲלוֹם אֲדַבֶּר־בּוֹ:
7 לֹא־כֵן עַבְדִּי מֹשֶׁה בְּכָל־בֵּיתִי נֶאֱמָן הוּא:
8 פֶּה אֶל־פֶּה אֲדַבֶּר־בּוֹ וּמַרְאֶה וְלֹא בְחִידֹת וּתְמֻנַת יְהוָה יַבִּיט
וּמַדּוּעַ לֹא יְרֵאתֶם לְדַבֵּר בְּעַבְדִּי בְמֹשֶׁה:
9 וַיִּחַר־אַף יְהוָה בָּם וַיֵּלַךְ:
10 וְהֶעָנָן סָר מֵעַל הָאֹהֶל וְהִנֵּה מִרְיָם מְצֹרַעַת כַּשָּׁלֶג וַיִּפֶן אַהֲרֹן
אֶל־מִרְיָם וְהִנֵּה מְצֹרָעַת:
11 וַיֹּאמֶר אַהֲרֹן אֶל־מֹשֶׁה בִּי אֲדֹנִי אַל־נָא תָשֵׁת עָלֵינוּ חַטָּאת אֲשֶׁר
נוֹאַלְנוּ וַאֲשֶׁר חָטָאנוּ:
12 אַל־נָא תְהִי כַּמֵּת אֲשֶׁר בְּצֵאתוֹ מֵרֶחֶם אִמּוֹ וַיֵּאָכֵל חֲצִי בְשָׂרוֹ:
13 וַיִּצְעַק מֹשֶׁה אֶל־יְהוָה לֵאמֹר אֵל נָא רְפָא נָא לָהּ:
14 וַיֹּאמֶר יְהוָה אֶל־מֹשֶׁה וְאָבִיהָ יָרֹק יָרַק בְּפָנֶיהָ הֲלֹא תִכָּלֵם שִׁבְעַת
יָמִים תִּסָּגֵר שִׁבְעַת יָמִים מִחוּץ לַמַּחֲנֶה וְאַחַר תֵּאָסֵף:
15 וַתִּסָּגֵר מִרְיָם מִחוּץ לַמַּחֲנֶה שִׁבְעַת יָמִים וְהָעָם לֹא נָסַע
עַד־הֵאָסֵף מִרְיָם:

And Miriam and Aaron spake against Moses because of the
Ethiopian woman whom he had married: for he had married
an Ethiopian woman. And they said, Hath the Lord indeed
spoken only by Moses? hath he not spoken also by us? And
the Lord heard it. (Now the man Moses was very meek, above
all the men which were upon the face of the earth.) And the
Lord spake suddenly unto Moses, and unto Aaron, and unto
Miriam, Come out ye three unto the tabernacle of the congre-

gation. And they three came out. And the Lord came down in the pillar of the cloud, and stood in the door of the tabernacle, and called Aaron and Miriam: and they both came forth. And He said, Hear now my words: If there be a prophet among you, I the Lord will make myself known unto him in a vision, and will speak unto him in a dream. My servant Moses is not so, who is faithful in all mine house. With him will I speak mouth to mouth, even apparently, and not in dark speeches; and the similitude of the Lord shall he behold: wherefore then were ye not afraid to speak against my servant Moses? And the anger of the Lord was kindled against them; and he departed. And the cloud departed from off the tabernacle; and, behold, Miriam became leprous, white as snow: and Aaron looked upon Miriam, and, behold, she was leprous. And Aaron said unto Moses, Alas, my lord, I beseech thee, lay not the sin upon us, wherein we have done foolishly, and wherein we have sinned. Let her not be as one dead, of whom the flesh is half consumed when he cometh out of his mother's womb. And Moses cried unto the Lord, saying, Heal her now, O God, I beseech thee. And the Lord said unto Moses, If her father had but spit in her face, should she not be ashamed seven days? let her be shut out from the camp seven days, and after that let her be received in again. And Miriam was shut out from the camp seven days: and the people journeyed not till Miriam was brought in again.

The jealousy which this episode deals with is evident in the reservations Miriam and Aaron express concerning the special status of Moses' discourse. "Hath the Lord indeed spoken only by Moses?" they protest, calling into question Moses' privileged relationship with the Father. In this drama of sibling rivalry,[13] God reaffirms His favoritism and punishes Miriam for seeking an equal footing with her brother. Exclusion from the canon is not necessarily a female issue, and yet the fact that Miriam alone is struck with leprosy while Aaron is spared makes clear that the Law has even less sympathy for jealous women.

God's punishment of Miriam is strikingly harsh, so much so that Aaron pleads on her behalf: "Let her not be as one dead, of whom the flesh is half consumed when he cometh out of his mother's womb" (Num. 12:12). If Miriam plays a maternal role both in watching over Moses in Exodus 2 and later—on a national level—in leading the women in Exodus 15, the leprosy, as Aaron's simile makes clear, reverses her position: the mother figure of the nation becomes as a child, even a dead child or an aborted fetus, whose flesh is eaten away.

In response to Moses' intercession, God justifies His punishment, reiterating the belittling of Miriam, for now she is compared to a shameful daughter: "And the Lord said unto Moses, If her father had but spit in her face, should she not be ashamed seven days? let her be shut out from the camp seven days" (Num. 12:14). The analogy God draws is quite astounding. Miriam's demand for greater expression seems to be synonymous with lewdness, and leprosy turns out to be the punitive spitting of the Father.

Although Miriam is brought back to the camp after being "shut out" for seven days, we hear nothing from her after this harsh incident. She dies shortly after without saying a word: "And the children of Israel . . . came into the wilderness of Zin in the first month . . . and Miriam died there, and was buried there" (Num.20:1).

Miriam's unsuccessful struggle with the Father is a fine reminder of the different lots of male poets and female poets. Miriam's challenge, unlike that of her brother, involves a critique of patriarchy—the very basis of the Father's rule—and as such it is far more difficult and far more dangerous. Moreover, if we expand on Bloom's family romance and take into consideration the respective struggles of the female poet and male poet with their siblings—that is, with their contemporaries (and in Numbers the struggle with the Father is clearly interconnected with sibling rivalry)—here too Miriam's disadvantages are evident. Aaron's rivalry with Moses is not doomed at the outset. As a man, he has the theoretical chance of being the Father's primary representative. By contrast, "penis envy," Freud's controversial term for the sister's jealousy vis-à-vis her brother (which Luce Irigaray [1985, 56] aptly redefines as "representative of woman's desire to enter into symbolic exchange as a subject"[14]) is, by definition, incurable in patriarchal society. For a woman in Moses' day with the gift of prophecy would have had to be silenced and then buried in the wilderness for daring to demand a central cultural position.[15]

In Bat-Miriam's poem, this complex biblical family drama is radically modified as a hitherto unknown mother-daughter relationship comes to the foreground. Bat-Miriam undoes the Father's punishment by restoring Miriam to her maternal role and "fleshing out" the prophetess's admiring descendant. If it is Miriam who responds to her daughter's address in the fifth stanza, she adjures her follower to turn jealousy and leprosy into a source of power and creativity, which is perhaps the ultimate undoing of the spit of the Father.

> (17) – I shall tell jealous and leprous,
> (18) I shall tell complaining of myself.

(19) I adjure you in your monasticism not surrendering,
(20) In your resplendent isolation do live!

From her experience, Miriam knows only too well that the marginality
of feminine discourse requires a capacity to endure solitude. Bat-Miriam
makes the uniqueness of such solitude conspicuous through the distor-
tion of the cliché "splendid isolation" (*bedidut zoheret*). A "resplendent
isolation" (*bedidut zehurah*) is nothing like the pretentious Romantic solitude so commonly attributed to poets. Rather, it is a disturbing noncanonical isolation which may serve as a source of inspiration only for
those who can avoid surrendering.[16]

Miriam's final words to her daughter (line 20) echo Ezekiel's famous
address to Zion (16:5-6):

לֹא־חָסָה עָלַיִךְ עַיִן לַעֲשׂוֹת לָךְ אַחַת מֵאֵלֶּה
לְחֻמְלָה עָלָיִךְ וַתֻּשְׁלְכִי אֶל־פְּנֵי הַשָּׂדֶה בְּגֹעַל נַפְשֵׁךְ
בְּיוֹם הֻלֶּדֶת אֹתָךְ: וָאֶעֱבֹר עָלַיִךְ וָאֶרְאֵךְ מִתְבּוֹסֶסֶת
בְּדָמָיִךְ וָאֹמַר לָךְ בְּדָמַיִךְ חֲיִי וָאֹמַר לָךְ בְּדָמַיִךְ חֲיִי:

No eye pitied thee, to do any of these unto thee, to have
compassion upon thee; but thou wast cast out in the open
field, to the lothing of thy person, in the day that thou wast
born. And when I passed by thee, and saw thee polluted in
thine own blood, I said unto thee when thou wast in thy blood,
Live; yea, I said unto thee when thou wast in thy blood, Live.

The prophetess seems to encourage her follower to struggle like Zion, to
live in spite of her lonely birth, to attain womanhood in spite of the hardships. In contrast to Ezekiel, however, where the daughter's maturation
takes place, rather problematically, "under the Father's wing," here it is
the mother who assists the daughter.

The foremother Bat-Miriam raises is surely an empowering precursor;
one who can offer her daughter the kind of backing she herself did not
have when struggling with literary male authorities. But here, as before, I
should suggest another reading. It may be the daughter who is giving
the advice in the fifth stanza, adjuring the outcast Miriam to return to life
and struggle so as to empower herself and her leprous/marginal
descendant. In any case, the union of the two enables them to join forces
against the canon's exclusion of feminine discourse.

Note that similar adjuring between women who converse while they
sing appears time and again in the dialogues of the beloved and the
daughters of Jerusalem in the Song of Songs. To give but one example:" I
charge you [הִשְׁבַּעְתִּי], O daughters of Jerusalem, If ye find my beloved,

That ye tell him, I am sick of love" (5:8). Yet while the beloved is love-sick, Miriam's disease is rather "monastic "and unpleasant.

What makes leprosy attractive for Bat-Miriam is not only its capacity to characterize the noncanonical status of the matrilineal tradition she attempts to reconstruct, but also leprosy's metaphorical use in the writings of other members of her generation. Shlonsky, in particular, often uses leprosy as a metaphor for creativity. In fact, one could argue that the fifth stanza alludes to Shlonsky's poem "Tsara'at" [Leprosy]. In "Tsara'at," humanity, struck with leprosy, tries to struggle with this disease in various ways; but, insofar as leprosy is the very core of existence, it remains incurable. The poem ends with the "black amen" of the crow crying: "In your evil-leprosy do live!" (betsara'atkhem hayu)[17] to the suffering masses. Rebelling against the false redemption that religion offers humankind, Shlonsky calls for the uncovering of the morbid Truth: there is no redemption; there is no peace-bearing dove. Accordingly the black crow, with his jarring cry, is the appropriate messenger of Truth. The crow's only advice is to turn leprosy and evil into a source of life. But perhaps a passage from one of Shlonsky's manifestos (written in 1923) would best clarify the implications of this metaphor for him (1973b, 157).

לאליפזים אסור לדבר. אסור בהחלט! אבל איוב לא שתק.
איוב לא יכול היה לשתוק. כי לאיוב "גדול הכאב מאד".
זהו! והמשורר איוב הוא... כי לא את זולתו ישיר המשורר
אלא את עצמו, נגעי עצמו. ומי שלא הוכה בשחין בשרו –
אינו אמן, באשר אינו ה א ד ם, באשר אינו ה כ ו א ב.

> Eliphazes must not speak. Definitely not! But Job was not silent. Job was incapable of remaining silent. Because for Job "pain was immense." That's it! The poet is Job. . . . Because the poet does not sing the suffering of the other, but rather his own afflictions/diseases. And he who is not struck by boils—is not an artist, insofar as he is not *mankind*, insofar as he is not *the sufferer*.

For Shlonsky, the poet, like Job, is the nonconformist who can neither save his skin nor refrain from challenging authority. Boils (which are analogous to leprosy) assure that his writing is about authentic pain and suffering, a cry of the daring outsider. One could argue that Bat-Miriam attempts to develop a feminine model that would be analogous to Job. Miriam, no doubt, is a fine female leper. But there is a significant differ-ence between these two biblical figures. Job is allowed to complain at length—a whole book is named after him—while Miriam's discourse is a marginal, mitigated discourse within the Book of Moses. Miriam, like Job, could not remain silent but, unlike him, she was eventually silenced. Both Shlonsky and Bat-Miriam intensify subversive trends in the Bible[18]; yet, while Shlonsky can rely on a well-established rebel, Bat-Miriam has to reconstruct a model from bits and pieces, and this is precisely what makes her project far more urgent and far more difficult.

IV. The Ark Revisited

In the last stanza which opens, like the first one, with the word ʿamdah (she stood), we return to the opening scene by the Nile; only now a baby, albeit unnamed, is mentioned. It seems as if all that has happened between the first and last stanzas may have been the strange prophetic dream of a spellbound Miriam, facing the fervor of reeds and waves. In any case, mothering this nameless baby is what the prophetess now seems to regard as her "vow," "decree," "redemption," and "fate." Big words. Bat-Miriam allows them to occupy the space of four lines, breaking the strict quadrate strophic structure of the previous stanzas and imitating, visually, the action of bending over a baby. This iconographic message participates in the concretization of the abstract nouns, blurring the distinction between the baby and words, turning motherhood into a metaphor for feminine creativity. Yet, in accordance with the fluidity mentioned above concerning the roles of mother and daughter, this metaphor is not unidirectional. Miriam guards the baby/work and vice versa. Thus it is not surprising that the prophetess does not rock the baby, as one would expect, but rather she herself is magically "rocked" (menudnedet).

V. The National Profession

The final big prophetic words at the end of the poem, especially "redemption," suggest that "Miriam" has more in common with the Song of the Sea than one would initially suspect. In the last stanza it becomes evident that Miriam's national role is essential to the understanding of Bat-Miriam's choice of precursor.[19] The motherly figure in line 20 seems to be concerned not only with the deliverance of the baby/work but also with the redemption of the nation as a whole. What augments this notion is Bat-Miriam's elusive allusion to the midrashic interpretation of Exod. 2:4.

> Why did Miriam stand afar off? Rabbi Amram in the name of Rab said: Because Miriam prophesied, 'My mother is destined to give birth to a son who will save Israel'. . . . This is why it

says: And his sister stood afar off, to know what would be the
outcome of her prophecy (*Shemot Rabbah* I: 22).

In contrast to *Shemot Rabbah*, however, the national redemption Bat-
Miriam's Miriam envisions as she stands by the Nile is only vaguely
related to Moses. Moses' name remains conspicuously absent throughout
the poem. The birth of the nation in "Miriam" is primarily a female
endeavor.

Assuming the role of the national prophet is a temptation no modern
Hebrew poet seems able to resist. Bialik, Uri Tsvi Greenberg, and even
Shlonsky, in his playful treatment of the homonyms "seer" and
"shepherd" (רואה – רועה), have made use of the prophetic calling. Bat-
Miriam, apparently, is not innocent of such desires either. To some
extent, through Miriam, she takes part in the formation of a Zionist pioneer literature, following the exigencies of the period.[20] Her nationalism,
however, is idiosyncratic. After all, Bat-Miriam's exemplary national
prophetess has pagan tendencies and, above all, the projected birth of the
nation in "Miriam" brings about no clear individuation. Egypt and
Zion/Goshen blend in the background, showing no respect for national
borders. Natan Alterman aptly described a similar phenomenon in an
article he wrote in honor of the publication of Bat-Miriam's collected
poems in 1963.

"רכב אש בין הררי תבל", כך עולה ארץ ישראל מן הספר
הזה, אך מהות זו, על אף עוצמת הביטוי האין-שני שהיא
זכתה לו כאן, ועל אף להט הקנאות הקם מתוכה, אינה
נהפכת בכך לכח סגור ומובדל. יחד איתו, ובמקביל לו,
וברגמת מתח ולהט לא פחותות אולי משלו, נמצאות בספר הזה
גם סופות הנהי והזמר והכבלים והדגלים שבשירי רוסיה.
אכן כפילות זו... היא מסימני – החיכר הבולטים ביותר של
משוררי הדור... אך כאן אתה חש את טעמיה של הכפילות
הזאת, לא על דרך הצרימה והדיסונאנס והדגשת הקרעים,
כדרך שזימרוה אחרים. כאן אתה חש... את הטרגיות האחרת,
אולי העמוקה יותר... שבהארמוניה הגורלית, שבה הן
מתמזגות יחד בנפש האחת.

"A chariot of fire among the hills of the world," this is how the
Land of Israel rises from this book, but this essence, despite the
unique form of its expression, and despite its fervent zeal, does
not turn into a closed and isolated power. With it, and parallel
to it. . .the storms of sorrow and singing and fetters and flags
of Russia's poems/songs rise. In fact, such duality. . . is one of
the most conspicuous characteristics of the poets of this
generation'. . . But here you feel this duality not through
jarring dissonance and an emphasis ongaps, as others sang it.

Here you sense. . .a different kind of tragedy, maybe the
deeper one. . . in that fateful harmony, in which the two blend
in one soul. . . .

Just as Bat-Miriam's yearnings for the Land of Israel and for Russia
are not mutually exclusive, so Egypt and Zion do not represent opposi-
tional entities. If in reading the first stanzas of the poem such national
blending seems to contradict the possibility of "Zionism," at the poem's
end one realizes that a different kind of nationalism is at stake, a nationalism that fits no conventional categories.

What makes Bat-Miriam's nationalism even more exceptional is its
refutation of the boundaries between the private and the public.[21] This is
evident not only in the last stanza where the word "redemption" relates
to both spheres. In retrospect, the allusion to Ezekiel in line 20 may be
defined as the initial point where the birth of the daughter/mother/work
is inseparable from the (re)birth of Zion. The fact that Zion is portrayed
in the Bible both as a daughter and as a mother makes "her" wholly
compatible with the fluid mother-daughter bond in this poem. A few
stanzas from Bat-Miriam's poem *"Erets Yisraʾel"* [The Land of Israel] may
clarify the intimacy with which Bat-Miriam relates to the Land of Israel
in her work and to the interchangeability of the roles of mother and
daughter in this respect.

מְבוּכָה, חָזוֹן וָפַחַד
וְהוֹד מְאֻכְזָב, מְדֻלְדָּל.
אַתְּ כְּמוֹתֵךְ רַק זוֹרַחַת
תּוֹחֶלֶת יְאוּשִׁי לֹא נִגְאָל...

מַעְגָּל תּוֹךְ מַעְגָּל מְסֻגֶּרֶת
עוֹנָה מִתְעַקֶּפָה תּוֹךְ עוֹנָה,
אַתְּ עַל פָּנַיִךְ נִקְשֶׁרֶת
וְחָנָה כְּלוֹת-נַפְשִׁי כְּחוּנָה—

וְקוֹרְאָה בְּחֵד לְלֹא דֶרֶךְ.
וְקוֹרְאָה בְּשָׁכוֹל וְאֵימָה,
אָסְפִינִי, סָגְרִינִי נָא בְּתִפְאֶרֶת
כְּנָפֵךְ דַּלָּה עֵירֻמָּה...

עַד אֶמְצָאֵךְ וְאַתְּ בּוֹכָה וְנוֹהֶרֶת
בְּחֵיקִי כְּנָמוּל בָּאוֹרוֹת,
הַפְּשׁוּטָה, הַדַּלָּה וּמְצֹעֶרֶת
עַד לִבְכּוֹת עַל עָנְיֵךְ וְלִבְכּוֹת—

Bewilderment, prophecy and fear
and a disappointed, impoverished glory.
With you like you only shining
the hope of my despair not redeemed . . .

A circle within a circle enclosed
an orbit spinning within an orbit,
with you I am tied upon your face
encompassing my yearning as a compass—

And calling with aimless echo.
And calling with bereavement and dread,
take me in, do enclose me in the splendor of
your wing, poor and naked— . . .

Till I find you and you are crying and glowing
in my bosom as a weaned child in lights,
the simple, poor and paltry one
to weep for your impoverishment to weep— . . .

                              (1972, 47-51)

The similarities are striking: here, as in the poem "Miriam," the speaker fervently wishes to join her female addressee (note the repetition of the word *itakh*—with you), driven by an unattainable desire to know her. Here, too, as a circle within a circle, mother and daughter are interchangeable: the daughter who seeks the protection of Zion's motherly wing can equally offer her own bosom as refuge to her mother. Here, too, the mother and daughter are on the margins, impoverished and isolated. Clearly, the presence of the Land of Israel in the poem "Miriam" is rather latent. National references in "Miriam" are primarily used to characterize the mother-daughter relationship and not vice versa, as is the case in the poem *"Erets Yisra'el."* And yet the Hebrew matrilineal poetic/prophetic tradition which Bat-Miriam shapes in this poem seems to depend on such a landscape. Zion nurtures this literary female bonding and, in turn, the foremother and her descendant take part in the formation of Zion.

VI. A Global Consideration

Now that we can view the allusive patterning of the poem as a whole, it becomes clear that Bat-Miriam is a thorough necromancer. She evokes all the Pentateuchal episodes in which Miriam is mentioned in chronological order (except for Num. 20:1, where Miriam's death is recounted laconically). She begins with an allusion to Miriam's standing by the Nile (Exod. 2:4), goes on to invoke the prophetess's singing of the Song of the Sea (Exod. 15:20), and then she reinterprets Miriam's leprosy and jealousy (Num. 12). The linear, chronological order is broken only in the final stanza of "Miriam," where we are led back to the initial scene by the Nile. This circular ending may be considered the ultimate subverting of biblical norms, one final pagan mythical touch that calls into question the exclusivity of monotheistic values.[22] By using and misusing the far too few verses alloted to Miriam in the Bible, Bat-Miriam thus manages to conjure up a strong foremother, an exemplary female symbolist, magician, rebel, outcast; a model national prophetess with dual nationality; and, above all, a precursor who can, in turn, empower her descendant.

VII. The Name of the Mother-Daughter Literary Bond

Let me conclude by returning to the question of psycholiterary models with which I began. I propose that Elizabeth Abel's use of Nancy Chodorow's psychoanalytic concepts is far more applicable to the literary mother-daughter relationship depicted in Bat-Miriam's work than Bloom's model. In "(E)merging Identities" (1981, 433), Abel astutely shows that the willingness of the female poet "to absorb (female) literary influence instead of defending the poetic self from it" is consistent with the flexible ego boundaries and relational self-definition presented in Chodorow's analysis of the mother-daughter relationship. Just as the girl, in Chodorow's adaptation of object-relations theory, never really achieves total separation from the mother nor gives up her earliest relational mode of primary identification, so the female poet tends to experience a sense of oneness and continuity with her foremother. Let me add that such conflation or exchangeability of roles both in the literary and the familial realms has to do with the fact that neither the mother nor the daughter represents cultural authority in patriarchal society.

The name of Yocheved Bat-Miriam miraculously captures the very essence of this fluid literary mother-daughter relationship. If one bears in mind that Yocheved is the name of the mother of Miriam in the Bible, then Yocheved Bat-Miriam is the mother who is the daughter of the daughter. Challenging the authoritarian structure of the patronym whose function is, as Freud (1939, 150-151) and Lacan (1977, 198-199) suggest, to prove and mark the father's paternity, the matronym floats between the mother and the daughter upon the black waves of the Nile (see "*Kifsukim hayamim*"), taking part in the (e)merging of both. But let us avoid idealizing this mother-daughter literary bond. If the Name of the Father, as Lacan would have it, is the paternal metaphor which marks the child's entry into the realm of the father, into the register of the symbolic, of culture, then the name of the mother, in Bat-Miriam's terms, is a "shaky" name on the margins of culture (the Nile is no place for weaned monotheists). It is a name which, like the dark reflection of the mother, rises and falls time and again.

NOTES

1. I am greatly indebted to Elizabeth Abel, Robert Alter, Zali Gurevich, Hanan Hever, and Chana Kronfeld for their inspiring suggestions and criticisms.

2. This quotation, as well as the following exchange between Frankel and Sadan appears in Dov Sadan's *Orḥot ushevilim* (1977, 50). Translations of Hebrew texts throughout the article are mine.

3. I am indebted to Dan Miron for providing me with biographical information on Yocheved Bat-Miriam. The lack of accounts concerning Bat-Miriam's life is astounding. Dan Miron's beautiful article, "*Hitvadᶜut limshoreret*," is a notable exception.

4. The inescapable question which is beyond the scope of this article is: Why wasn't the lot of Leah Goldberg similar to that of Bat-Miriam? That is, how could Goldberg—also a female member of this literary circle—have attained such renown? This is a complex issue involving many socioliterary factors (e.g., Goldberg's prominent status in the academic critical community). One aspect that is relevant to our discussion is that Leah Goldberg's poetry, unlike the work of Bat Miriam, has quite easily lent itself to stereotypical readings of "feminist poetry." That such readings disregard the often subversive subtext of Goldberg's poems is another issue that awaits further examination.

5. To mention but two examples from this series (*Bein ḥol veshemesh*) Bat-Miriam authored a poem on Eve and another on Hagar.

6. I am trying to avoid the criticism put forth by Jonathan Culler vis-à-vis Bloom's application of Freudian concepts to literary genealogies. "Bloom's theory," Culler writes, "looks like an account of intertextuality and presupposition, but when intertextuality is narrowed to this point, where it is a relationship between a given poem and a single great precursor poem, one begins to have doubts" (1981, 109-110). Although I tend to agree with Culler's presentation of intertextuality "as an open series of acts, both identifiable and lost"(ibid.), I find his reading of Bloom too literal. Bloom does not refute the existence of nontraceable precursors; rather, his psychoanalytic approach, which involves "practical criticism," is meant to account only for the primary identifiable precursors in literary works. Nor does Bloom so rigidly adhere to the notion that the ephebe has but one poetic father. In *The Anxiety of Influence,* he does not hesitate to mention both Nietzsche and Freud as "the prime influences" upon his theory of influence.

7. I am using Ziva Ben-Porat's term.

8. The profusion of odd participles contributes to the characterization of this lack of boundaries. Participles such as *rodemet* (sleeping) and *mutsᶜad* (marched) create a hesitation between a present continuous form of the verb and nominal adjectives, the result being a blurring of boundaries between stasis and action. For more on the blurring of distinctions in the poetry of Bat-Miriam, see Kartun-Blum's comprehensive analysis (1977, 33-70).

9. Although a well and the incantation "Rise up, O well" are mentioned in Num. 21:17, it is only in the Midrash that this well is attributed to Miriam. The rabbis base their observations upon the resemblance between this incantation and Miriam's singing of the Song of the Sea.

10. All biblical citations are from the King James Version.

11. The word "timbrel" in modern Hebrew, *tof Miriam*, literally means "the drum of Miriam."

12. It is noteworthy that the very fact that the Song of the Sea incorporates narrative elements (it renders the whole story of God's parting of the sea and the subsequent destruction of the Egyptians) is indicative of its polytheistic origin. Biblical poetry, as Shemaryahu Talmon (1978) points out, tends to avoid narrative. This avoidance, he claims, needs to be seen as a rejection of pagan mythology, which in Mesopotamia was primarily expressed in the form of epic poetry. For an insightful analysis of the question of narrative in biblical poetry, see Alter (1985, 27-61). For a feminist consideration of this issue, see Bal's *Murder and Difference* (1988).

13. For more on sibling rivalry in this context, see Zeligs (1986, 225-238).

14. According to Freud, penis envy can be only partially resolved when the wish for a penis is replaced by one for a baby and a baby boy in particular. For a critique of Freud's observations in this respect, see Irigaray (1985, 83).

15. I am alluding to Virginia Woolf's brilliant account of "what would have happened had Shakespeare had a wonderfully gifted sister" (1929, 48-51).

16. In his otherwise illuminating discussion of Bat-Miriam's work in *Imahot meyasdot, aḥayot ḥorgot*, Dan Miron misrepresents Bat-Miriam's relation to resistance. He depicts her early poems as daring and powerful (though somewhat immature) and goes on to suggest that she gradually yields to the conventions of "female poetry" in writing "impoverished submissive poetry," after the model of Rahel Blaustein's work. (Although Miron seems to have a different notion of the character of Bat-Miriam's later poems, he doesn't devote much time to them). Let me suggest, contra Miron, that throughout Bat-Miriam's work there is an immense tension between a desire for power and a realization of the disturbingly impoverished condition of woman. This tension is poignantly represented in the fifth stanza of "Miriam," where the speaker's cry "not to surrender" is accompanied by an acknowledgement of the isolation and poverty that are part and parcel of the life of a female poet.

17. Note the neologism which combines the words "leprosy and "evil" (צררעת). This poem clearly reflects the existential character of Shlonsky's revolutionary stance. For more on this topic, see Kurzweil (1966, 170-180).

18. Alterman's heavy reliance on Ecclesiastes throughout his depiction of the wandering stranger in *Simḥat ʿaniyim* may be seen as an analogous phenomenon.

19. For more on the biblical Miriam's role as a female redeemer, see Trible (1989).

20. For an extensive analysis of the national commitment of Third Aliyah writers, see Shaked (1983, 237-269).

21. For more on the blurring of the private and public in Bat-Miriam's work, see Alterman's *Kamah devarim* (1963), and Dan Miron's *Shiratah shel Yokheved Bat-Miriam* (1963).

22. See Alter's discussion of the linear, chronological order in the Bible (1981, 23-46).

WORKS CITED

Abel, Elizabeth. 1981. "(E)merging Identities: The Dynamics of Female Friendship in Contemporary Fiction by Women." *Signs* 6(31): 413-435.

Alter, Robert. 1981. *The Art of Biblical Narrative*. New York: Basic Books.

———. 1985. *The Art of Biblical Poetry*. New York: Basic Books.

Alterman, Natan. 1940. *Simḥat ʿaniyim*. Tel Aviv: Mahberot Lesifrut.

———. 1963. *"Kamah devarim beshaʿah gedolah leshiratenu"* [Some Remarks at a Great Moment in Our Poetry]. *Davar* 25 (January).

Bal, Mieke. 1988. *Murder and Difference*. Bloomington: Indiana Univ. Press.

Bat Miriam, Yocheved. 1972. *Shirim* [Poems]. 2nd ed. Tel Aviv: Sifriat Poalim.

———. 1985. *Meraḥok* [From a Distance]. 2nd ed. Tel Aviv: Hakibbutz Hameuhad.

Ben-Porat, Ziva. 1976. "The Poetics of Literary Allusion." *PTL* 1: 105-128.

Bloom, Harold. 1973. *The Anxiety of Influence*. New York: Oxford Univ. Press.

———. 1975. *The Map of Misreading*. New York: Oxford Univ. Press.

Cassuto, Umberto. 1951. *Commentary on Exodus*. Jerusalem: Magness.

Chodorow, Nancy. 1978. *The Reproduction of Mothering: Psychoanalysis and the Psychology of Gender*. Berkeley: California Univ. Press.

Culler, Jonathan. 1981*The Pursuit of Signs: Semiotics, Literature, and Deconstruction*. Ithaca N.Y.: Cornell Univ. Press.

Freud, Sigmund. 1939. *Moses and Monotheism*. Trans. Katherine Jones. New York: Vintage.

Gilbert, Sandra and Susan Gubar. 1979. *The Madwoman in the Attic: The Woman Writer and the Nineteenth-Century Literary Imagination*. New Haven, Conn: Yale Univ. Press.

Irigaray, Luce. 1985. *Speculum of the Other Woman*. Trans. Gillian C. Gill. Ithaca N.Y.: Cornell Univ. Press.

Kartun-Blum, Ruth. 1977. *Bamerḥak haneʿelam: ʿiyunim beshirat Yokheved Bat-Miriam* [Receding Horizons: Studies on the Poetry of Yocheved Bat-Miriam]. Tel Aviv: Massada.

Kurzweil, Baruch. 1966. *"Ḥazut hamavet veharat ʿolam beshirei Avraham Shlonsky"* [The Vision of Death in Shlonsky's Poetry]. *Bein ḥazon levein haʾabsurdi* [Between Vision and the Absurd]. Jerusalem: Schocken Books.

Lacan, Jacques. 1977. *Écrits.*. Trans. Alan Sheridan. New York: W.W. Norton and Company.

Miron, Dan. 1963. *"Shiratah shel Yokheved Bat-Miriam"* [The Poetry of Yokheved Bat-Miriam]. *Haʾarets*, 22 February.

———. 1980. *"Hitvadʿut limshoreret"* [Getting to Know a Woman Poet]. *Maḥbarot lesifrut, leḥevrah, ulevikoret* 2 (February): 7-12.

———. 1989 and 1990. *"Imahot meyasdot, ahayot horgot"* [Founding Mothers, Stepsisters]. *Alpayim* 1: 29-58 and *Alpayim* 2:121-177.

Sadan, Dov. 1977. *Orhot ushevilim* [Ways and Paths]. Tel Aviv: Am Oved.

Shaked, Gershon. 1983. *Hasiporet ha^civrit 1880-1980 II* [Hebrew Narrative Fiction]. Tel Aviv: Hakibbutz Hameuhad.

Shlonsky, Abraham. 1965. *"Tsara^cat"* [Leprosy]. *Shirim* [Poems]. Tel Aviv: Sifriat Poalim.

———. 1973a. *"Hamelitsah"* [Melitsah]. *Yorshei hasimbolizm bashirah ha^ɔEropit vehaYehudit* [Heirs of Symbolism in European and Jewish Literature. Ed. Binyamin Hrushovski. Tel Aviv: Tel Aviv Univ. Press.

———. 1973b. *"Ra^cananut"* [Freshness]. *Yorshei hasimbolizm bashirah ha^ɔEropit vehayehudit* [Heirs of Symbolism in European and Jewish Literature]. Ed. Binyamin Hrushovski. Tel Aviv: Tel Aviv Univ Press.

Spence, Lewis. 1915. *Myths and Legends of Ancient Egypt*. London: Harrap.

Talmon, Shemaryahu. 1978. "The Comparative Method in Biblical Interpretation—Principles and Problems." *Göttingen Congress Volume*.

Trible, Phyllis. 1989. "Bringing Miriam Out of the Shadows." *Bible Review* 5, 1: 14-25.

Woolf, Virginia. 1929. *A Room of One's Own*. New York: Harcourt, Brace, Jovanovich.

Zeligs, Dorothy. 1986. *Moses: A Psychodynamic Study*. New York: Human Sciences.

Why Was There No Women's Poetry in Hebrew Before 1920?

∽ DAN MIRON ∽

I.

Women's poetry in Hebrew—namely, poetry written by women in the framework of ongoing creative activity, motivated by full literary, emotive, and intellectual intentions—entered the world between 1920 and 1922.[1] Before that time, during the nineteenth century, there were incidental cases of educated women whose circumstances and thirst for learning brought them to acquire a knowledge of Bible, Midrash or even Gemara, and who wrote poems for certain occasions: for instance, sonnets in honor of weddings or births, epitaphs, or riddles in verse. However, even the best known of these, Rachel Morpurgo (1790-1881), was a minor poetic talent. Only her letters and her prefatory comments to her poems are readable today. The praise showered on her poems in her own time—like the interest shown in her at later times by historians, scholars, and critics—resulted from the oddity of her being a woman Hebrew rhymester. Poetic efforts by her and others could not have predicted the powerful lyric breakthroughs associated with the appearance of the first women Hebrew poets in the years after World War I.

This was a sudden and surprising phenomenon, which in its time aroused amazement and wonder. From the 1920s on, women poets established a special preserve within the growing body of Hebrew lyric poetry. There emerged a more or less consecutive tradition of women's creativity in poetry, in contrast to most of the European literatures (English, for instance), where women's writing was centered primarily in the novel. And yet, at the beginning of the twentieth century, precisely at

- 65 -

the time of Hebrew poetry's great entrance into the era of modern writing—thanks to the efforts of Hayyim Nahman Bialik, Saul Tschernihovsky, and their disciples—there was not one Hebrew woman poet, even as a token curiosity. This absence of women prevailed from the 1890s to the end of the second decade of the twentieth century. During this period of the Hebrew Revival the seeds of Hebrew fiction by women were sown, primarily in Eretz Yisrael (the Land of Israel). There, in addition to the outstanding Devorah Baron, five or six other women authors were at work (Nehama Puchachewsky, Hemdah Ben-Yehuda, Itta Yellin, Yehudit Hararit, and others). There even appeared during that time the first Hebrew woman critic and essayist, Havah Shapira, whose articles and reviews were printed under the pseudonym "The Mother of All the Living." But the appearance of a woman poet apparently was impossible. At the beginning of the 1920s, suddenly, it was not only possible, but timely. All at once, some obstacle was lifted, and gates that had been locked were opened wide.

Within two years, not more, there appeared on the literary stage four outstanding woman poets: Rahel Blaustein and Esther Raab in Eretz Yisrael, Elisheva Zirkova-Bikhovsky and Yocheved Bat-Miriam (Zhelezniak) in Eastern Europe. At their side there appeared as well others who left a less lasting impression: Bat-Hamah (Malka Schechtman), Miriam Wilenski (Yalan Shtekelis, known primarily for her children's verse), and Mira Yarhi.

A series of factors fostered this sea change in women's creativity in Hebrew literature. First, a revolutionary social ambience encouraged the literary expression of cultural elements that until then had been marginalized or silent. Significantly, in this regard, women's poetry emerged in only two of the five or six centers in which Hebrew belles lettres flourished at this time: the Soviet Union (after the October Revolution) and Eretz Yisrael (at the height of the Third Aliyah). Both locations were characterized by a period of stormy upheaval and by ideologies supporting liberation for the oppressed. This atmosphere coincided with a weakening of the old hierarchies in the literary establishment. Bialik's poetics, which had held such powerful sway over the Hebrew Renaissance, were now openly challenged and new voices—young voices, in particular—began to be heard. The new social and literary norms of this period, the artistic forms to which they gave rise, the ways women's writing related to and also diverged from the modernism which replaced Bialik's poetics—these issues provide fertile ground for the historian of literature. In order to understand these phenomena, though, it is crucial to explain the complete absence of women poets in Hebrew from 1890 to 1920, the era of the Hebrew Renaissance. That conundrum is the focus of this current essay.

II.

The absence of women's voices from the poetry of the Hebrew Renaissance places this literature in cultural isolation among world literatures, as well as among other Jewish writing of the period. In most of the European literatures women writers became an increasingly prominent and permanent presence during the nineteenth century and at the beginning of the twentieth. For example, in Russian poetry—which in the era of Bialik and Tschernihovsky provided a model emulated by many Hebrew poets—the presence of women writers increased gradually from the first half of the nineteenth century (Carolina Pavlova) by way of symbolism and decadence (Zinaida Gippius), through the post-symbolist trends of the years before World War I and the revolution (Anna Akhmatova, Marina Tsvetayeva).

To be sure, the Hebrew poets at the beginning of the century made eclectic use of the Russian models and turned simultaneously to different historical strata of Russian poetry for guidance (starting with the Romantics, Pushkin and Lermontov, and ending with the contemporary Symbolists). But this eclecticism does not explain why they completely overlooked the "feminine" component that existed in one measure or another in all strata of the Russian model. Especially striking, then, is the absolute difference between the Russian "literary republic" of 1900-1914 and the parallel Hebrew one. While the climate of the former encouraged writing by young women—including many Jewish ones—the climate of the latter impeded it, to the point where being a woman and writing poetry in Hebrew became a contradiction in terms.

Take, for instance, the case of U.N. Gnessin, who created women poets as characters in two of his stories (Milly in *Beterem*, [Not Yet,] and Dina Barabash in *Etsel*, [Alongside]).[2] It is not by chance that, when he wished to quote a poem of Dina's as part of the story, he relied on a Russian poem written by his friend, Celia Levin Dropkin. (This is the same Celia Dropkin who later emerged as a prominent Yiddish poet in the United States). Gnessin reworked this verse in a Hebrew version (*"Vehayah ki yashuv minudo"* [If He Comes Back From His Wanderings]; in the Russian and Yiddish versions the title is "The Kiss"). When he imagined another woman poet (the protagonist of a story he never finished), he resorted to even stranger tactics. He wrote the poem himself, in Russian, and then entrusted it to a friend, the poet A. Hofnstein, to be translated into Hebrew. In this translation (*"Ani ta'iti 'al penei sadot"* [I Wandered over the Fields], called also simply *"Shirah"* [Singing] or [Poetry]), there remains one of the author's last works—certainly, the last example of verse that he wrote. In both of these cases Gnessin's behavior testifies that his creative intuition recoiled from relying on the figure of a Hebrew woman writer, or on a poem written by a woman, without the mediation of Russian. This was considered a "natural" creative language for a young, educated (i.e. assimilated or semi-assimilated) Jewish woman. Hebrew, in contrast, could not be described as a tool of poetic expression for such a girl.

The lack of Hebrew women poets is even more striking in comparison with contemporary Yiddish poetry. At the time in question the distance between the two Jewish literatures was not yet very great. Dominating the literary landscape of both were the figures of the bilingual founding fathers (Sh.Y. Abramovitch, Y.L. Peretz, David Frishman) who contributed definitively to the development of each one. Most of the outstanding fiction writers of the time composed in both languages, and a respectable portion of the Hebrew poets, including Bialik himself, assisted notably in the crystallization of the modern Yiddish lyric. This broad bilingualism in poetry and prose led to considerable similarity between the two literatures in terms of shared thematic, formal, and ideational features. And yet, this similarity did not extend to the phenomenon of poetry by women. While absent entirely from Hebrew, women's voices became pronounced and central to Yiddish belles-lettres over the course of the twentieth century.

In 1928, in Chicago, the poet and cultural entrepreneur Ezra Korman published a thick, handsome volume, with the name *Yidishe dikhterins*. This comprehensive anthology of Yiddish poems by women included a small selection of liturgical poetry (supplicatory poems: *tkhines* and *maneloshn)* written in the seventeenth and eighteenth centuries. In addition, it contained hundreds of pages of texts by approximately seventy women poets whose work had been published since 1888. To be sure, as is the way with cultural apologists, Korman made an effort to swell his selection in order to prove that numerous women had turned to poetry in the *mameloshn*, the mother tongue. Many of those represented in the book are hardly worthy of the title "poet." Nonetheless, the anthology shows not only impressive numbers but also quite a few authentic creative personalities (including Miriam Ulinover, Celia Dropkin, Roshelle Veprinsky, Shifra Kholodenko, Devorah Chorchel, Malka Lee, Kadya

Molodowsky, Rikude Potash-Fuchs, Rokhel Korn, Sarah Reyzen, Esther Shuymatsher, Fradl Shtok, and others).

It demonstrates, too, the openness of the Yiddish press to women poets. Well known is the story of Yankev Glatshteyn's beginnings in poetry—as a woman. He was to reveal himself eventually as one of the chief spokesmen of modernism in American Yiddish poetry, but in the years 1915-1916 Glatshteyn had difficulty publishing his first poems. He did not overcome the skepticism of the editors until he sent them his rejected poems under a feminine pseudonym (Klara Blum).[3] This openness to women's poems later characterized the Hebrew periodicals of the 1920s, as well. In the first two decades of the century, when no women's poetic voices were yet heard in Hebrew, it was this openness and receptivity which made it possible for the seventy women poets in Korman's book, and many more as well, to present their work before the Yiddish-reading public.

How is it possible to explain this sharp difference between Hebrew poetry and, on the one hand Russian poetry, or, on the other hand, Yiddish poetry? It is advisable to exercise a certain caution in this matter and not to give too easy an answer—for example, the technical, linguistic excuse. At first glance it might seem possible to attribute the difference entirely to language proficiency. According to this line of thinking, Jewish women had access to Yiddish, the mother tongue, or to an education in foreign languages; but the holy tongue was closed to them, for two reasons. Traditional Jewish education excluded them from male ritual and scholarship, and then modern assimilationist education emphasized European languages rather than Hebrew.

Certainly, there is an element of truth in this explanation, but also grounds for its refutation. First, it is not true that young women never learned Hebrew. Some did, especially those from homes imbued with a Zionist/nationalist atmosphere. There were, no doubt, many hundreds of Hebrew *maskilot* such as those described in the stories of Y. Bershadsky (*Neged ha-zerem*, [Against the Stream]) and A.A. Kabak (*Levadah*, [By Herself]), who studied Hebrew and were among the readers of contemporary Hebrew literature. Second, why was there a rabbi's daughter, like Devorah Baron, who attained enough mastery of the language to create narrative art in prose, but no counterpart who turned to poetry? (It is widely recognized that prose is no easier to write than poetry; often the opposite is true.) Third, how can this technical, linguistic excuse apply to the literary reality that developed in Eretz Yisrael, where girls and boys took equal part in the revival of Hebrew speech and the study of the language? Why did no local poetry by women emerge in that surrounding, in parallel with the narratives written by women of the *moshavot* and of maskilic households in Jerusalem and Jaffa? Above all, we should note that Rahel, Elisheva, and Bat-Miriam—at least at the beginning of their efforts as poets—had no better command of Hebrew than did many women at the turn of the century. But after 1920 they were not denied the literary publication that had been impossible ten years earlier. What made it possible at the later date was not a sudden improvement in their mastery of the language, but rather a profound change in the relation of the literature and the culture as a whole to poetic language. Significantly, there came about a renunciation or diminishment of the linguistic demands placed on poetry.

By the same token, it is important not to get caught in the shallow, simplistic reasoning which blames each and every deficiency in women's status on intentional discrimination, or on attempts to preserve a male monopoly on power and prestige. In the case of Hebrew, the declared national ideology of the period considered the literary presence of women a desideratum and a cultural goal of the highest order. Time and again, the poets and critics expressed their sorrow at the lack of a strong feminine element in Hebrew culture. They saw this phenomenon as a spiritual defect of the first degree and blamed a variety of social and cultural ills on it. The concept of cultural revival, which stood at the center of that literature's self-awareness, was based on the (unfounded) assumption expressed by Frishman in the following way: "We [i.e., the exponents of Hebrew literary culture] have a people, we have a revival, everyone is reading, women have started to read, we have a new continent of readers" (1901, 1).

In short, misogyny and male chauvinism are not the issue here. Editors would have welcomed a woman poet had one sent them work that could meet the standards of their poetics. Such texts were not submitted, whether because the women who tried to write could not conform to the norms of reigning tastes, or because an atmosphere was created in Hebrew literature which dissuaded women from even attempting to stand the test and brave the criticism of influential editors such as Frishman and Bialik, Brenner and Klausner.

The discrimination, if it existed, was not in the ill will of the literary establishment. Instead it manifested itself in the cultural and aesthetic tastes, and in the norms and restrictions these determined. So, for example, throughout all the long years of his work as editor of *Hashiloah* (beginning in 1903), Yosef Klausner never published even a single poem by a woman until 1920. However, in 1920, that same Yosef Klausner published Rahel's first poem, and several years later he published poems by Yocheved Bat-Miriam. It was not a change in Klausner's approach to women that caused this turnabout, but rather his observations as a critic and as an editor alert to the winds of change. These heralded a new era in Hebrew literature and a poetics which granted these poems the right to exist. It was his discriminating taste, in this sense, which also brought Klausner to open the doors of *Hashiloah* to Avraham Shlonsky and David Fogel, M. Temkin and A. Solodar—all poets who for one reason or another did not win the backing of Bialik. Altogether, an understanding of the historical episode under discussion here requires insight into the inhibiting taste that governed Hebrew poetry till the First World War, and the liberating changes that occurred thereafter.

III.

Women's poetry met with several obstacles that are not easy to describe or localize, but there is no doubt about their cumulative impact.

These obstacles might at first seem unlikely. At the beginning of the century the thematic and generic domains of Hebrew poetry had widened tremendously in comparison with those of the Haskalah and the Hibbat Zion periods. Among other things, this expansion made possible (and even required) the distancing or the removal of the "poetic I" from the pose of the universal, philosophical observer typically found in neoclassical poetry. Likewise, the "lyric I" abandoned the (no less generalized) pose of the sensitive man of feeling, typically found in the emotional, declamatory poetry—whether personal or national—of the sentimentalist poets of Hibbat Zion. Now the "poetic I" could present himself in autobiographical concreteness, telling in a direct and detailed way about his past, about the experiences that shaped the course of his life, and about his spiritual inner world, including erotic or sexual experience.

The question then becomes: what prevented the appearance of a female "poetic I" in this corpus? Relations between the sexes received concrete expression with an abundance of nuances; yearning for love, revulsion or fear of love, desire, its fulfillment, unrequited love, war between the sexes, appeasement, separation, longing, feelings of loss and bitterness—all these became common currency in Hebrew poetry, but all were presented only from the point of view of the male poet. To be sure, the contemporary male poets—Bialik, Tschernihovsky, Yakov Fichman, Yakov Steinberg, and others—wrote not a few poems in which they adopted female speakers. These gave expression, as it were, to the "feminine" viewpoint on relations between the sexes in all their complexity and diversity. But these poems established or strengthened a masculine self-image by means of the poet's projections onto the soul of imagined women. Even in those poems, where the words of a female speaker were set opposite the words of a male speaker, as if in a confrontation, the opposition was not a real one. The encounter was merely a camouflaged confirmation of the male, and so a complementary corroboration of his outlook.

It is possible to explain this self-containment within the realm of "masculine" experience as a matter of moral-ethical reluctance to disclose female sensual experience, especially erotic experience. Operating here, then, is the familiar double standard. What was permissible in male writing was intolerable as a confession heard from the lips of a chaste daughter of Israel. And yet, as a sole or even primary explanation for women's delayed entrance into Hebrew poetry, this reasoning leaves too many questions unanswered. First, we must understand why the treatment of female eroticism was permissible in Hebrew poems of a folkloristic genre in which the speaker is, supposedly, an unsophisticated, rustic, or shtetl girl: for example, in Bialik's "Bein nehar Prat unehar Hidekel" [Between the Tigris and the Euphrates] or "Yesh li gan" [I Have a Garden]; Yakov Steinberg's "Shir shel baḥurah" [Song of a Young Lass]; or Fichman's "Shir naʿarah ʿazuvah" [Song of an Abandoned Girl]).

Second, we must ask why the same openness permitted in prose was not permitted in poetry. In the period discussed here, outstanding authors (Bershadsky, Berdichevsky, Gnessin, Shofman, Berkowitz, Yakov Steinberg, A.A. Kabak, and even Bialik in Meʾaḥorei hagader [Over the Fence]—not to speak of Devorah Baron), did dare to depict concrete female experiences, including many that were erotic and sexual. In narrative it was possible to portray characters driven by desire such as Gnessin's Milly, Zina Adler, Dina Barabash, and Ruhama, and even to cite their poems of longing (written in Russian). But it was not possible for the Dinas and Zinas to express themselves directly as Hebrew poets. This means that the moral sensitivities of that generation were genre-specific, and lessened in the transition from poetry to prose.

Third, Yiddish poetry of the time sprang from a social/cultural world not terribly different from the world of Hebrew poetry. Here, too, female eroticism was more acceptable in prose than in poetry (in, for example, Mary by Sholem Asch; Nokh aleman [When All Is Said and Done] by Dovid Bergelson; and the stories of Yonah Rosenfeld). However, Yiddish poetry tolerated the appearance of a poet such as Fradl Shtok, who at the beginning of the second decade of this century published "decadent" erotic poems marked by ambivalences of love and hate, desire and revulsion. Yiddish poetry in that decade even absorbed the uninhibited Celia Dropkin, who published poems filled with transparent sexuality (e.g., "The Circus Lady") in such central periodicals as *Di tsukunft*.

These questions force us to turn away from explanations which rely on a simplistic claim of double standards. Even if they touch on a historical truth, such explanations must be integrated with a more complex literary explanation—one which uncovers the root of the problem not just in the area of cultural sensibilities, ideational concepts, and social conventions, but primarily *within* the poetic and stylistic systems that organized and regulated the process of literary development in that period.

The poetics of the lyric during the Hebrew Revival stemmed from the accomplishments of Bialik and Tschernihovsky, in the 1890s, and crystallized at the beginning of the twentieth century as a system of thematic, generic, stylistic, and formal norms (prosody, rhyme, and structures). These norms were both firm enough and flexible enough to allow dozens of poets—each with an individual complexion—and members of several generations or literary schools, to function and develop their art without a sense of coercion. Of most immediate importance for this discussion are two fundamental rules of Bialikean poetics with which women's poetry was not prepared to deal: (a) the poem must relay a private, personal experience as if it also contained national/universal content; (b) the poem must present a rich, dense, multilayered expression, springing from a literary culture of great depth and resonance. It was possible to publish poems in Hebrew which did not fully comply with one of these criteria, especially the first (although this failure relegated the poet, or at least the "defective" poem, to a rank of secondary importance). However, failure to comply with both criteria assured immediate rejection.

This, apparently, is one of the principal roots of the difficulty met by Hebrew women's poetry at the beginning of the century. The literature of the period almost entirely lacks representations of the "new young Hebrew woman" who exposes through her life an aspect of the national, collective experience. In this writing, the life of the Jewish girl unfolds mainly as a personal, private experience, whereas the opposite is true of male characters. The life of the young man is presented as a metonymy of collective Jewish experience—a national symbolic drama par excellence.

Hebrew poetry, of course, was familiar with classical uses of feminine figures as collective symbols. The Jewish mother as the nation, the *shekhinah,* and the muse of national poetry at one and the same time; the daughter of Israel, innocent and modest, embodying the purity of the national psyche—this was safe territory for the modern poet. The same could not be said, however, the moment this poet wished to go beyond stereotypes and portray his contemporary, modern Jewish young woman as an individual. In his poems Bialik could develop female figures as symbols quite naturally—as a mother of the nation, a *shekhinah,* and as a daughter of Israel. In his "folk" poems (adaptations of authentic Yiddish folk poems and original imitations), he did not flinch from developing the character of the naive, innocent lass, unembarrassed to tell her beloved about her pillow burning beneath her flesh ("*mitaḥat livnat besari*") each night. Whether or not she is aware of the psychological content of her imagery when she says, "I have a garden and a well I have," she does not break out beyond the accepted bounds of folk innocence. Once those boundaries are breached, the poet can no longer present the desires of a young woman so sympathetically.

The difference between Yiddish poetry and Hebrew poetry in this context manifests itself primarily in the fact that the analogic national element does not serve as a compulsory norm in the former, while in the latter it does. Indeed, it is a central axis in the structure of the poetic foundation. Yiddish literature at the beginning of the century was engaged in a major struggle to free itself from the collective, communal context that was established for it in the prose writing of the nineteenth-century classics (Sh.Y. Abramovitch, Sholem Aleichem, and their predecessors) and from the collective class context established in the socialist-proletarian poetry that emerged primarily in the immigrant milieu of the West. Both in prose and in poetry Yiddish literature strove for individualism, for psychological characterization, and lyrical expression. In poetry the departure from collective experience and analogy became the cornerstone of the principal modernist schools: the symbolism of *Di yunge* (the Young) and the postsymbolism of the *Inzikhistn* (the Introspective Poets who searched within themselves, within their own consciousness and experiences, for the contents, forms, and language of their poetry). Therefore, even though national symbols and themes were often incorporated freely into Yiddish poetry, this same corpus of work absorbed, without difficulty, expressions of personal experience that were not expanded into historical or national meaning. This openness made it possible for Yiddish literature to accept women's poetry while also distancing itself from the principles of the traditional feminine folk poem. However, the stylistic criteria of Hebrew poetry, as differentiated from those of Yiddish, were by far more inhibiting than the cultural/thematic ones.

IV.

In order to clarify the stylistic norms that blocked the way for women's poetry in the era of Bialik, it is instructive to examine in more depth a case already mentioned—the poem by Celia Dropkin that was incorporated, in a Hebrew version, into Gnessin's story *Etsel* [Alongside].

Young Dropkin was in love with Gnessin. She even attempted suicide on his account, as is recounted in the story *Beterem* (Dropkin served as the model for the poetess Milly). She sent Gnessin her love poem as a kind of gift or personal communication. He, as is known, drew it into his story without any indication of the fact that this poem was not the product of his own pen (which tells us something about the sociology and ethics of cultural/literary relations between men and women at the beginning of this century). The poem was for many years considered an original work of Gnessin's—indeed, his one outstanding contribution in the realm of the lyric. The poem was rightly considered revolutionary, and so the modernist poets of the thirties and forties (Shlonsky, Leah Goldberg, Natan Alterman) and their circle welcomed it as one of the early blossoms of modernism in Hebrew verse.

In the poetic/historical circumstances in which it was published (in 1913, several months after Gnessin's death), this was an exceptional and innovative poem both in thematic and in formal or stylistic terms. Thematically, it was surprisingly bold in the unconcealed eroticism of the female speaker; she tells openly not only of her desire for the man and about her willingness to share her bed with him but also about her enormous erotic rage, her willingness to drink the "blood of his heart." This is no longer the woman speaker whose soul is ready to accompany the man in his wanderings through the desert or to a deserted island as a saintly distant presence (as in Bialik's love poetry). Instead, she is a flesh-and-blood woman "howling like a she-wolf in her den, pining for love" (*meyalelet kiz'evah beḥorah beyisurim le'ahavah*). She displays feigned indifference toward the man who reappears in her city and her house but craves his blood "to quench my thirst."

From a formal/stylistic point of view, the poem demonstrated rare liberty, despite being metrically balanced (in the Ashkenazic accentuation, of course), thanks to "varied line length, sliding syntax, and lack of rhyme" as well as "sensual, expressionistic direct discourse" (Binyamin, 240). It also had just a touch of a prosaic quality, which suited Gnessin's fictitious speaker—a character known for her emotional directness throughout the story.

Nonetheless, Gnessin could in no way truly sever himself from the stylistic and rhetorical norms of Hebrew verse at that time. When he came to adapt the Russian text of Celia Dropkin, he suited it to the laws of Bialik's poetics. In the process he changed the poem fundamentally. A comparison of the original (in an almost literal translation) with Gnessin's version may, therefore, shed light on that normative stylistic and rhetorical stratum which was "lacking" in the original and which Gnessin added to it. This he did so that the text—despite all its innovations—would function as a poetic text according to the conceptions of the Hebrew reader of that period; that is to say, so that it would appear to the reader as a "genuine poem." This move was necessary in order to strengthen the dramatic effect of an encounter between Ephraim Margolis and Dina Barabash, and also in order to enhance Dina's characterization as a sincere, passionate soul who, through her tragic love, rises to true poetic heights.

Here, then, is Celia Dropkin's original version of "A Kiss" (translated from the Russian):

> If he comes back to my town
> I'll be calm;
> If I see him
> I'll be calm;
> If he looks into my eyes
> I'll clothe them with the calm of darkness;
> If he offers me his hand,
> Lightly and freely I'll shake it.
>
> But if, by chance, he spends the night
> With me in the same house,
> Quietly, stealthily I'll creep to his bed.
> And as he, unknowing, trembling in his dream
> Lies in front of me
> I shall kiss him on the chest.
> I shall raise the cover and kiss him on the chest.

And my kiss will be murderous.
I'll drink his blood, his heart with my kiss.
And the blood will satisfy to saturation
My sick, my lonely desire;
A desire which knew no tenderness
And which never kissed from the day of birth
To the day of withering.[4]

And here, the rendering of the poem by Gnessin, both in its Hebrew original and in a verbatim nonpoetic English translation:

וְהָיָה כִּי יָשׁוּב מִנְּדוֹ וְיָבוֹא אֶל אַרְצִי,
אֲנִי אֶהְיֶה שְׁלֵוָה.
וְכִי יִפְקוֹד בֵּית אִמִּי וַאֲנִי אֶרְאֶה בְּפָנָיו—
שׁוּב אֶרְאֶה בְּפָנָיו
אֲנִי אֶהְיֶה שְׁלֵוָה.
וְכִי יַבִּיט אֵלִי
גַּם כִּי יַבִּיט אֵלִי וְאֶל מִסְתָּרֵי נַפְשִׁי כְּשֶׁהִבִּיט,
בְּרַחֲמָיו הָרְחוֹקִים וּבְתוּגַת הַנֶּפֶשׁ הַגְּדוֹלָה שֶׁל גֶּבֶר—
כִּגְבוֹר הַלּוֹבֵשׁ אֶת מַדָּיו, אֲנִי אֶלְבַּשׁ שַׁלְוָה אֲפֵלָה.
וְכִי יוֹשֵׁט לִי יָדוֹ לְשָׁלוֹם—
אֲקַבֵּל בְּרוּחַ שׁוֹקֵטָה אֶת יָדוֹ הַגְּדוֹלָה,
אֶת יָדוֹ הַחַמָּה, הַחוֹבֶקֶת וְדוֹחָה בַּטּוּחוֹת,
וְזֵכֶר לֹא יִהְיֶה לְאוֹתוֹ הָרֶטֶט הַנּוֹאָל שֶׁבְּכַפִּי שֶׁלִּי,
אֲנִי אֶהְיֶה שְׁלֵוָה.

וְאוּלָם
אִם יִגְרֹם מַזָּלִי וְהוּא יִפְקֹד אֶת נָוִי וְגַם יִשְׁכַּב בַּלַּיְלָה
אִתִּי וּבְצֵל קוֹרָה אַחַת – בֵּית אִמִּי
אָז אָקוּם בַּדְּמָמָה בַּלַּיְלָה וַאֲגַשֵׁשׁ בַּלָּאט וּבִכְהוֹנוֹת
רַגְלַיִם יְחֵפוֹת
וְאֶמְצָא מִשְׁכָּבוֹ בָּאֹפֶל—
אֲנִי אֶמְצָא מִשְׁכָּבוֹ בָּאֹפֶל!
וְהָיָה בִּהְיוֹתוֹ סָרוּחַ לְפָנַי, וְאָחוּז בְּתֹהוּ תַרְדֵּמָה,
וְיִצּוּרָיו חֲרֵדִים מֵחֶרְדַּת הַמְּנוּחָה כִּי גָבְרָה,
לֹא יַכִּיר וְלֹא יָחוּשׁ וְנַפְשׁוֹ לֹא תַחֲלוֹם קָרְבָתִי,
אֶשְׁתַּחֲוֶה וְאֶשַּׁק לוֹ בְּחָזֵהוּ—
אָסִירָה בַּלָּאט קְצֵה הַשְּׂמִיכָה וְאֶשַּׁק לוֹ בְּחָזֵהוּ...

וּתְהֵא זוֹ הַנְּשִׁיקָה נְשִׁיקַת הָאִישׁ הָרוֹצֵחַ אֶת הַנֶּפֶשׁ:
אֶת דָּמוֹ אֶסְבָּאָה בַּנְּשִׁיקָה הַלֵּזוּ!
וִיהֵא זֶה הַדָּם לִי לְהַשְׁקִיט בּוֹ צְמָאִי.
וְלִרְפָאוּת יְהֵא לִי, לְהַשְׁקִיט בָּהּ אֶת תַּאֲוַת נֶפֶשׁ
גַּלְמוּדָה וְחוֹלָה,

מְיַלְלָה כִּזְאֵבָה בְּחוֹרָה, בְּיִסּוּרִים לְאַהֲבָה
וְחוֹבְקָה אֲבָנִים דּוֹמֲמוֹת,
נֶפֶשׁ חֲרֵדָה וְנִשְׂרֶפֶת בְּלַהֲבָה לִנְשִׁיקָה שֶׁבְּאַהֲבָה
וְנָשֹׁק לֹא נָשְׁקָה — —
לְמִיּוֹם גִּיחָהּ לְצָמָא וְלַחֲלוֹת לְאוֹר שֶׁמֶשׁ —
וְאֶל אַחֲרֵי בְּלוֹתָהּ.

(1982, 243)

And if it comes to pass and he will return from his wandering to my country,
I shall be calm.
And if he visits my mother's house and I shall see his face—
Once again I shall see his face,
I shall be calm.
And if he looks at me—
Even if he looks at me and into the secret places of my soul, like he used to,
With his distant compassion and the great sadness of a man—
Like a hero who dons his uniform I shall, put on dark calm
And if he offers me his hand in greeting—
I shall peacefully take his big hand,
His warm hand, which is both embracing and decisively rejecting,
And there will not be even a hint of that silly tremor in my hand,
I shall be calm.

But
If my luck wills it and he visits my abode and also sleeps in the night
With me, under one roof, in my mother's house,
Then I shall quietly get up in the night and noiselessly grope with the toes
Of my naked feet
Until I find his couch in the darkness—
I *shall* find his couch in the darkness!
And when he is prostrated before me, a prisoner in the void of slumber,
His limbs quivering with the pleasure of overwhelming rest
And devoid of recognition and sensation his soul would not even dream of my
　　closeness,
I shall kneel and kiss him on his chest—
I shall stealthily raise the fringe of the blanket and kiss him on his chest . . .

And this kiss will be the kiss of a murderer:
I shall guzzle his blood with this very kiss!
And I shall use the blood to quench my thirst
And as medicine for soothing the desire of
A soul sick and lonely,
Howling like a she-wolf in her den, pining for love
And embracing still stones;
A soul trembling, burning for a kiss of love,
Which never kissed—

From the day she was born to thirst and pine for sunlight—
Till after she withers away . . .

It is clear from even an initial, superficial examination that Gnessin's version is not a translation so much as a free reworking of Dropkin's poem. In it can be discerned three mutually reinforcing tendencies: (a) rhetorical heightening of the emotive level of the poem; (b) lengthenings, plus some omissions, which add figurative and thematic fullness to the poem (the number of lines increases by 50 percent, the number of words doubles); (c) the short, direct syntax of most of the original lines is exchanged for complex syntax; in H. Binyamin's words, for a "baroque, repetitious circumlocution" (240).

To these initial observations it is possible to add another: Gnessin's inclination to forgo the narrative divisions that split the original poem into three stanzas—stanzas that resemble three chapters of a hypothetical story (the man's return and his expected meeting with the woman; the kiss on the chest that will take place after renewed sexual contact between the two; revelation of the kiss's meaning and of the woman's unrealized, and until now unmentioned, love). Gnessin recasts the poem as a continuous, massive block, split open at one point: the empty line at the end of which appears the word *ulam* (But). This makes for a single, tension-filled break in the thirty-five line poem, as if a crack suddenly opened under mounting pressure. Clearly, Gnessin wanted to raise the tension and present the poem's speaker in a heightened and more complex emotional state than that indicated by the simplicity of the original. The continuous structure reinforces this effect, for it presents the words like a confession streaming out of a febrile soul, freezing for a moment before the turning point *ulam* and then flowing from here until the end in a mighty rhetorical outpouring from the heart.

The syntactic complexities and the reinforced rhetoric Gnessin introduced, along with the filling-in of descriptive and metaphoric material, imbue the event described with heightened drama. It's possible to say that Gnessin wanted to turn the poem of a somewhat naive young girl (Celia Dropkin was 18 when she wrote the Russian version) into the poem of a mature, experienced woman more conscious of the true content of her words about a wasted life ("from the day of birth to the day of withering"). This emphasis would be appropriate for a protagonist like Dina Barabash, whose poem must explain the background for a potential suicide. It's also possible to say, to the contrary, that Gnessin rejected a simple, candid poem that went right to the heart of drastic matters, and that he reworked it in a softer, more Romantic version.

So far our observations refer just to the general, surface characteristics of Gnessin's version. At issue more specifically are a number of expansions or intensifications of elements found in the original. For example, where Gnessin finds repetition in Dropkin's poetry (the doubling of "I shall be calm" and "I shall kiss him on his chest"), he retains this feature and at times makes it even more conspicuous. "I shall be calm" he triples; "I shall kiss him on his chest" he repeats twice, as in the original. Yet he also adds repetitions not found in the Russian: "I shall see his face," "and if he looks at me," "my mother's house," and most important, "until I find his couch in the darkness—/I *shall* find his couch in the darkness." This last repetition puts an additional emphasis on both the determination behind the speaker's decision and the expected difficulty of its execution.

Similarly, Gnessin found near the end of the poem examples of anaphora (repetition of a word or words at the beginning of successive lines in a poem) or epiphora (repetition of a word or words at the end of successive lines): "a soul, sick and lonely/a soul trembling, burning for a kiss of love"; "and my kiss will be murderous/I'll drink his blood, his heart/with my kiss." Gnessin retained and reinforced these effects by creating a triple anaphora (*"utehe* zo *haneshikah*. . ./*viyhe* zeh hadam li . . . /*ulerif'ut yehe* li") and by intensifying the epiphora of "pining for love . . . for a kiss of love." He introduces anaphoric and epiphoric imagery into the earlier sections of the poem as well ("his big hand—his warm hand"; " the kiss—with this kiss"). When he found a simple metaphor without much tension ("If he looks into my eyes/I'll clothe them with the calm of darkness"), Gnessin doubled its force by adding an accompanying simile which creates a distinct tension: "like a hero who dons his uniform I shall put on dark calm." Thus the woman's seemingly cool, impassive reaction to meeting the eyes of her lover is figured as an effort, a battle. Moreover, "calm of darkness" does not carry the fateful tension of *"shalvah afelah"* (dark calm). The "calm of darkness" may speak of a darkness that comes with tranquillity, but Gnessin's is a calm in which there inheres a dark, i.e., threatening or unfathomable aspect.

Gnessin also elaborates on generalized descriptions of a situation, for example, Dropkin's "quietly, stealthily, I'll slip into his bed." He adds tangible details full of dramatic tension: silence, slow seeking, bare toes. On the other hand, Gnessin muted and weakened several things in the original version. For example, where he encounters a sentence that possesses a clear opposition ("If I see him, I'll be calm"), he dampens its effect with a complicated rendering: "And if he visits my mother's house and I shall see his face—/Once again I shall see his face,/I shall be calm." The repetition may add excitement and dramatic detail to the narrative plot (the meeting between the speaker and the man will be a second encounter, a return meeting), but Gnessin gains these effects at the price of the lost contrast. Another example comes at the end of the poem, where Gnessin found a generalization that emphatically introduces to the poem an existential consciousness: "from the day of birth born/to the day of withering." Gnessin embarks here on a metaphoric journey: "from the day she was born to thirst and pine for the sunlight—/Till after she withers away." This rendition offers artistic riches and emotive force, representing thirst both as hope and disease, but the Ecclesiastes-like existential awareness almost disappears in the abundant imagery.

A further examination of Gnessin's text reveals that his rendition also introduces altogether *new* elements into the poem, and it is precisely these elements that constitute the main "poetic" touch added to the original. The effect already is notable in the opening lines, which describe the man's projected return to the speaker's town. On reading these lines and comparing them to their parallel verses in the short, economical original, we should ask ourselves first of all why the man in Gnessin's version must "return from his wandering." We hear nothing in Dropkin's poem about his being some sort of Cain figure, who sojourns in "the land of Nod" or who has sentenced himself to exile. According to Dropkin, it's possible that during his entire separation from the speaker he resided peacefully in another city, or that he has been out and about his business or other affairs. Essentially all that matters to the "poetic I" is that the male protagonist is not with her, not near her; the rest does not concern her. Second, why must he come to her "country," and not to her city? What good will it do her if he comes to her country but not to her town, the only place where the return meeting between them can possibly occur? Third, there is the line "And if he visits my mother's house." Dropkin's "lyric I" speaks merely of a meeting, one which might take place on the street, in the drugstore, or in the home of a mutual acquaintance. And, if the meeting does take place in her home, why should that home be called her mother's house and not her father's or simply her own? While "my mother's house" adds a female backdrop, a mother-daughter connection, to the narrator's confessions in the poem, and presents her home as one of women only to which this one man, alone, will arrive, it is doubtful whether this is the only reason, or even the main reason, that the construction "my mother's house" appears in Gnessin's rendition.

Finally, what is the basis for the profound pity and deep-felt suffering of the man, which appears in the dramatic glance he casts not to the woman's eyes, but to the "secret places of [her] soul"? Celia Dropkin says not a word about this pity and suffering, neither of which is even manifested in the man's actions. It is doubtful that she would have been willing, without objection, to accept such pity or pain. It seems, too, that her "poetic I" would not have been able to deal with these emotions without anger. But then, this figure is not the least interested in knowing the man's feelings. She is concerned only with her own feelings and her ability to hide them behind a screen of feigned carefree composure.

Gnessin's version, then, has altered Dropkin's poem in two parallel ways. Thematically, he has transferred the poem's emotional focus from the female speaker and her tormented love into an interpersonal realm between the narrator and the man, who himself, it seems, is also suffering. Gnessin paints a positive picture of the man in his version, lending him romantic stature and splendor. In so doing, he also implies that the man's special "fate," rather than his insufficient response to the narrator's love, is what somehow compels him to distance himself from her. He is the marked Cain, a sinner who has sentenced himself to wandering or to a quest which obliges him to leave his home and country for a lengthy exile. He is not merely an indifferent lover, for when he meets the woman (still in love with him) he will look "into the secret places of [her] soul" knowing, suffering, and pitying her. His compassion, though, like that of God, will be from a great distance.

For her part, the "poetic I" will once again experience his male magnetism (unmentioned in the original). His pity and suffering are those of a "real man"—restrained, well-concealed, "manly." Hence these qualities also distance him from her. His hand is "large" and "warm," a suitably masculine hand, which, covering a woman's small hands, triggers a "silly tremor," as it assures her not only of shelter and warmth but also of that feeling associated with the strength of a man's hand in the act of love itself. And if we transfer this strength from the synecdoche—the hand—to the essence it represents—the man's whole body—then the woman's "silly tremor" also spreads throughout her body and represents, synechdocally, her bodily craving for the man's "strong" and "warm" embrace. Yet this same hand is at once "embracing" and "rejecting." That is, the woman already senses the decision of the man not to allow the relationship between them to become lasting and permanent. This touch makes clear to her that, if her "luck wills it"—that is, if he stays the evening and sleeps with her—he will then quickly vanish. Condemned as he is to a life of wandering, he will abandon her to her miserable love—as, indeed, is the case in the story of Ephraim Margolis and Dina Barabash in *Etsel*.

In short, whereas Celia Dropkin writes a poem about her female speaker, Gnessin writes less about the speaker than about her lover: the doomed, suffering, Romantic male, the lone wanderer who is at once fascinating and desperate, seductive and spurning, sorrowful yet distant; the man who, mounted on a high pedestal before her eyes, causes the woman to tremble and to gaze at him with longing and love while despairing of its fulfillment. That is to say, Gnessin uproots the poem from its authentic domain of women's poetry and places it in the realm of quasi-feminine, poetry where male poets adopt female speakers to glorify themselves and to define the terms of their own "mission" to the world. As in the poetry of Bialik and his disciples, the man here too pushes the woman from the center to the margin. She becomes a wretched spectator, witnessing the drama of his life, in which her part is so small and peripheral. Her eyes and her soul are exploited for the aggrandizement of this drama and its hero. Basically, in other words, we have returned to literature in which the young man has a fate full of meaning, and the young woman is allowed only a supporting role.

These thematic changes are part of a larger transformation expressed in the very words Gnessin chooses. In Dropkin's poem, words are remarkable for their expositional functionality. They are few, simple, and stripped of literary figures (in the entire first stanza there is only one metaphor: "I'll clothe them with the calm of darkness.") Gnessin's words reinforce the emotive register of the poem. They are more numerous, syntactically complex, literary, and, most notably, full of allusions and fragmented quotations. In many lines what drives the words is not their referential function, but rather another force entirely. Otherwise, why would Gnessin twice mention the concept of "my mother's house"—and in the second instance with a multiple emphasis ("If my luck wills it and he visits my abode and also sleeps in the night/With me, under one roof, in my mother's house,")—if not to raise in the reader's memory two key texts as well as several other minor ones? The main texts are, first, two verses from the Song of Songs and, second, Bialik's 1896 poem *"Mishut bamerhakim"* (From Wandering in Distant Places).

It was but a little that I passed from then, but I
found him whom my soul loveth: I held him, and
would not let him go, until I had brought him into
my mother's house, and into the chamber of her
that conceived me (Song of Songs 3:4).

I would lead thee, and bring thee into my mother's
house, who would instruct me: I would cause thee
to drink of the spiced wine of my pomegranate
(Song of Songs 8:2).

מָשׁוּט בַּמֶּרְחַקִּים. מִמְּקוֹמוֹת נָדַדְתִּי,
כְּצִפּוֹר מִיָּם אֶל בֵּית־אִמִּי חָרַדְתִּי.
(1966, 12)

From wandering in distant places. From the places of my wandering
Like a seabird I turned, toward my mother's house.

In this last text are found both the moment of the man's return from
wandering and his visit to the mother's house. There are numerous less
central textual fragments, a few which bear noting: "Send me away, that
I may go unto mine own place, and to my country" (Gen. 30:25); "And it
shall come to pass when ye have come to the land" (Exod. 12:25),
together with the rest of the verses beginning with "And it shall come to
pass" (*Vehayah ki*); "and thou shalt visit thy habitation, and shalt not sin"
(Job 5:24); "Therefore he shall lie with thee tonight" (Gen. 30:15);[5] "The
luck of the day does not hold, but the luck of the hour does" (*Shabbat*
156a); and, above all, "My luck did not cause me to be lost with you—
from your threshold I have departed" (Bialik, *"Hamatmid"* [The Eternal
Student], 1898).

It is clear that we are not looking at a miscellany of minor source bor-
rowings like the *melitsah* (the high florid diction) of the *maskilim* who
used a pastiche of scriptural fragments for the sake of their stylistic
beauty and also, quite simply, because the writers themselves lacked the
basic linguistic material to mold their perceptions. They were forced to
take their texts piece by piece from within the Bible, but this use of quotation and allusion was discredited by Bialik's poetics; in its place came a
dialectical usage which developed the quotes and references into an echo
chamber that magnified the resonance of experiences described or lent
them a contrastive background. Gnessin was fully capable of creating
verses and prose free of such allusive layering—for instance, in the poem
before us, in the line "and there will not be even a hint of that silly

tremor in my hand" or "And if he looks at me—/Even if he looks at me and into the secret places of my soul. . ./With his distant compassion and the great sadness of a man."

Yet Gnessin *wants* to anchor the bulk of the poem in the linguistic materials drawn from the Bible and from Bialik (to whom poets of that generation alluded nearly as much as they alluded to the Bible).[6] He does so because he chooses to arrange his theme around several archetypes: most centrally, the archetype of the loving biblical woman, longing in the night for her soul's love, seeking him and dreaming of meeting him in her mother's house, in the room where she was conceived. There she will suckle him on "the spiced wine of [her] pomegranate." We find one of the unhappier versions of this archetype in the figure of Leah, the neglected and unloved woman. Leah's sister promises her that, in exchange for some mandrakes, her husband Jacob will lie with her. By means of this archetype, Gnessin lends to the love story of the poem's speaker, i.e., of the fictitious Dina Barabash, a rich and resonant echo, an ancient echo, and so a universality coupled with a nationalistic, messianic undertone of hope for redemption. The second archetype is that of the great wanderer. It is built primarily from allusions to Bialik's poem, "From Wandering in Distant Places." Implied here is reference to the personal/national nomad featured in that text: the youth returning from the Volozhin yeshiva and from Odessa to his birthplace, Zhitomir, who is also the Jewish people returning, uncertain, to their historical origins, "the house of their mother." (See also Bialik's *"Basadeh"* [In the Field]: "For all that you became precious to me, fields—since you recall to me my distant brothers, working in my mother's house"). This archetype enriches the figure of the man in "The Kiss," casting his fate as that of the wandering Jew.

Gnessin thus uproots Dropkin's poem from the poetics of candor and replants it in what has been called *The Poetry of Allusion* (Brower 1959). In this sort of lyric a text cannot stand alone as a poetic statement without clear assistance from some other poetic text. Obviously, such verse is intended almost exclusively for those who are capable of recognizing the sources alluded to behind the veil of the explicit poetic text. Into such an elitist poetics, dependent on the mutual erudition of the poet and a select community of readers, Gnessin introduces Dropkin's straightforward and honest poem. This stylistic change goes hand in hand with the thematic transformation that shifts the poem's central focus from the woman to the man, for it is by means of these parallel shifts that Gnessin succeeds, according to his aesthetic criteria, in redeeming Celia

Dropkin's verses from the status of a nonliterary text. He turns her poetry into a deeply layered, dense, and heavy text charged with meaning on top of meaning; in short, the poem of a "true" poet.

Similar shifts also mark that portion of the text which in Dropkin's original centered around the second stanza. The depiction of the intimate night undergoes a major revision, one which elaborates on the archetypal figure of the man "sprawling" or "stretched out" ("*saruah*") on his bed after the pleasures of intercourse. In Dropkin's poem, the man is not sprawling, he is simply lying asleep, dreaming. His body twitches in a dream tremor, which distances him from the woman at his side and expresses his commitment to his own world. In Gnessin's version the man is a "prisoner in the void of slumber" and his limbs are "quivering with the pleasure of overwhelming rest." He lies at night with the woman and beside her, under the roof of her mother's house, after he has drunk the wine of her pomegranate, and his soul "would not even dream" of her presence. He lies beneath a blanket (a "*semikhah*"), and not a cover, as in the original. The woman then draws down the blanket in order to execute upon him the act of the kiss—the kiss on his chest and not on his face. This is a ritual act, hence it is done by her bowing down (something never even hinted at in the original).

It is apparent that in Gnessin's text there emerges an analogous relationship between the act of kissing in the dark, as it is portrayed in the poem, and a whole series of parallel literary events: Jael covers Sisera with a blanket (a "*semikhah*") after she has quenched his thirst with milk. And then, when he sinks into a deep sleep, she uncovers him and drives a peg through his temple. Adam, too, sinks into a deep sleep, one which the Lord casts upon him in order to remove from his breast the lump of flesh that will become Eve ("and the Lord caused a deep sleep to fall upon Adam [Gen. 2:21]). Gnessin's phrase "*tohu tardemah*" also recalls other verses, such as: "when deep sleep falleth on men" (Job 4:13; 33:15) and "a deep sleep from the Lord was fallen upon them" (1 Sam. 26:12). In Gnessin's rendition, the "void of slumber" is the drunken sleep that follows lovemaking. Therefore the man is stretched out *(saruah)* on the bed, recalling additional passages, such as: "[those] that lie upon beds of ivory and stretch themselves upon their couches"; "and the banquet of them that stretched themselves shall be removed" (Amos 6:4,7). Sated with pleasures and relaxation, this figure has lost all sense of danger and of moral duty.

In contrast with the man given over to his dream in Dropkin's poem, the man here is given over to the experience of pleasure and total relaxation, and it is therefore appropriate to speak of him in the same terms Jacob applies to Issachar "And he saw that rest was good, and the land that it was pleasant; and bowed his shoulder to bear, and became a servant unto tribute" (Gen.49: 15). As the limbs of the man in Gnessin's poem "subside in the pleasure of overwhelming rest" danger hovers over him. Bialik described the process of his own self-consecration to the mission of the poet/prophet as a process of recognizing the closeness of the Prince of Night: "I will know you in all your secrets, Prince of Night—your soul I will feel, your thoughts I will understand ("*Razei laylah*" [Night Mysteries]); but the man in Gnessin's poem does not understand the nocturnal mysteries nor does he recognize the figure that approaches him in the dark: "and he will be devoid of recognition and sensation."

Gnessin here utilizes the very strategy that Bialik favored, drawing new life from familiar textual fragments, for example: "and all my members are as a shadow" (Job 17:7); and "and he saw that rest was good" (Gen. 49:15); and so forth. He makes cunning use of the various polysemic possibilities contained in these intertexts in order to create what is at once a logical and paradoxical set of meanings. In the case before us, this spectrum of significance is based upon the polysemy of the root *h.r.d.*, which can mean physical quivering or fear. Gnessin uses the first sense when he describes the man as one whose members are still quivering with pleasure. He uses the second sense in order to introduce into the picture a moment of threat and fear. The combination of dread with restfulness, and of fear with sweetness seems contradictory, yet it is precisely for this reason that the combination is lively and suggestive.[7] In the end the man, in spending a pleasure-filled night in the speaker's bed, has "betrayed" his calling of solitary wandering. He exposes himself to a ritual symbolic act in which the woman serves as a priestess and makes of him a sacrifical offering at the altar of the religion of love.

The priestess drinks the blood of her victim in the third stanza of Dropkin's original as well, but in the original there is not a single mention of the word "love" (*ahavah*). Instead, the word "desire" stands out, repeated with the extra force of the anaphora. The speaker does not "love" the estranged man; she only desires him. She cries out her "sick" desires which have not been kindly answered and decries the affront of kisses she has never had "from the day she was born until the day she withers." Gnessin, too, mentions a soul, sick and lonely, but he shifts the focus of the poem in this concluding section by speaking about the torments of love ("*yisurim le'ahavah*") and "a kiss of love" ("*neshikah shebe'ahavah"*). His reliance on Bialik's poetry here is explicit, even as the biblical sources reverberate clearly: "for I am sick of love" (Song of Songs 2:5); "It shall be health to thy navel, and marrow to thy bones" (Prov. 3:8); "as if it had issued out of the womb" (Job 38:8); "After I am waxed old, shall I have pleasure" (Gen. 18:12). Gnessin's audience would have heard in the inner rhyme of the line "a soul trembling, burning for a kiss of love" (*"nefesh haredah venisrefet belahavah linshikah shebe'ahavah"*) echoes of *lahavah/ahavah* in the famous stanza from *"Hakhnisini tahat kenafekh"* [Take Me Under Your Wing](1905):

וְעוֹד רָז אֶחָד לָךְ אֶתְוַדֶּה:
נַפְשִׁי נִשְׂרְפָה בְלַהֲבָהּ;
אוֹמְרִים אַהֲבָה יֵשׁ בָּעוֹלָם—
מַה־זֹּאת אַהֲבָה?
(1966, 138)

And one last secret I'll confess to you
My soul was consumed in its flame;
They say there is love in the world—
What is this thing, love?

In addition there are heard here echoes of dozens of typical Bialik lines, from which arise the same "accompanying melody" of internal rhyme described so exactly and delicately by Dov Sadan (1936, 111-115). Gnessin's readers also would have identified the following famous lines from Bialik's *"Holekhet at me'imi"* [You Go Away from Me] (1907) as a source for the image "howling. . . pining for love/ And embracing still stones":

וּקְלוּיֵי תַאֲוָה וַאֲכוּלֵי חֵשֶׁק
אִישׁ אִישׁ בִּרְעָבוֹ וּבִצְמָאוֹ יֵצֵא,
יְנַשֵּׁשׁ קִיר כְּעִוֵּר, יַחְבֹּק אָבֶן.
(1966, 192)

And seared with lust, eaten with desire
Each man with his hunger and thirst will leave,
Will grope the wall like a blind man, will embrace
                                              a stone.

The image of the soul thirsting for the sunlight of love is connected not only to lines from Bialik's *"'Im shemesh"* [At Sunrise] (1903): ("and he rose up and shook himself, your brother of yesterday—/ and thirsted for the sun") but also to the description of the bright-eyed youth in "*Megilat ha'esh*" [The Scroll of Fire] (1905), whose imprisoned desires "burst forth all of a sudden like vipers crushed in their holes, with half their bodies pulled out and writhing, hungering and thirsting to confront you, to face you."

It is clear that Gnessin has laced the entire poem with Bialik's ethos of love, and also with traces of his poetic language, creating the sense of a visionary poem. Here is a poem that translates a naked depiction of an emotional event (an event unto itself in the original Russian text) into symbolic language and into the mythos of calling and redemption. The fate of wandering and cultural crisis manifest themselves here as a desperate seeking for love. In Gnessin's rendition the man is transformed into the youth from "The Scroll of Fire" who falls with his lover into the Lethe of sensuality and loses both his mission and true love. What is more, everything here becomes more fateful, more emotional, more complex, more symbolic, and more ritualistic. In short, Gnessin added to the poem all the elements that Bialik's poetics demanded from a Hebrew lyric text.

The question remains whether Gnessin's character, Dina Barabash, could have written such a poem. The answer has a number of ramifications. It's not just that Dina is not well-versed in Bible and in Bialik's poetry, but also that she would not be able to imagine her fate and life the way they are defined—in the poem, through scripture, and through Bialik's verse. The entire mental world of the poem, supposedly the fruit of her creativity, the essence of her searing love, is alien to her; that is, the poem that Dina Barabash could truly have written would have had to be very similar to the Russian poem by Celia Dropkin (if not identical with it).

But such a poem would not have been acceptable to the Hebrew reader of that day. If Gnessin had translated the Russian text sent to him word for word, his Dina would have appeared to the reader not as a poet but as a young woman of meager learning and culture, compromising herself by declaring her "naked" desire while scribbling lines of a weak and shallow lyric; this text would have been read as a meaningless story of a lustful kiss in the night with no content, no universal truth, no Jewish and human tragedy—in short, containing nothing. This is exactly why a young woman like Dina, even had she learned Hebrew, would never have been able to publish such a text in a Hebrew periodical. The lack of layeredness which characterizes her sentences would have been dismissed out of hand as unpoetic.

It is, therefore, almost certain that no young woman like Dina ever wrote a Hebrew poem like the Russian one Celia Dropkin sent to Gnessin. If a woman ever produced something similar to it in the pages of her diary, she never showed it to anyone. In order to be a female Hebrew poet, Dina the woman would have had to let her poem be translated into the poetic Hebrew of her generation by a male saturated with ancient Hebrew texts and stuffed to the gills with passages from Bialik. And if to be a woman poet she would have had to be a male poet, what would have been the point of dealing with poetry at all, at least in Hebrew? She thus refrained from writing Hebrew verse—refrained completely. As a result, not a single Hebrew poem written by a woman was published during the entire thirty years of the Hebrew Renaissance when Bialik dominated the literary horizon. Only when this star dimmed, marking the end of an era in Hebrew verse, could a few women begin to raise their heads and to make their voices heard. This happened in the years 1920-22, and not one year sooner.

— Translated by Naomi Sokoloff and Michael Yogev

NOTES

1. This essay is excerpted from my monograph "Founding Mothers, Stepsisters" which discusses at length the factors that fostered the appearance of women Hebrew poets in the 1920s.

2. In Vol. 2 of the collected works of Gnessin (1982, 47-48).

3. See Hadda (1980, 13-14).

4. The English translations of these poems are by Dan Miron.

5. All biblical citations are from the King James version. However, references are made to the "Song of Songs" and not to the "Song of Solomon."

6. For comments on the affinity which fiction writers of Hebrew felt for Bialik's poems at the turn of the century, see my book *Bodedim bemoʿadam* (224-51). For a discussion of Gnessin's special affinity for Bialik, see my article "*Ḥaḥim beʾapo shel hanetsaḥ.*"

7. In Bialik's poetry the same technique appears in various texts. Examples connected with the root *h.r.d.*, to tremble, include: "Crowned with splendor, like a bird I will tremble" ("*Zohar*" [Splendor]); "and myriad rays—they trembled" ("*Mishomrim laboker*" [Of Those Who Watch for the Dawn]); and especially "And your souls trembled before every stirring of beauty" ("*Yehi ḥelki ʿimakhem*" [Let My Share Be With You]).

WORKS CITED

Bialik, Hayyim Nahman. 1966. *Kol shirei Ḥ. N. Bialik* [Collected Poems of H. N. Bialik]. Tel Aviv: Dvir.

Binyamin, H. 1981. "Tsili shel Gnessin," *Siman kriʾah* 12/13: 240-43.

Brower, Reuben Arthur. 1959. *The Poetry of Allusion*. London: Oxford Univ. Press.

Frishman, David. 1901. "*Meʾeit haʿorekh* [From the Editor]. *Hador* 1,50 (26 Decmber): 11.

Gnessin, U.N. 1982. *Kol kitvei Uri Nisan Gnessin*. [Collected Works of Uri Nisan Gnessin]. Ed. Dan Miron and Yisrael Zemora. Tel Aviv: Hakibbutz Hameuhad.

Hadda, Janet R. 1980. *Yankev Glatshteyn*. Boston: Twayne Publishers.

Korman, Ezra. 1928. *Yidishe dikhterins: antologye* [Yiddish Women Poets: An Anthology]. Chicago: Farlag L.M. Shteyn.

Miron, Dan. 1986. "*Ḥaḥim beʾapo shel hanetsaḥ*" [Rings in the Nose of Eternity]. In *Uri Nisan Gnessin: meḥkarim uteʿudot*, [Uri Nisan Gnessin: Studies and Documents], eds. Dan Miron and Dan Laor, 231-368. Jerusalem: Mossad Bialik.

———— 1987. *Bodedim bemoʿadam* [When Loners Come Together]. Tel Aviv: Am Oved.

———— 1991. *Imahot meyasdot, aḥayot ḥorgot* [Founding Mothers/Stepsisters]. Tel Aviv: Hakibbutz Hameuhad. An earlier version appeared in two installments in *Alpayim* 1(1989): 29-58, and 2(1990): 120-177.

Sadan, Dov. 1936. "*Neginat levai—lederekh haḥarizah hapenimit beshirat Bialik*" [Background Music: Internal Rhyme in Bialik's Poetry]. *Knesset* 1 (1936.): 111-115.

The Eyes Have It:
Celia Dropkin's Love Poetry

∽ JANET HADDA ∾

This paper concerns the love poetry of Celia Dropkin[1] and, especially,
the entangled mesh of feeling that forms its matrix: conflict, powerful
erotic longing, and forlorn loneliness. I will suggest a way of reading
Dropkin's deep yet accessible poetic oeuvre that I hope will both unify
these disparate thematic moods and shed light on Dropkin's view of the
nature and meaning of love. In doing so, I also will suggest some biographical connections.

An examination of Dropkin's love poetry is overdue. Criticism has
neglected her, for a variety of reasons, but all—significantly—are related
to the fact that she was a woman. Dropkin was, on certain occasions,
maligned in her own time. She was ignored subsequently by a generation of critics who did not typically concentrate on women; more
recently, feminist critics who have dealt with specific Jewish experience
have tended not to focus on her because her concerns with Jewishness
are not uppermost.

I am deeply committed to the psychoanalytic theoretical views of self-
psychology and its most recent development, intersubjectivity (For further elaboration on these concepts see note 4 , as well as Stolorow et al.,
1987). My approach leads me to understand that my personal reaction to
a work is not insignificant to the way I will discuss it. In other words, I
interact with the text at a fundamental level, and this should be discussed. Hence the mention of my introduction to Dropkin's work.
Similarly, I believe the artist stands in intersubjective relation to his/her

own work. Hence my decision to view Dropkin's "I" as connected to, although not equal with, her autobiographical self.

The way in which I became acquainted with Celia Dropkin's work deserves mention, because it illustrates a certain neglect she has suffered. I was already a faculty member at UCLA, having completed my graduate work in Yiddish literature at Columbia. I considered myself well versed in the subject, particularly with respect to American Yiddish poetry. I was teaching a translation course, and one of my female students came to me one day, complaining that we weren't reading any women poets (which was true) and suggesting that we read the two available poems in our anthology by Celia Dropkin. "Who?" I asked. I had never heard of her. I read the anthologized poems. One in particular mesmerized me. Here it is, as it appears in the Howe and Greenberg *Treasury of Yiddish Poetry* (1972, 168-169), in a translation by Adrienne Rich:

> I haven't yet seen you
> asleep.
> I'd like to see
> how you sleep,
> when you've lost your power
> over yourself, over me.
> I'd like to see you
> helpless, strung-out, dumb.
> I'd like to see you
> with your eyes shut,
> breathless.
> I'd like to see you
> dead.

Fascinated, I began to discover who Celia Dropkin was. I learned that she had been born in Bobroysk, White Russia, in 1888, that she had come to this country to be with her husband, the Bundist Shmaye Dropkin, who had been forced to leave Russia because of his politics. I found out that she had begun writing in Russian; that, while studying in Kiev, she had developed a profoundly important personal relationship with the Hebrew writer U. N. Gnessin, until his untimely death; and that she had begun to write Yiddish only after she arrived in the United States. I learned that she had published one volume of poetry during her lifetime, *In heysn vint* [In the Hot Wind], which appeared in 1935,[2] and that her five children had reissued this volume (*In heysn vint: Poems, Stories and Pictures*, 1959) after her death, adding to it previously unpublished material, as well as copies of some of the poet's painting—an activity that had occupied her in the years before her death in 1956.

I was amazed, moreover, to discover that while I had never heard Celia Dropkin's name in any of my many Yiddish literature courses, my ignorance of her was not actually from want of exposure: she had appeared in the first issue of *In zikh,* the poetry magazine, which I must have had in my hands dozens, if not hundreds, of times during my dissertation research on the *In zikh* poet, Yankev Glatshteyn (1920, *In zikh,* I,i [January]:11). Clearly, I had been deeply, if unconsciously, affected by an academic education that gave me to understand, without ever saying so explicitly, of course, that only men counted.[3]

Despite my own ignorance, Celia Dropkin's love poetry had not gone unnoticed in the world of Yiddish letters, where its searing immediacy and unveiled sexuality had caused considerable discomfort. Critics at the time—who were male—tended to deprecate her and minimize the importance of her writing: consider the words of Arn Glants-Leyeles, writing in the *Tog-morgn zhurnal* after Dropkin's death in 1956. This is Glants-Leyeles's explanation for Dropkin's switch from poetry to her new creative passion—painting—which she pursued energetically during the last several years of her life (1956, 5):

> Internal growth means: in spirit, in thought, in ideas . . . Celia Dropkin remained the young girl, the young woman, who lived and fevered only with feelings and the thirsts of her body. Ideas, thought, the vibrant relationship to the world and to life, all of which enrich the personality and make it stronger than the five senses, were not her "métier". She didn't even have an organic relationship to the language of her poetry, so she could not grow internally, creatively. (Translation mine.)

More recent female and feminist critics have acknowledged Dropkin but not granted her much focused attention. On the surface, this lack of concentration appears to result from her disinterest in grappling with the issue of specifically Jewish female expression; i.e., she rarely uses the imagery of Jewish life—neither religion nor Eastern European folk tradition. But I suggest that the nature of her subject matter has had more to do with the relative silence around her than might at first be evident.

Even when a modern feminist critic does discuss Dropkin's life and work, there is a peculiar lack of the feminist perspective that we have come to expect for non-Yiddish writers. How, otherwise, can one explain the strange reference by Norma Fain Pratt in her 1980 article in *American Jewish History* to marriage as an emblem of the ordinary: "Margolin's life was unconventional. She had lovers, was twice married, and left an infant son in the permanent care of its father . . . Celia Dropkin's life was more conventional. She married, reared five children and kept house . . . ." (83-84)

In fact, as both John Dropkin and Esther Unger (two of Celia's children) report, the Dropkin household was highly unconventional. Daily life was vibrant and functional; both John and Esther remember their mother as fulfilling their needs well. Yet, at the same time, Shmaye evidently did much of the housework, and Celia was capable of sitting in the kitchen with pots boiling over and burning, writing poetry, totally oblivious to her surroundings. Esther Unger reports that her father taught her to iron when she was six years old, so that she would be assured of a proper dress to wear. And, finally, to cite one of the most appealing anecdotes I was told, it was a somewhat zany environment: one day, Esther came home to find her mother surrounded by a group of women poets, all of whom, except for her mother, were smoking. Without missing a beat, Esther turned to her questioning playmates and said with aplomb: "It's in memory of their dead husbands."

Close inspection of Dropkin's love poetry reveals that, while she certainly does not shrink from descriptions of erotic moments—her "Shpatsirndik iber vayse volkns" [Strolling Over White Clouds] (53) is a splendid example—and while the basic currency of her language is highly emotional, the essence of her daring is her utter openness about her extramarital liaisons. Although the bond between Celia and Shmaye was close and loving, the existence of these affairs was not a secret. Both John and Esther confirmed what is perfectly clear from the poetry. I connect life and poetry, although I do not equate them. To suggest that the "I" in her writing is somehow unrelated to the woman and her feelings denies the essential lyric quality of Dropkin's work in the service of a literary myth. At the same time, I do not intend to dwell on, or even speculate about, who these lovers may have been, or about when and how often in her life her affairs took place. Instead, I want to probe the meaning of those connections for Celia Dropkin: Why did she look outside her marriage? What was she looking for? What can be learned about the nature of love for her? What, if anything, was the benefit to her of these relationships?

I argue here that Celia Dropkin, who in very early childhood suffered the loss of her father, engaged in a lifelong search for the nurture that was lost to her at that early moment. She had the added misfortune to be raised among relatives who did not welcome her—quite the contrary—

and her mother, whom she idealized, was, from other accounts, a rather rigid and ungiving individual. Love for Dropkin meant a combination of adult closeness and acceptance, combined with a freeing sexual contact. However, because of her early experiences, she also needed to be comforted and protected as if she were still a child. Moreover, any hint of nonacceptance, or, indeed, of inattention, could throw her into a state of profound melancholy and even depression. And all of these shifting affect states were articulated by the poet through her writing, which, if we are to understand the lines of her famous poem "*Mayn mame*" [My Mother], served to define her as a woman of full sexuality and spirit, even as it allowed her to explore, and grieve over, the ways in which she had not reached such a state:

מיין מאַמע איז צו קיינעם א ווייב ניט געוואָרן,
נאָר אַלע פּילטשעניקע,
פּיליאָריקע, פּילנאָכטיקע זיפצן
פון איר יונגן און ליבענדן וועזן,
פון איר בענקנדיק בלוט,
האָב איך מיט מיין קינדערשן האַרצן פאַרנומען,
טיף אין זיך איינגעזאַפט. [...]
איצט שפּריצט פון מיר אָפן,
מיין מאַמעס זודיקער, הייליקער,
טיף־פאַרבאַהאַלטענער באַגער.

My mother became wife to no-one,
But all the sighs of many days,
Many years, many nights
Sighs of her young and loving being,
Of her longing blood,
I perceived with my childish heart,
Soaked it all in deeply.
. . . Now from me springs openly,
My mother's hot, holy,
Deeply-hid desire.

(48)

Clearly, the entire issue of creativity and fluid expression is tied to sexuality for Dropkin. I will confine my comments to approximately one dozen poems that deal with the larger subject of love within which sexuality is subsumed, although my choice by no means exhausts the available examples. From these love poems, what emerges most clearly is a predominant mood of unhappiness and longing; a forlorn quality dominates, although, to be sure, there are also poems in which the poet's words are strong and confident.

Both Pratt and Kathryn Hellerstein have pointed out the ambivalence that can be found in Dropkin's work; Hellerstein (1988, 221) calls it "[t]he speaker's ambivalent desire for the Other . . . whether the Other is defined as exotic, obsolete, or male." Pratt (84) sees the ambivalence as having to do with "anticipating freedom and fearing its consequences."

I certainly would not dispute that there are individual cases in which Dropkin grapples with ambivalence. Yet, when I concentrated on the love poems as an entity, I discovered, instead, a prominent tendency towards powerful evocations of several clear themes: the longing to be cherished, sometimes with hope of achievement, sometimes not; the idealization of the lover, often with accompanying deprecating self-evaluation; the outcry of sadness and depression, mainly due to the absence or withdrawal of the needed love. And throughout, as an expressive vehicle, the most obvious image is that of the lover's eyes, either focused on her with kindness, or averted, or—not infrequently—looking upon her with condescension and coldness.

These diverse articulations actually form a coherent pattern when explored from a psychoanalytic perspective. The psychoanalyst Heinz Kohut tells us that, where development proceeds smoothly, the child will look for two essential qualities in the parental environment: a source of mirroring for his or her feelings and experiences of mastery, lovability, and innate value; and a source of idealization, the knowledge that there is safety and solace in the world. Put perhaps somewhat simplistically, the conclusion of the first experience is, "I believe I am great, and you think so too, so it must be true"; whereas that of the second one is, "You are great, and you let me be with you, so I gain some luster from this connection." Kohut, in what I view as a rather sexist formulation, indicates the mother as the source of mirroring for the growing child, and the father as the source of idealization. In my view, and also in my clinical experience, what is important is the function itself, and not the gender of the person providing it.[4]

In Dropkin's case, there was from a very early age only one person to do the major parental providing , namely, her mother. It is natural and common for a child who fails to receive the necessary developmental supplies from one parent to turn to the other parent in the hope of fulfillment. Dropkin had only her mother, who seems to have been too absorbed in her own world to be truly available to her daughter. This may help explain why Dropkin came to feel herself so dependent on men: her father had disappeared through death, but while this was a profound abandonment, it was not the sustained and repeated disappointment that she apparently encountered with her mother. At the same time, however, any sense that the man was rejecting or distant could reproduce in her the early experience of traumatic loss.

In her adult life, the relationship took a dramatic turn, when Dropkin brought her mother over from Russia to live with her. The mother, from Esther Unger's account, disrupted her daughter's home with her demands and stinginess, to which Celia responded alternately with anger and remorseful self-abasement. At this point, moreover, Shmaye, Celia's husband, truly withdrew from his involvement in the household—this according to Esther.

In my assessment, there was one person who, in Dropkin's young womanhood, provided her with a deep fulfillment of her most basic needs, the Hebrew writer U. N. Gnessin. Gnessin was, for her, an idealizable man who also mirrored her longing to be seen and appreciated as an artist. Gnessin urged the young Celia to write, and thereby eased her out of a writing inhibition to which she had been prey due to previous criticism (*Vint*, 1959, 264). At the same time, he evidently loved and welcomed her. In later years, long after the loss of Gnessin, the memory of his acceptance and encouragement remained strong reminders to Dropkin of what had been, as well as of what no longer existed.

In the following pages, I will explore the link between sexuality and idealization in Dropkin's poetry, showing that, even when she feels lower than, or inferior to, her lover, she is nonetheless able to maintain her vitality as long as she knows that she has an intact bond with the admired man. Even when the connection seems to be ruptured, she is able to sustain herself as long as she can fantasize the existence of a loving relationship. When the internal sense of contact is lost, however, she is lost as well, dead inside.

Complicating this powerful dynamic is the poet's sense that her sexuality, which is the vehicle for achieving the tie in the first place, is shameful or even sinful. Finally, underlying the mix of idealization and passion is the deep wish to be cherished as a child, both to assure her that she will not be abandoned and as a way to reestablish the innocence she felt was lost through sexuality.

Dropkin reveals how she integrates idealization of a man with her own creativity in the following poem[5]:

דו, מיט אַ געזיכט פֿון אַפּאָלאָן,
מיט אַ קערפּער פֿון גאַנימעד,
וואָס פֿאַר אַ שאַרף אויג,
וואָס פֿאַר אַ חוש דו האָסט
ווי נאַריש, ווי אומבאַהאָלפֿן
בין איך אַנטקעגן דיר.

You, with a face like Apollo,
With a body like Ganymede,
What a sharp eye,
What a flair you have
How foolish, how incapable
I am next to you.

(31)

Here, the speaker sees herself as minor and unworthy next to the man
she so admires. Nonetheless, she retains the ability to create despite her
minimized state: this is obvious in her educated and literary choice of
imagery. So, too, in the poem *"Du host nit farzeyt a kind in mir"* [You
Didn't Sow a Child in Me], where the poet announces that her beloved
has sown himself in her body. His presence grows like a cancer rather
than a fetus; there is gradually less and less, rather than more and more
of the woman herself. Finally:

און מיין נשמה ליגט, ווי אַ הונט ביי זיינע פֿיס,
און ווערט אַלץ שוואַכער, שוואַכער,
נאָר שטאַרבנדיק דורך דיר,
זינג איך צו דיר, ווי פֿריער, סערענאַדן.

. . . my soul lies, like a dog, at your feet,
Growing ever weaker,
But dying because of you,
I serenade you, as before.

(54)

Even though she is destroyed by the internal experience of her love,
the speaker still functions as an artist, dredging out of herself the beautiful creation of poetry as she might a child, albeit at the expense of her
life.

The secret of the poet's ability to create despite feelings of inferiority
or even abdication of self lies in the fact of the bond itself, which invigo-
rates even as it destroys. The truth of this paradox emerges through
comparison with a contrasting experience, that of being abandoned.
Without any access to her beloved, the woman's creative impulse is lost,

because all energy and emotional effort must serve to regain the abandoning lover. Consider the following abject outcry:

איך וועל קושן די ערד, אויף וועלכער דו טרעטסט,
איך וועל שעפטשען די ווערטער, וועלכע דו רעדסט,
נאָר ווייז זיך צוריק אין מיין לעבן,
נאָר ווייז זיך צוריק אין מיין לעבן!

איך וועל שלינגען די שוים פון דיין ליבע צו מיר,
נאָר ווייז זיך צוריק אין דער ראָם פון מיין טיר,
וועל איך דיר מיין לעבן געבן,
וועל איך דיר מיין לעבן געבן!

> I will kiss the ground that you walk on
> I will whisper the words that you speak,
> Just turn up once again in my life!
> Just turn up once again in my life!

> I will gulp down the foam of your love for me,
> Just turn up once again at my door,
> And I'll give you my life,
> I'll give you my life!

(39)

The perfection of the man, especially his sexual potency, and the woman's concomitant utter lack of self-esteem are connected to his absence. Now there is no hope for mirroring, for affirmation of artistic and sexual creativity. However, although in this case the hunger for any acknowledgement of worth has been extinguished, some of Dropkin's most riveting poems recount the anguished process of realizing that mirroring has been withdrawn. Others reflect the pain of remembering how important such attention had been. In this way, Dropkin underscores the depth and magnitude of the loss. Notice how literally these poems focus on the mirroring gaze, especially when it isn't there.

On the best of occasions, when the relationship with the man contains both intimacy and sexual intensity, the woman retains some sense of herself in the face of possible rejection. The following poem describes the watchful attention the woman lavishes on the man in order to decipher the nuances of his mood, lest she lose his presence:

ווען דו האָסט שטיל געקושט און צערטלעך מיך געאָרעמט,
זיינען אומבאַוועגלעך מיטאַמאָל געוואָרן דיינע אויגן,
אָט האָבן זיי געלאַסטשעט מיך, געוואַרעמט,
און פּלוצלינג, ווי מיט אייז באַוועבט, פאַרצויגן.

איך האָב געדענקט אַז דו ביסט קראַנק געוואָרן,
ווייל מאָדנע אַנדערש איז געווען דיין קוק,
פאַרקוואַלעשט, ווי פון פּיין, ווי פון שרעק פאַרלאָרן,
איך האָב זיך שטיל געגעבן פון דיר אַ רוק.

נאָר דו האָסט מיך נאָך שטאַרקער איינגעקלאָמערט,
און נאָנט האָב איך דערזען די אויגן דיינע צוויי,
פאַרשטאַנען נאָר דיין האַרץ, ווי ס׳האָט געהאַמערט,
אַז עס קומט צו דיר דיין ליידנשאַפט אזוי.

When you quietly kissed me and embraced me tenderly,
All at once your eyes stopped moving,
Having just cuddled and warmed me,
They were now overcast, woven with ice.

I thought you were ill,
Since your gaze was strange and different,
Weakly, lost in pain and fear,
I pushed away in silence.

But you enclosed me still closer to you,
And I saw your two eyes near to me,
Perceived your heart, how it hammered
Understood that your passion arises this way.

(34)

This poem has a happy ending, for the speaker is not rejected, nor does she force herself away; the danger of no response has been averted, and the result is continuity based on understanding.

Unfortunately, things do not always turn out so satisfactorily. Still, there are occasions, such as the poem *"Mayn neshome in dayne hent"* [My Soul in Your Hands] when, although the answering gaze is removed, and the poet feels bereft, she is able to maintain a memory of sweeter moments:

דו דערנידעריקסט מיך היינט,
מיט דיין ניט קוקן אויף מיר,
מיט דיין שווייגן,
איך וואָלט וועלן,
זאָלסט ניט אראָפּנעמען
פון מיר דיינע אויגן
און עפּעס מיר שטיל דערצײלן

אוּן אִיךְ זָאל דִיךְ הערן,
זינקענדיק אִין דײַנע אוֹיגן.

קוּק אוֹיף מִיר, ווִי דאַן,
ווען אִיךְ הָאֲב דערפִילט,
ווִי מײַן נשמה נעמסטוּ אִין דײַנע הענט
אוּן קוּשסט זי שטיל.

You abase me today,
By not looking at me,
By your silence,
I wish,
You would not take
Your eyes from me
And would say
something softly to me
That I could hear you,
While sinking into your eyes.

Look at me, as then,
When I felt
You take my soul in your hands
And softly kiss it.

(43)

In psychoanalytic terms, the reactions displayed in this poem would
generally be viewed as healthy and mature, since the unhappy woman
retains her capacity to understand what is upsetting her, how circumstances might be different, and why the previous situation was preferable to her. Above all, she maintains the perception that her soul is worthy of embrace, even if she isn't receiving what she needs at the moment.
In other words, an overarching sense of value and completeness remains,
even under less than satisfying conditions.

The very next poem in the original *In heysn vint* betrays a completely
different mood, however. Here, the averted gaze of the beloved is tantamount to a death sentence:

אִיךְ בִּין אַ דערטרוּנקענע
אִין אַ טִיפן ברוֹנעם.
עם זעט נָאך מײַן אוֹיג דײַן בלוֹי אוֹיג פוּן אוֹיבן,
וואָס זוּכט מִיךְ אוּן ווִיל מִיךְ רעטן,
צוּ אפשר אִיז דָאס נָאר
אַ שטיקל בלוֹיער הִימל,
וואָס קוּקט, ווִי דײַנס אַ בלוֹי אוֹיג
אַרײַן אִין ברוֹנעם?

די פֿאַרשימלטע ברונעם־ווענט זײַנען גליטשיק,
און מײַנע הענט קענט פֿאַרלירן די קראַפֿט
פֿון באַרירונג מיט זײַ.
דו זעסט מיך שוין מער ניט,
דו נעמסט אַוועק דײַן בלוי אויג פֿון ברונעם.

> I am a drowned woman,
> In a deep well.
> My eye still sees your blue eye above,
> Which looks for me and wants to save me,
> Or maybe it is really
> A bit of blue sky,
> That gazes, like one of your blue eyes
> Into the well?

> The moldy well walls are slippery,
> And my hands lose the strength
> To hold on to them.
> You see me no more
> You remove your blue eye from the well.

(44)

The speaker is alone and isolated in her cold, confining space. All is lost: there is no room for hope, no vitality; indeed, it is impossible to live when no one is watching. The desperately needed response could save her life, could be like a blessed ray of light in a dark internal prison. But, with the confirmation of continued absence, there is no salvation, and Dropkin's poetic psyche cannot summon up a remembered holding atmosphere to sustain her. She must, instead, drown in her own longing.

While Dropkin's love relationships might have signified her attempts to achieve a necessary sense that she was innately cherishable, the arena in which they occurred was sexual. And, for her actions, she was subject to feelings of remorse and sinfulness. The regret is obvious, for example, in "Vi zaftig royte epl" [Like Juicy Red Apples], a poignant work in which the speaker compares herself to a ripe apple—beautiful and flourishing on the outside, but rotten and irredeemable inside. This poem contains all the power and emotional extravaganza of the more famous "Di tsirkus dame" [The Circus Lady] or "Vos ikh zog un tu" [Whatever I Say and Do], but it lacks their bravado, tentative and superficial though that bravado may have been. Here, despite its flaming cheeks, the apple barely manages to cling to the tree. And when an unsuspecting man, blinded by the sun-drenched fruit, finds it after it has fallen, he will be revolted:

וועט ער פֿול עקל און מיטלייד
מיך צוריק אַ וואָרף טאָן,
ווייל אויסגענאָגסן פֿון ווערים איז מיין האַרץ
און דער פעטער וואָרעם, — ליידנשאַפֿט,
קריכט קיינמאָל ניט אַרויס
פֿון מיין זאַפֿטיקן קערפער, —
אַ פֿאַרוואָרפֿענע וועט ער מיך צעפֿרעסן
ביז צום טויט.

Full of disgust and compassion
He will toss me back,
Because my heart is eaten up by worms,
And the bloated worm—passion
Will never crawl out
Of my juicy body,—
It will devour me, a cast-off
Till I die.

(69)

Although the biblical Fall is never mentioned, it provides the back-drop for the poem's aura of ruin and sexual depravity. Unlike the biblical original, however, the man is innocent, never partaking of the evil that brings about the everlasting connection with death. Moreover, the fault here lies not with forbidden knowledge, which might lead to lust and carnality, but rather with the experience of passion itself. That is, the very feeling causes all the decay and morbidity, but only the woman is cul-pable and therefore only she is punished.

Underlying this bold and agonized imagery is a depiction of the utter helplessness that results from the possession of or, perhaps more accu-rately, the being possessed by sexual passion. There is nothing that the poet can do but suffer the consequences of this hated quality, because her underlying needs are never fully met through sexual contact. Moreover, her feeling of self-disgust is only accentuated, because the outer manifes-tation—her body the vehicle for attracting the hoped-for response—betrays none of the inner ravagement and despair.

The sense of futility and entrapment appears elsewhere as well, although not always in as dramatically metaphoric a fashion. One of my favorite poems, because of its characteristic mix of linguistic simplicity and psychological perspicacity, is "An ovnt in merts" [An Evening in March]. This is a circumscribed yet deeply evocative discussion of one woman's inability to enjoy the world, because a necessary bond has never existed or has been withdrawn. It reminds me of the mood I perceive at times in patients who cannot invoke an inner feeling of connection when they are lonely or alone. The poet addresses herself, almost as if she hopes that, through such an internal conversation, she will manage to provide herself with the enlivening presence she so badly needs and without which she remains bereft.

The poem contains muted self-protest, as memory confronts the speaker: it is a wonderful spring evening, rainy and captivating; other women are busily moving about—just as she used to be able to do—welcoming the new season with eyes as light as springtime clouds, their faces made up brightly, *"vi letste shpurn fun zunfargang"* (like the final traces of sunset).

The poet, however, cannot participate in the gentle spirit of renewal and optimism:

אָך, דו אליין נאָר גייסט אַרום אַ בלייכע,
אַ גרוייער שאָטן אין לוסטיקן פאַרנאַכט,
נאָך אַלץ אין ווינטערדיקן הוט און מאַנטל;
און די גרוייסע אויגן זאָגן אויס דעם סוד,
און פון ליבע טראַכסטו נאָר, פון ליבע,
דו נאַרישע, דו אומגליקלעכע פרוי!

> Ah, you alone walk around so pale,
> A grey shadow in the cheerful dusk,
> Still in your wintry hat and coat;
> And your large eyes announce the secret,
> That you can think only of love, of love,
> You foolish, you unhappy woman!
>
> (67)

Both Esther Unger and John Dropkin spoke to me about their mother's tendency to feel depressed, or melancholy, and Esther reported that her mother had once, in her young years, attempted suicide, although this depth of misery had never been equaled after Celia married Shmaye Dropkin. I understand the depression and the lack of overt suicidality as forming a continuum: at a point when absolutely no one could help her know that she was not isolated, then the pain of life may have temporarily seemed unbearable; after she married and had children around, she was more stable and balanced, although, even then, the fear of being left was never completely banished.

Moreover, the very relationship she enjoyed with her children was, at the same time, linked to her struggle with love as an adult emotion. For, as is most often the case, Dropkin's experience as a parent raised unresolved issues about love that stemmed from her own childhood and adolescence.

The poem *"Ot azoy"* [That's It] (100) illustrates how precarious the mother-child bond can be. The speaker envisions merger with her child in a marvelous cocoon, but then she cannot help but continue the image, watching in her mind's eye how her child must, as part of a natural developmental process, sprout wings and fly away from her body and her love.

Dropkin makes quite plain in her poetry what she needs, and the poetic statements have some corroboration in her life as well. In a nutshell, she wants to feel that, as a woman, she is understood, given to, and tenderly regarded—as she imagines a young child would be loved, as she seems to have loved her own children, and, evidently, as she was never loved herself.

The longing to return to a childlike state of innocence and greater lovability is explicit in several poems, the most dramatic of which (because it also contains a suicide theme) is *"Baym fentster"* [At the Window]. The speaker looks out her fifth-floor window and, head bowed, finds her memory jogged by the street below, although at first the nature of the association eludes her. As she reflects, however, the connection becomes clearer:

דער טראָטואַר האָט געקוקט אױף מיר מיט מילדע, גרױע אױגן,
און װי אַ װאַרים בעט, װי ליבלעכע אָרעמס געצױגן,
דער טראָטואַר איז געװען אַזױ נאָנט, אַזױ נאָנט...
און אָן מײן װאַרים קינדעריש בעטל האָב איך מיך דערמאָנט.

> The sidewalk looked at me with mild, grey eyes,
> Like a warm bed, like loving arms outstretched,
> The sidewalk was so near, so near . . .
> And I recalled the warm little bed of my childhood.
>
> (75)

The sidewalk five stories below, offering probable if not certain death, seems inviting and responsive to the weary and lonely woman above. Moreover, it implies affection, safety, and warmth to her. Her connection of these associations with her childhood forms the strength and sadness of the metaphor; only a child whose comforts had been meager indeed would be likely to find a source of gratification and mirroring in as cold and potentially harmful a resting place as a concrete sidewalk.

The prospect of receiving the caring attention that childhood can allow attracts the poet of *"Baym fentster"* so irresistibly that she follows her urge at the end of the last stanza: *"Ikh hob zikh mer un mer aynge-boygn,/ Un tsu mayn opru, vi a foygl gefloygn"* (I bent over more and more,/ And flew, like a bird, to my rest) (75).

The poem *"Ikh tulye tsu mayn heysn shtern"* [I Press My Heated Brow], however, provides fuller information about the longing for childhood than *"Baym fentster"*. At the same time, it clarifies Dropkin's profound relationship with her children (which, together with her nature poetry, is a subject worthy of a separate study). This work links adulthood and sin; therefore, the wish for the earlier state emphasizes the poet's desire to rid herself of guilt and pain. In the simple caress between mother and child, the speaker finds herself absolved and released:

און מיין שווערקייט ווערט פֿאַרפֿאַלן,
ווען איך דריק מיין קאָפּ צום קינד,
שטילע טרערן לאָז איך פֿאַלן,
ס׳גייט אַוועק פֿון מיר מיין זינד.

ס׳פֿאַלן, ס׳פֿאַלן שטילע טרערן
פֿון דערלייזונג און פֿון גליק,
ס׳ווערט געקילט מיין הייסער שטערן
און אַ קינד ווער איך צוריק.

And my heaviness falls away,
When I press my head to my child,
I let quiet tears fall,
And my sin departs from me.

Quiet tears fall and fall,
Tears of salvation and of joy,
My heated brow grows cooler,
And I am a child again.

(97)

The poem *"Vi gut iz mir mit mayne kinder haynt"* [How Good I Feel With My Children Today] echoes the theme of regaining childhood innocence, and I will not go into it in detail here, except to indicate that the nature of the sin for which childhood could be the solution is particularly obvious in this case: it is her illicit love. As Dropkin puts it:

און רואיק זיץ איך מיט זיי, ווי אַ קינד,
און ווייס בין איך פֿון בענקעניש, פֿון זינד,
און ווייס בין איך פֿון דיר פֿון מיין שלעכטער פֿריינט,

And I sit calmly with them, like a child,
And I am far from longing and from sin,
And I am far from you, my bad friend. . . .
(106)

The children anchor her, remind her that she has a life apart from her world of love and longing outside the home. Moreover, their purity allows her to tap into something within herself, a feeling from her past, when she was not yet prey to the complications and miseries of her current existence, and when she was free from the self-censure that she expected, as well, from her social milieu.

If I am correct about the reason for her critical neglect, Dropkin was not wrong in her suspicions of others, even those who may have been too polite, cautious, or unaware to say that they were uncomfortable or disapproving of her overtly erotic articulations. Glants-Leyeles, for example, comments, with what seems like a sigh of relief, that *"Vi gut iz mir mit mayne kinder haynt"* is a nonerotic poem, representing *"an ekhte, vareme, muterlekhe shtub-shtimung"* (a genuine, warm, motherly, homey mood). Esther Unger told me that her mother "would smell a snub across the Atlantic Ocean." Her critics affected her deeply. Given her sensitivity, how much more painful it must have been for her to realize that even those closest to her could not always comprehend her thoughts and behavior. This anguished understanding is beautifully crystalized in *"Tayerer"* [Dear One], which illuminates Dropkin's feelings about the existence and meaning of her liaisons. Dedicated to *Sh. . . ,* whom I guess to be Shmaye, her husband, the poem's fourteen lines are technically a sonnet, but the distribution of lines is not standard. The form thus provides a backdrop for a discussion of love that will not proceed along predictable lines:

טײערער, טײערער, פֿאַרשטײ, אַז איך נאָר דיך ניט,
נאָר עס איז קראַנק אַזוי מײַן אָרימע זעל,
אַז אַלע זעען עס אַרויס פֿון מײַנע אויגן,
זײ זײַנען געוואָרן אַזוי לוסטיק און העל,
און איצט מיט אַ אומעט אַ ווײַסטן פֿאַרצויגן.

און עס טרײַבט מיך מײַן קראַנקע, מײַן אָרימע זעל
אַנטלויפֿן פֿון דײַן גוטן און לײַדענדן בליק.
וואוהין און צו וועמען? איך ווײַס און איך ווײַס ניט,
נאָר גלויב, איך געפֿין ניט קײן גליק.

לאָז פֿאַלן צו דיר אויף דײַן ערלעכער ברוסט
און וויינען, ווי אַ פֿאַרשולדיקט, פֿאַרבלאָנדזשעטע קינד.
ווי איך לײַד, ווי איך לײַד, ווען דו וואָלסט געוואוסט,
וואָלסטו ניט געשטראָפֿט מיך מיט רייד פֿאַר מײַן זינד,
וואָלסט צערטלעך פֿאַרוויגט, ווי אַ קינד.

Dear one, understand, that I'm not fooling you,
My poor soul is simply ill in this way,
Everyone sees it revealed in my eyes,
Which once were so cheerful and bright,
And are now overcast with bleak sadness.

And I'm chased by my sick, my poor soul
To run from your decent and suffering gaze.
Where and to whom? I know and I don't know,
But believe me, I cannot find joy.

Let me fall on your honest breast,
And cry, like a naughty, misguided child,
How I suffer, how I suffer, if only you knew
You'd not punish me with talk about sin,
Gently you'd rock me, like a child.

                        (66)

Everything is here: the longing to be treated with tenderness instead
of punishment for her supposed sexual sins, which may look bad but
actually are merely the unfortunate actions of someone lacking the capacity to behave differently; the hunger for the benign gaze of her beloved
and needed man is here, too, although in this case she feels compelled to
flee, seeking love elsewhere, always in vain.

Most important, however, is the clear and unambiguous statement
that this is the way she is and she hates it, but she can make no effort to
change—or even to promise that she might—because she knows that
such an attempt would be fruitless. The only hope for salvation is to be
understood. The sad part of the formulation is that, while pleading for
compassion from the outside, she is unable to muster any of it for herself.
That is, she still regards herself as sick and damaged, even if she realizes
that her behavior is not evil per se.

In the end, what can, or should, these poems mean for the reader? For
me, the answer is simple: they represent the unabashed decision—
whether taken self-consciously or out of creative need is immaterial—to
reveal the inner workings of a varied and troubled womanhood, which
nonetheless exults in being, even if that being involves pain, even if it
means humiliation. Fully exposed in her female sexuality, Dropkin

simultaneously accepts the paradox that her most childish needs and strivings persist. In this, her writings express what the psychoanalyst Ethel Person (1988, 24-25) cites as the transcendent hallmarks of the experience of love:

> Despite the general cautions of traditional wisdom and psychoanalytic theory, I am certain that romantic love is generally more enriching than it is depleting. It is a magnificently human condition, and yet not everyone will experience it. Despite its (usually) transient nature, it offers access to the unconscious, lights up the emotional life, and brings internal change in a way that often far outlives the experience itself. . . . Like so many other human gifts, romantic love has the potential for both good and evil, but it should not be judged by its corrupted forms or dismissed on account of its transience.[6]

What Celia Dropkin left behind, as part and parcel of her creative legacy, is a compassionate and sensitive view of the inevitable yet particular vicissitudes of love and sexuality, seen through the eyes of a woman who, while conveying common experience, knew herself to be artistically unique.

NOTES

1. I generally employ the rules of Yiddish transcription formulated by the YIVO Institute, in which case the poet's name would be rendered "Tsilye Drapkin." However, in a personal communication from John Dropkin (June 28, 1990), he indicated that his mother preferred her name to be spelled "Celia Dropkin" in English. Therefore, in deference to both him and her, I have changed my usual practice for purposes of this article. I wish to acknowledge the help of Celia Dropkin's son, John, and her daughter, Esther Unger, who kindly spent time and effort talking to me and answering my questions. I also received much valuable information from John's wife, Ruth, who came to know her mother-in-law after the fact, yet whose insights ring with truth for me.

2. *In heysn vint.* All page citations of poems discussed in this article appear in the body of the text and refer to the 1935 volume. However, I have compared the texts with the 1959 edition of Dropkin's work, and wherever there is a discrepancy, I have chosen the version that makes more sense. For example, in the poem *"Ven du host shtil gekusht un tsertlekh mikh georemt,"* the original penultimate line contains the word *nor.* A comparison with this poem in the 1959 edition shows that the latter edition contains instead *nokh.* Since the meaning of *nokh* is more in keeping with my general understanding of the poem, I cite this version in the text, even though it does not appear that way in the 1935 volume. Similarly, *"An ovnt in merts"* contains an *un* in the penultimate line in 1935, whereas the 1959 version uses *az.* All translations of Dropkin's poetry into English are my own.

3. I want to say that Irving Howe and Eliezer Greenberg admirably diverge from this mold in their anthology since they include, in addition to Celia Dropkin,

the poets Anna Margolin, Rashelle Veprinsky, Devorah Fogel, Reyzel Zychlinska, Kadya Molodowsky, Roza Gutman-Jasny, Rokhel Korn, and Rikude Potash-Fuchs. (See note number 1.)

4. For an introduction to Kohut's work see, e.g., *The Restoration of the Self* (1977).

5. Where no title is cited together with the text of a poem, the poem is untitled and cited in the index of both the 1935 and 1959 editions by its first line.

6. Person's use of the concept "romantic love" does not refer solely to happy or fulfilled love, but rather encompasses as well the kinds of conflict and unhappiness that Dropkin describes. Indeed, it is because of this broad view that Person's conclusions are so striking.

WORKS CITED

Dropkin, Celia. 1920. "*Du derniderikst mikh haynt*" [You Abase Me Today] and "*Mayne hent*" [My Hands]. *In zikh* 1, 1 (January) 11.

——— 1935. *In heysn vint: lider* [In the Hot Wind: Poems]. New York: Posy-Shulson Press.

——— 1959. *In heysn vint: Poems, Stories and Pictures*. New York: Published by her children.

Glants-Leyeles, Arn. 1956. *Tog-morgn zhurnal*, 1 September, 5.

Hellerstein, Kathryn. 1988. "A Question of Tradition: Women Poets in Yiddish." In *Handbook of American-Jewish Literature: an Analytical Guide to Topics, Themes, and Sources*, ed. Lewis Fried. New York: Greenwood Press.

Howe, Irving and Eliezer Greenberg, eds. 1969. *A Treasury of Yiddish Poetry*. New York: Holt, Rinehart and Winston. First Holt paperback edition, 1972.

Kohut, Heinz, 1977. *The Restoration of the Self*. New York: International Universities Press.

Person, Ethel Spector. 1988. *Dreams of Love and Fateful Encounters: the Power of Romantic Passion*. New York: W.W. Norton and Company.

Pratt, Norma Fain. 1980. "Culture and Radical Politics: Yiddish Women Writers, 1890-1940." *American Jewish History* 70: 83-84.

Stolorow, Robert D., Bernard Brandchaft, and George E. Atwood. 1987. *Psycho-Analytic Treatment: An Intersubjective Approach*. Hillsdale, N.J.: The Analytic Press.

From "Ikh" to "Zikh": A Journey From "I" to "Self" in Yiddish Poems by Women

ᡣ KATHRYN HELLERSTEIN ᡣ

When speaking about poetry, the difference between the Yiddish words *ikh* and *zikh* involves more than simply the presence of one letter or another. The term "*ikh*," the "I," raises questions of poetics: How does a poet present his or her voice as a speaker or persona in a poem? How does that presentation affect the poem's dynamics? In contrast, the problem of "*zikh*" or "self" relates to the intersection of psychology and autobiography: How is the self constructed in a poem? How does the self, as a presence, represent aspects of its author's life? Whereas the "*ikh*" emphasizes the poem and its voice, the "*zikh*" stresses the person who wrote the poem.[1] For women writing poetry in Yiddish, particularly in the twentieth century, the movement from "*ikh*" to "*zikh*," from the assertion of the first person singular pronoun "I" to the evolution of a self on paper is one issue that shaped what I will call a tradition beside the mainstream.[2]

For most Yiddish poets since the Haskalah or Jewish Enlightenment, one of the central problems has been how to voice the first person pronoun. Yiddish poetry as a self-conscious, secular literature and the idea of the individual person with a unique, inner life both developed in response to the Haskalah. With its intoxicating ideology of political rights and worldly knowledge, the Haskalah disrupted traditional religious explanations for the order of things. The initial impulse of a Yiddish poet of the late nineteenth century was to speak for the collective, to stand as a spokesman able to articulate the injustices suffered by the mute masses of Jewish workers. The poems of Dovid Edelstat exem-

plify the communal nature of such a speaker. When an "I" appears in
Edelstat's poems, it usually allies itself with the first person plural, with
the poet assuming a Romantic posture as a redeemer for the collective.
These poems are couched in conventional poeticisms, in the Labor
movement clichés of enslavement, battle, bloodshed, and heroism. Even
in poems by a more accomplished writer such as Morris Rosenfeld, the
voice is an implied collective, dramatizing the plights of particular characters. The work-worn father, the exhausted mother, the hungry child,
the orphaned girl on the street corner are all types, not individuals; their
situations in the world represent the predicaments of many others. So,
too, in the Yiddish folk song, where the anonymity of the lyric's author
veils any autobiographical referent for the "I," and the use of standard
phrasing and motifs converts the personal voice into an archetype, a collective voice. Even as the Yiddish poem entered modernity, emphasizing
the individuality of the poet and his vision, the poetic "I" remained a
problem.

Between the turn of this century and the 1940s, poets within the various Yiddish modernist movements strove to create an individual, aesthetic "*ikh*," but always to counterpose the collective "I." This dualism
between the collective "we" and the personal "I" emerged in the aestheticism of the first modernist poets in New York, known as the *Yunge*
(Young Upstarts) and led to a productive tension in the works of some of
its major poets, such as Moyshe-Leyb Halpern and Mani Leyb: where the
former deflated and made ironic the Romantic poet-speaker, the latter
brought him into a clearer focus.[3] The individuation of the first person
speaker was further sharpened and then fragmented by the influence of
psychoanalytic thought and by contact with American and European
modernist poetics in the works of the *Inzikhistn* (Introspectivists), a group
of slightly younger poets (led by Yankev Glatshteyn and Arn Glants-
Leyeles) who reacted against the Romantic bent of the *Yunge*.[4] Although
distinctive poetic speakers emerged from Mani Leyb's lyricism and
Halpern's mad improvisations, the splintered poetics of the *Inzikhistn*
produced an "I" mirroring the workings of memory and sensation to the
extent that external events and political issues were transformed into
purely internal experiences. In the aftermath of the Holocaust, much
Yiddish poetry turned away from individualism back to the voicing of
collective experience as a means of coming to terms with the devastation
of Europe's Jews. What I have just sketched were the characteristic tendencies of poets writing in the "mainstream" of Yiddish poetry; these

were mostly male poets publishing in the urban centers of *yidishkayt* in America and Europe—New York, Warsaw, and Vilna.

For women poets, writing in the margins of Yiddish culture, the individuation of the "I" raised other problems. These problems stemmed from the complex status of women within Jewish law and life and the ways the Haskalah challenged this status.[5] Conforming unconsciously to the demarcated gender roles in traditional Judaism, male Yiddish poets initially rebelled against religious communality by shifting the communal voice of Hebrew prayer first to the vernacular language of Yiddish and the secular terms of politics or nationalism, and then to individualism. Women did not participate in communal prayer, according to the strict separation of the sexes in traditional Jewish worship, but merely observed it from behind the screen, the *mekhitse*. Instead, women recited prayers privately, and many of these prayers were supplicatory prayers, *tkhines*, composed in the Yiddish vernacular, specifically for women (Weissler 1987, 245-52). Because of the overwhelmingly private and often solitary nature of their worship, one can argue, Jewish women literally lacked a communal voice in the traditional practice. Emerging, albeit rebelliously, from this context, women Yiddish poets, unlike their male peers, wrote secular poetry out of a tradition of private Yiddish rather than communal Hebrew prayer. For these women poets, the Haskalah's secularizing shift from prayer to poetry required neither a great leap from sacred to secular language nor from the congregational text to that of an individual. Paradoxically, then, traditional women's practice of Jewish prayer prepared "enlightened" women poets for the individualizing direction taken by modern Yiddish poetry. Women thus made a more gradual progression into the individual poetic voice than men did, and when they broke with Jewish tradition as writers, it was more in substance than in form.

That women were culturally more accustomed to the solitary voice of private prayer may explain why many Yiddish poems written by women across the twentieth century exhibit an internal counterpoint of self-definition. Women poets, of course, wrote many other kinds of poems as well. There are obvious examples of women who modeled their poetry after the mainstream, such as Roza Goldshteyn (born 1870), whose political protests and nationalist addresses are standard Labor fare. There may well be poems by men that conform to the marginal paradigm of self-definition. What this study seeks to establish is the existence of the dualism between *ikh* and *zikh* in a small selection of poems by women. In these poems, the voices fluctuate between the *ikh* and the *zikh*, between

the establishment of a poetic "I" and the revelation of an autobiographical "self." From this fluctuation results, not ambivalence, but resistance
to self-revelation.

Any resistance to autobiographical confession in poems by women
would have seemed puzzling to the poets' contemporary Yiddish critics.
These men—women did not publish literary criticism or book reviews in
the 1920s (Novershtern 1990, 459)—saw nothing complex in the poetic
presences of women. Whatever their particular vantage points, the
Yiddish critics tended to group together women poets and characterize
their work as instinctual, emotional, sentimental, and ultimately anonymous. For example, in 1915, A. Glants (later known as Glants-Leyeles, a
leader of the *Inzikhistn*) urged women to enrich an overly cerebral
Yiddish poetry with their intuitive and emotional talents, proclaiming,
"And if Woman is meant to play a significant role in the culture . . . she
must find her*self*. . . she must stop imitating Man." Yet for Glants, a
woman poet's search for self had little to do with introspection and
would result chiefly in external benefits for male writers: "Women's
poetry will create a new world and become a blessing for men" (1915, 4-
5).[6]

More antagonistically, in 1927, the Warsaw modernist Melekh Ravitsh
published a vicious group review of books by women poets, whom he
coyly refused to identify, attacking them as a homogeneous group for
not fulfilling his ideal role of women poets as the peacemakers and
homebodies of Yiddish literature (1927, 395-6). And even the conservative critic Sh. Niger, attempting in 1928 to write constructively about
what he dubbed "*froyen lirik*" (women's lyrical poetry), praised "the chief
virtue" of the "many gifted Yiddish women poets" as being "that they
are *women* in their poetry" and found their work to lack the "artistic universalism in which we sense more the personality of the poet than the
collective to which he [sic] belongs" (909). Although Niger denied the
presence of the individual in such poems by women, he discerned in
them the "feminine disposition." In what he called a "group poetry, a
type of folklore of the female sex," Niger located qualities that he considered benign and even praiseworthy, although hopelessly outdated: it
was a "sincere and straightforward" poetry that preserved an "element
of feeling," the "intimate tone" of longing, and "naive moods." In "the
'old' erotic motif" and love poems that he claimed dominated the wom-
en's writing, Niger assumed an unmediated expression of emotion. If not
revealing of an individual self or personality, the first-person speaker in

poems by women was, for Niger, "eternally womanly, eternally lyrical," and guilelessly revealed the placid, faceless, female self.

Such grouping together of women poets by male Yiddish critics was based on assumptions that subjectivity, emotionalism, intuition, and tenderness dominated both the poems and the selves of women. These critics seemed blind to the paradox that these very qualities are all essential to the self-definition and self-knowledge of each individual person, female or male. Furthermore, the male critics apparently equated unquestioningly what they deemed an undistinguished poetry with the people who wrote it. Against the prejudiced assumptions of their male contemporaries stands a remarkable tendency of poems by women, while appearing to reflect autobiographical experience, actually to veil or mask the identities of the authors. The poems resist rather than invite revelation.

This resistance to self-revelation in poems by women contradicts the underlying ideas in some current feminist work on autobiography. Most relevant is the essay "Women's Poetry and Autobiography," by Celeste Schenck, which argues, against conventional divisions of literary genre, that women's autobiography and poetry can be read as "coextensive, recuperative, not necessarily unified discourses of female subjectivity" (1988, 305). Schenck persuasively challenges the standard critical assumption that literary genres are determined purely by aesthetic criteria, and thus are not subject to the hierarchial and exclusionary influences of gender and class. For evidence, she reads the oeuvres of Emily Dickinson and Adrienne Rich as revealing a "female selfhood" engaged in a dialectic between power and exile and as resulting in "a refusal of a totalized, unitary selfhood" (294). According to Schenck, both poets defy the displacement of the woman writer from cultural history and reclaim their place there by portraying a divided self, in contrast to the "masculine unified subject" (295-296). Schenck bases her argument on the assumption (which, as she acknowledges, male writers have often used to dismiss or demean poetry by women, and which here she reevaluates) that a poet reveals her self through poetry. It is this assumption that the following Yiddish poems by women challenge.[7]

The first poet to consider is Rokhl Bernshteyn, a Russian poet who wrote under the pen name Yehudis (1869-?). One poem of 1907, "*Breyte himlen*" [Ample Heavens], opens as a complaint of Romantic ennui. The voice is one of generalized despair:

ברייטע הימלען

ברייטע הימלען, ערד א גרויסע
און א שיינע זון א הייסע—
אַלע אייביג שטום...

און פערמאַטערטע, פערוויענטע,
ווי די ווערים האלב־צודריקטע,
קריכן מיר אַרום...

קריכן... ווי א וואָרים פיהלען,
מיט א טרעהר דעם צאָרן שטילען...
צאָרנען ווי א פליג...

ליעבען, האָפען, האַסען, בייניקען...
און פערמאַטערט, אַלעס שענקען?...

_____

ניין! זאָל זיין גענוג!

איך וויל לאַכען, שד׳יש לאַכען,
כ׳וויל פון אַלעס חוזק מאַכען,
לאַכען, לאַכען הויך!

עס זאָל דונערן און בליצען,
פון געלעכטער זאָלען שפריצען
פייער־פלאַמען, רויך!

און די הימלען זאָלען ברומען,
זאָלען ריידען, — זייער שטומען
לייד איך שוין ניט מעהר!

רעדט! כ׳וויל הערען, וועלכער רוח,
וועלכער טייוועל, וועלכער כח
האַלט אייך ביז אהער!...

(1928, 63-64)

Ample Heavens

Ample heavens, earth enormous
And a sun so hot and gorgeous—
All forever mute . . .

And as weary and as woeful
As the worms half-crushed and doleful,
So we creep about . . .

Creeping . . . like an earthworm feeling,
With a tear our sorrow stilling . . .
Raging like a fly . . .

Loving, hoping, hating, longing . . .
Wearily excusing all things? . . .

———————

No! Enough! That'll do!

I want laughter, demon laughter,
Want to mock all forever after,
Laughing, laughing loud!

Let it thunder, let it lightning,
Laughter shall spew forth a frightening
Fire-flame and smoke-cloud!

And the skies shall roar and bellow,
They shall speak,—for their mute wallow
Suffer I no more!

Speak! I want to hear which specter,
And which devil, and which power
Holds you hitherto! . . .[8]

The implicit transition from "we" to "I" in the outburst at the end of
stanza four is so dramatic that it severs the triplet (although the braided
rhyme scheme continues, creating a tension with the narrated revolt).
The poet's "I," intruding suddenly and explicitly in the metrically
stressed first syllable of stanza 5, accompanies her finding a voice. This
voice, born of derisive laughter, causes all the silence of heaven and earth
(that the meek, forgiving "we" have taken for granted) to erupt into a
force that, though destructive, is necessary to open communication. The
mute heavens, the devils and ghosts, the fire and smoke may connote
any one of the following: unsatisfying religious constraints, an oppressive social system, an inaccessibly remote natural world. Whichever
these connote, what matters is that the "I" coincides with the speaker's
assumption of a voice in an act of rebellion.

Who is this "I"? Is it the poet herself, an individual distinct from all
others? Is it the poet speaking for her generation? Against it?[9] The impa-
tience, the anger, and the celebratory rebellion in "*Breyte himlen*" give
Yehudis's poetic "I" a freshness and unruliness that overcome the standard rhymes and the formulaic language of her poem. The forcefulness
of this "I" is almost overwhelming. Perhaps such raw power, steam-
rolling any subtlety, was necessary in order for Yehudis to be able to
assert her "I" through her own adherence to the language of poetic convention—the numbing clichés of melancholy and the communal shouts
of protest poetry. "*Breyte himlen*" is an innovative poem, because its
author applies the force of a political protest poem to the mood and

feeling of the pseudo-Romantic poem. This application of the popular form to the fashionable subject results in the rebellious poetic "I."

Although the assertion of the first person singular in Yehudis's poem has a nascent force, the power of the rebellion is, in the end, impersonal and unrevealing. This "I" is neither explicitly female nor rooted in a particular social place or time. External factors of gender and setting, which might contextualize the speaker's vocalization of rebellion and give the reader an anchor, are absent from this poem. Here, the poet does not characterize the actors; they are abstractions of human beings and nature. Although the poetic speaker's expectation that the natural world ought to respond to human feeling appears to be the Romantic pathetic fallacy, this speaker is unlike Romantic poets in projecting an unreflecting "I," an "I" that eerily has no memory, no history, no self. The unselfconsciousness of this "I" is transparent, because it lacks any identity or substance but its universality, and such abstraction obscures the speaker.

Reflecting the poetics of mainstream modernism, Anna Margolin (1887-1952) consciously crafted a poetic "I" that masked the personal self. An audacious example of such masking is the persona poem that opens her 1929 book of poems, *Lider*:

איך בין געווען אַ מאָל אַ ייִנגלינג

איך בין געווען אַ מאָל אַ ייִנגלינג,
געהערט אין פּאָרטיקאָס סאָקראַטן,
עס האָט מיין בוזעם־פֿריינד, מיין ליבלינג,
געהאַט דעם שענסטן טאָרס אין אַטען.

געייעזן צעזאַר. און אַ העלע וועלט
געבויט פֿון מאַרמאָר, איך דער לעצטער,
און פֿאַר אַ וויַיב מיר אויסדערוויילט
מיַין שטאָלצע שוועסטער.

אין רויזנקראַנץ ביַים ווייַן ביז שפּעט
געהערט אין הויכמוטיקן פֿרידן
וועגן שוואַכלינג פֿון נאַזאַרעט
און ווילדע מעשיות וועגן ייִדן.

(5)

I Was Once a Boy

I was once a boy, a stripling,
Listening in Socrates' portico,
My bosom-buddy, my sweet darling,
Had Athens' most stunning torso.

Was Caesar. And from marble constructed
A glistening world, I the last there,

And for my own wife selected
My stately sister.

Rose-garlanded, nursing wine all night,
Heard tell in high-spirited lull of booze
About the weakling from Nazareth
And wild tales about Jews.

Margolin startles her reader with this opening poem, for the woman poet here takes on the dramatic personae first of a favored boy in the porticoes of Socrates and then of the Emperor Caesar in his marble cities.[10] In the erotically charged and hedonistic world of the Greeks and the Romans, where homosexuality and incest are the norms, the speaker—this stripling (*yingling*) who evolves into the most powerful and ultimately doomed of classical men—is seduced as much by these cultures' philosophy and architecture as by eroticism. Empowered through his ambiguous sexuality, the speaker of the poem reclines at the center of his pagan world, and, unbeknownst to him, at the edge of his civilization. Bedecked with roses,[11] in drunken revelry, he overhears, as only remote, fantastic gossip, news of the event that will change the order of his world: the rise of Christianity among the Jews. Through the perception of this persona, the poem offers an ironic view of the relative scale of historical significance.

This persona, male and classical, establishes the parameters for Margolin's poetry. By assuming this persona at the beginning of her book, Margolin asserts that her poetry is far from the slight, cliché-ridden, first-person lyrics that critics such as Sh. Niger and Melekh Ravitsh characterized as *"froyen lyrik"* in the late 1920s, or from the collective voicings of protest by the previous generation of Yiddish poets (Niger, 909-10; Ravitsh, 395-6). By making the fictional speaker male and allying him with a pagan, classical past alien to Yiddish literature, Margolin consciously distinguishes between the poetic "I" and a literally autobiographical "I" in a poem that poses as self-definition or autobiography. She thus upsets her readers' assumptions that the speakers of subsequent poems in her book represent an authorial self; instead, her strategy emphasizes the fictional or inventive dimension of poetry. Yet this emphasis on the imagined in poetry draws attention away from the person of the poet and toward the act of the imagination in the poem.

There arises, then, a distinction between the author's invention of a persona through whom she speaks and the author herself. In fact, rather than the dramatic persona representing the authorial self, this invented "I" obscures the author. All we know of its author from this poem is that she/he invents a fictional "I" in order to reconstruct a history that marginalizes the very culture from which she/he is writing the poem. In this ironic move, the poetic "I" of "I Was Once a Boy" diminishes the culture-language matrix of the poem and negates the self of the poet.

The ironic strategy of Margolin's poetic "I" sets her reader on guard. It introduces an opacity in what might otherwise be construed as transparent autobiography in the poem, *"In kafe"* [In the Café]:[12]

אין קאַפֿע

1

איצט אַליין און קאַפֿע,
װען עס לעשן זיך שטימען און װיאַנען,
װען פֿערלדיק צינדן זיך לאָמפּן
און שװימען אַרױס פֿון קאַפֿע
װי לױכטנדע שװאָנען
איבער דער גאַס—

—קעלנער, שװאַרצע קאַװע—דעמיטאַס.

איצט אַליין אין קאַפֿע,
װען עס שאָרכן די רגעס װי זײַד,
הײב איך אױף צו דער גאַס, צו דער װײַט
מײַן שװאָרצן און דופֿטיקן װײַן.
און װי אַ געזאַנג איז דער געדאַנק,
אַז ס׳פֿאַלט פֿון מיר אין טונקלקײט
אַ װײַסער שײַן.

2

און אַלע פּנימער אין רױך װי מאַסקן.
אַ װיץ, אָן אַקסלצוק, אַ בליק אַ טריבער,
און פֿאַלשע װערטער צינדן זיך, פֿאַרבלאָסן.
האָב איך דיר װיי געטאָן, מײַן ליבער?

מיר טראָגן אַלע דאָ פֿאַראָכטלעך קאַלטע מאַסקן.
מיט קלונער אירראָניע פֿאַרשטעלן מיר דעם פֿיבער
און טרײזנט שמײַכלען, און געשרײַען, און גרימאַסן.
האָב איך דיר װיי געטאָן, מײַן ליבער?

3

מיטן פֿראָסטיקן שײַן פֿון די לאָמפּן
און בליקן, און שטימען
שװימט דיר אַקעגן מײַן שװײַגן—
אַ געהײַמער און ליכטיקער סימן.
קרײַזט װי אַ זומערװינט אַרום דיר.
רעדט ציטערדיק צו דיר
װענן דיר און מיר.
אָ, שטילע, שטילע װערטער

וועגן דיר און מיר.
און שווייגט.
און וויגט דיך מיט בענקענדע הענט.
און נעמט דיך מיט ווייַסע און צוקנדע הענט.

(82-84)

In the Café

1

Now alone in the café,
When voices extinguish and fade,
When pearly lamps kindle
And float out of the café
Like shining swans
Over the street—

—Waiter, black coffee—demitasse.—

Now alone in the café,
When the moments rustle like silk,
I raise to the street, to the distance
My black and perfumed wine.
And like a song is the thought
That there falls from me in the dimness
A white light.

2

And all the faces in smoke, like masks.
A joke, a shrug of the shoulder, a dreary glance,
And false words kindle, grow pale.
Have I hurt you, my lover?

Here we all wear contemptible cold masks.
With clever irony we disguise the fever
And a thousand smiles, and shouts, and grimaces.
Have I hurt you, my lover?

3

With the frosty light from the lamps
And glances, and voices[,]
Across from you floats my silence—
A covert and luminous sign.
Curls like a summer wind around you.
Speaks tremblingly to you
About you and me.
O, quiet, quiet words
About you and me.
And stays silent.
And rocks you with longing hands.
And takes you with white and twitching hands.

The poem is set explicitly in the present moment—part 1 opens with the word "Now"—in a familiar urban place, a literary café, and appears to be spoken by a woman to her lover. Although the material may be closer to home, the speaker's monologue to the lover is disjointed. Ultimately, in part 3, it becomes an address to the unspoken words themselves. She describes her silence speaking ("O, quiet, quiet words/ About you and me") and acts upon the lover—rocking him, taking him. In this movement, a deliberately constructed poetic "I" exists only in the poem. The primary relationship in this poem is between the speaker and her words. The "you" becomes an object upon which the word-filled silence, replacing the physical woman, acts.

Each section of this poem contradicts itself by combining the descriptive mood piece with a dramatic interaction between the lovers. These contradictions in turn create the sense of disjuncture between the poet and the speaker. Thus, in part 1, the "I" appears directly only in the second stanza, although it is implied in the word "alone" and in the line of directly quoted dialogue. This "I" sees itself simultaneously from within and from without. The sensation of being within the subjectivity of the "I" is conveyed in the first stanza's catalog of perceived sensation—the fading of voices and the kindling of lamps; but as the light swims out "like shining swans/ Over the street," the center of the speaker also disperses, and her order to the waiter—itself a fragmented sentence—comes as if from outside the speaker. This process of distancing grows even more disjointed when the "I" appears in the second stanza, transforming the small cup of black coffee into a strange, black wine in a toast to the street. Her gesture bridges the inner and the outer worlds jarringly, for the "I" has a thought about herself that she likens to a song. With this thought, the speaker finds a second metaphor for herself—a source of light in the obscurity—which connects her to the lights migrating from the café into the street in the previous stanza.

In part 2, the literal solitude of the speaker gives way to an emotional solitude in the café's smoky atmosphere, where all the faces are "like masks" and where words are false. The speaker likens the kindling and fading of these false words to the voices and lamps in part 1. Human gestures—"A joke, a shrug of the shoulder, a dreary glance" and "a thousand smiles, and shouts, and grimaces"—are fragmented, and either inexpressive or deceptive. The masklike smoke enveloping the faces in the first stanza of part 2 is transformed, in the second stanza, into "contemptible cold masks." By describing the absence of genuine feeling or expression of feeling, the speaker distorts the refrain of directly quoted speech. The affectless context charges the query, "Have I hurt you, my lover?" with an irony that drains away authentic emotion.

In part 3, the speaker's communication with the lover ceases, as the poem shifts into an interior monologue. The speaker describes the scene as if from underwater, conveying a feeling of dreamlike unreality. In the cool, "frosty" light of lamps and looks, voices act upon the addressee—"you" (du)—and make him float opposite to the speaker's silence, like the lamps floating into the street in part 1. For this intimate "du," silence now becomes "A covert and luminous sign." The conversion of silence from a dramatic action to a symbol transforms the poem as well as the dramatic situation. Now language itself—not the café atmosphere, not love gone wrong—is the subject of the poem. Ceasing to address the listener, the speaker turns to the silence. The speaker's lack of words in the dramatic setting of the poem replaces actual communication between the characters. Emphasizing this irony, her silence is animated and displaces the woman by enacting her erotic gestures. At the moment when animated silence displaces the woman, the poem recoils into itself as if it were a black hole in space sucking stars into a self-created vacuum. This self-consuming poem draws attention to the distinctly poetic nature of the speaker, who cannot exist beyond the words of the poem.

In contrast to "I Was Once a Boy," the speaker in Margolin's "In the Café" may initially seem to correspond more closely to the author Anna Margolin's autobiography. In fact, the subject matter of the poem has little to do with the proximity of the poet to the poetic "I." One cannot take for granted the identity of the poet at all. In fact, "Anna Margolin" is one of the many pseudonymns that the journalist, writer, and poet Roza Lebensboym assumed (Novershtern 1990, 435; 1991, 1-3). The issue of pseudonymity is complex for Yiddish writers. Dan Miron describes the tradition of pseudonymous writing in Yiddish, from the early maskilic writers to Mendele Moykhr Sforim, Sholem Aleichem, and beyond, as one in which an author assumed a pen name—and often a folksy persona who narrated the stories—in order to protect his actual identity from the stigma of writing in Yiddish (Miron 1973,14-18; 273, notes 42-43).

Women poets at the turn of the century occasionally took pseudonyms, although for different reasons and to different effect. Compounding what Miron calls the "promiscuity" of writing in Yiddish was the convention of feminine discretion or modesty. But the pseudonyms adopted by women also lent an air of elegance and even authority to their Yiddish authorship. The poet Rokhl Bernshteyn (whose poem "Breyte himlen" I discussed earlier) may have assumed her pen name in somewhat the same spirit as the famous and popular prose male writers, but, standing alone, the name "Yehudis" is not folksy, but rather grand. This pseudonym embodies Bernshteyn's own transitional place in the evolution of an individual poetic voice, for the name denotes "Jewess," making the woman who assumes it a generic representative for all Jewish women; at the same time it refers to the distinctive and courageous poet-heroine of the apocryphal Book of Judith, whose deeds deliver her nation from the enemy and whose praise-song heralds a return to Jerusalem. By adopting the name "Yehudis," Bernshteyn elevates her Yiddish poems by linking them to classical (if noncanonical) Hebrew writings and empowers herself as a poet by establishing her lineage from this legendary namesake.

The pseudonym "Anna Margolin" is of a different order. The first and last names sound contemporary and plausible for someone living in a twentieth-century American city. Anna is not a Yiddish name; although it derives from the Hebrew *Hana* and means "gracious, merciful," it has Christian connotations (Kolatch 1982, 165). Margolin appears to derive from the Hebrew noun, *margolit*, which means "gem, jewel, pearl," and connotes the Hebrew idiom for an eloquent person, *pe meifik margoliot*. "Anna Margolin" is the perfect pseudonym for a Yiddish poet who wants to emphasize her worldliness, eloquence, and aestheticism. Lebensboym's use of the pseudonymn creates a poetic identity that corresponds to the elegant, crafted poems she wrote. Although her actual surname, meaning "life's tree," has its own poetic charm, "Roza Lebensboym" connotes Eastern European *yidishkayt*, rather than literary sophistication.[13] Of the women poets, Margolin most consciously imposes the distance between the authorial self and her poetic "I,"—not through an alliance with a collective identity, but by shaping words into masks.

In 1922, in Warsaw, Miriam Ulinover published a book of poems spoken by a very different kind of poetic persona. Ulinover (1890-1944) is often treated as a naive, almost guileless poet. Her apparent unself-consciousness suggests the literal equation of the poem's "I" with the poet's self, for most of her readers have taken her to be a pious folk poet. This view results from the thematic focus in Ulinover's poems on the folk customs of a great-grandmother so immersed in traditional shtetl life that she lacks any inkling of the modern world. Yet Ulinover's Yiddish critics—almost all of them admirers—have tended to overlook the deliberate nature of the poet's choice and the delimitations of the poems. Ulinover crafted as opaque a poetic "I" as Margolin. Take, for example, the poem "*Putern-broyt*" [Buttered Bread]:

פּוטערן=ברויט

ווען ס'פיטערן=ברויט פאַלט אויף דער ערד מיר אַראָב,
דאָ נעמט זיך צעששאָקלען דער באָבעשיס קאָפ:

‎- אַ סימן, מיין לעבען, אַ סימן, מיין קינד,
דער חתן איז ערגעץ=וואו הונגעריג אַצינד ָ.

אָ, ווידער זעהן וואָלט איך דער באָבעשיס קאָפ
זיך שאָקלען, ווען ס'פּוטערן=ברויט פאַלט מיר אַראָב,

דער באָבעשיס חנ'דעל, אין שטערן דעם קנייטש,
צי הערען דעם ליבען, דעם היימישען טייטש!

(5)

Buttered Bread

When onto the floor falls my bread-and-butter,
Then starts the head-shaking of grandmother:

"A sign, my darling, my dear child, a sign,
Your bridegroom goes hungry, without food or wine."

Oh, could I see grandmother shaking her head
Whenever I let fall my butter-and-bread,

Grandmother's coquettishly wrinkled-up brow,
Or hear her dear, homely sense of it now!

Like Margolin's "In the Café," Ulinover's eight-line poem introduces
the "I" obliquely. *Mir,* in line 1, is a first-person dative of reference connected to the verb *aropfaln* [to fall down] in an idiom, difficult to reproduce in English, that indicates all the ramifications of the speaker's
responsibility for letting the bread fall. The first person, then, appears in
the first half of the poem indirectly and passively, as a grammatical
object. With this indirect presentation of the first person, the speaker sets
in the foreground the actions of both the bread falling and the grandmother responding, but allows her own presence to stand shadowed in
the background.

When the *ikh* speaks directly in line 5, more than halfway through the
poem, the active "I" steps center stage and breaks through the veil of
memory. Placing this *ikh* alongside the conditional mood of the verb "to
see," the poet distinguishes between the past moment in which the
grandmother interpreted the bread's falling and the present time of the
speaker's vision, when the grandmother is gone. The appearance of the

ikh makes the reader aware of how time has imposed itself between the action in the first stanza and the voicing of the poem.

The repeated phrases around *"bobeshis kop"* (lines 1-2 and 5-6) mark the temporal distance between the speaker and what has transpired. The repetition of both phrasing and rhyme words (a repetition varied with an untranslatable subtlety) is disproportionate to the poem's brevity: four of the poem's eight lines are nearly identical, resulting in a sensation of stasis, as the poem appears to start over again in the middle. Thus, in the penultimate line, the description of the grandmother—her coquettish mien, her wrinkled brow—is a talisman of what has been lost, for only after the grandmother and her world—in which such explanations make sense—have disappeared, can the speaker recall those details that characterize the grandmother's physical presence, details that were not noticed *in medias res*. With regret for the inevitable change, the poem ends by sentimentally characterizing the grandmother's sayings, as *"libn"* and *"heymishn"* (dear and familiar), whereas in the moment of action, the grandmother's interpretive words filled all of reality. For the regretful modern speaker, these words are now *"taytsh"*—the interpretation of small accidents of everyday life as if they were Holy Scripture.

This speaker's remembered past defines a world of females, in which males and the speaker's own sexuality are but a distant promise, or threat. The old woman's explanation for the dropping of buttered bread gives the young girl a means by which to anticipate the onset of her womanhood. Her yet-unknown but predestined bridegroom goes hungry when the girl is clumsy with precious food. But the grandmother sheds no light on whether her carelessness inadvertently causes his hunger and the girl should feel guilty, or whether it is simply a sign that she should worry for him, even before a domestic situation appropriate for such concern yet exists. Yet in the world of the grandmother's saying, the actual guilt or worry is abstract and distant. In contrast, the speaker's present world is implicitly one in which worry is immediate, responsibility rests its full weight on the speaker, and there is little promise of what is to come. The grandmother's folk saying, while connoting the negative feelings of reprimand, suggests a positive sense of certainty for the future that the grown, modern speaker no longer has.

The simplicity of the couplets, the idiomatic quality of the language, the extensive repetition, and the apparently unmediated moment of folk interpretation all seem to indicate the poem's simple naiveté. However, Ulinover's careful withholding and then pressing forth of the first person pronoun signal a carefully crafted poetic "I."

Celia Dropkin (1888-1956) differs from both Margolin and Ulinover. One of the few women published in the journals and anthologies of both the *Yunge* and *In zikh*, Dropkin wrote love poems in which it is natural to assume that the poetic "I" corresponds transparently to the woman writing the poem.[14] This transparency is deceptive, however. Take, for example, *"Odem"* [Adam], which seems to be a poem confessing to an erotic passion. The poem is not a straightforward confession, though, for it narrates the encounter through a persona that distances the poetic "I" from the poet's self and makes a larger statement about sexual politics. The biblical name, Adam, is a device signaling the poem's ironic play against the story of creation in Genesis. This allusion results in a subversive appropriation of the traditional story that creates a distinctly invented poetic "I."

אָדם

אַ צעלאָזענעם,
אַן אויסגעצערטלטן פֿון פֿילע פֿרויען־הענט,
האָב איך דיך אויף מיַין וועג געטראָפֿן,
יונגער אָדם.
און אײדער איך האָב צונעלייגט צו דיר מיַינע ליפּן,
האָסטו מיך געבעטן
מיט אַ פּנים, בלאַסער און צאַרטער
פֿון דער צאַרטסטער ליליע:
— ניט בייַס מיך, ניט בייַס מיך.
איך האָב דערזען, אַז דיַין ליַיב
איז אין גאַנצן באַדעקט מיט צייכנס פֿון ציינער,
אַ פֿאַרציטערטע האָב איך זיך אין דיר איַינגעביסן.
דו האָסט פֿונאַנדערגעבלאָזן איבער מיר
דיַינע דינע נאָזלעכער,
און האָסט זיך צוגערוקט צו מיר,
ווי אַ הייסער האָריזאָנט צום פֿעלד.

(1959, 26)

Adam

Spoiled,
Stroked by many women's hands,
I met you on my way,
Young Adam.
And before I had placed my lips on you,
You begged me
With a face more pale and delicate
Than the most delicate lily:
—Don't bite me, don't bite me.
I saw that your body

Was entirely covered with teeth marks,
So tremblingly, I bit into you.
Above me, you flared
Your narrow nostrils,
And drew nearer to me,
Like a hot horizon to the field.[15]

This poem presents the creation of man through a woman's sensuality. The "young Adam" has already been fondled by other female hands and bitten by other female teeth. Because the name *odem* in Yiddish is also a noun denoting "man" in general, it suggests that his predicament is the archetypical condition of all men. The image of biting alludes to Eve, who (in Gen. 3:6-7) bites the fruit of the Tree of Knowledge of good and evil and determines what she and Adam will know of sexuality (and thus of mortality) by opening their eyes to their own nakedness. Yet in Dropkin's poem, Eve is not the speaker: she is not the first woman, nor even the second (after the midrashic Lilith), for many other women have handled this Adam, this first man. In terms of the biblical story, it is not at all clear who the speaker is; in terms of the human condition, the speaker offers her story as an archetype.

Here, too, the fruit of the Tree of Knowledge merges with Adam himself, now not the partaker with Eve, but himself the fruit. This merging suggests that the woman speaker has power over the knowledge of good and evil. Adam is not the subject or victim of her temptation (as some traditional interpretations have it) but the tempting object of desire. In addition to being the fruit, Adam takes over the role of God from the Genesis story. When he pleads, repeatedly, "Don't bite," his words echo perversely, weakly, God's command in Gen. 2:16-17:

"Of every tree of the garden thou mayest freely eat; but of the
tree of the knowledge of good and evil, thou shalt not eat of it;
for in the day that thou eatest thereof thou shalt surely die."

Because this Adam is a sensualized version of both fruit and God, in the poem, man, fruit, and God are all at the mercy of the woman speaker. She is all-powerful; she goes ahead and bites. But hers is an ambiguous power: the woman bites "tremblingly," making her move in trepidation, as though desire controls her.

When she bites into Adam, the relationship of power changes. As Adam's nostrils flare with breath, he appears to be positioned above her, and in their coupling, his nearness becomes oppressive, like the horizon on a hot day. From the overturning of conventional power earlier, the poem reverts to archetypal gender metaphors—the woman as earth, the man as sky, and the dominance of sky over earth. Yet in contrast to the archetype, this woman/earth is not fertile, this man is not a sky full of seminal, life-giving rains, but instead the neutral line where earth and sky meet. By focusing on the neutrality of the horizon, rather than the complementary qualities of earth and sky, Dropkin stresses the irony of how, in the sexual act, the powerless young Adam acquires only an apparent power, an ambiguous dominance.

Dropkin revises the Genesis story by replacing the traditional centers of power—God's decrees and Adam's dominion—with female-centered sensuality. She thus undermines traditional readings, which rationalize woman's service as the procreative vessel for humanity, at the mercy of God and man. Dropkin appropriates the biblical allusion for her own agenda of sensuality and eroticism. The "I"—a particular woman who takes on the voice of an archetype—participates in the actions of "many women" and thus, in the moment of her own unstable sexual intimacy, comes to speak for the power of women, outside of traditional Jewish definitions and roles.

The final poet I will consider, Malka Heifetz Tussman (1893-1987), attempted a radical redefinition of the poetic "I" for a Yiddish poem.[16] Her 1949 poem *"Ikh bin froy"* [I Am Woman] is essentially a list of self-contained verses, in each of which the speaker proclaims her identity as various legendary or traditional types of Jewish women of the Diaspora, from Rabbi Akiba's luminous wife, Rachel, who encouraged him to study,[17] to the Woman of Valor to the shtetl bride to the anarchist revolutionary, the Zionist pioneer, and the Yiddish teacher in America:

איך בין פֿרוי

איך בין די עקזולטירטע רחל וועמעס ליבע האָט באַלויכטן דעם וועג
פֿון די רבי עקיבאס.

איך בין דאָם קליינע, שעמעוודיקע דאָרף־מיידל וואָם איז צווישן הויכע
טאָפּאַלן געוואָקסן און זיך גערויטלט ביים ים גוט מאָרגן ֿ פֿון ברודערס
מלמד.

איך בין דאָם פֿרומע מיידל וואָם האָט זיך געבלייכט ביי דער מאַמעס
ציטערדיקע פֿינגער אויף די אויגן אַנטקעגן די בענטשליכט.

איך בין דאָם געהאַרכזאַם כלה־מיידל וואָם האָט די הכנעהדיק דאָם קעפּל
אונטערגעטראָגן צום שער ערב חופה.

איך בין די אשת־חיל וואָם האָט זיך אונטערגענומען געבערן און שפּייזן
פֿאַר אַביסעלע צונעזאָנט גן עדן־ליכט.

איך בין די אויסגעאיידלטע בת תלמיד חכם וואָם האָט מיט איר
אָפּנעהיט לייב אַ שטאַט אַ יידישע מציל געווען און נאָכדעם מיט
אייגענע העגט זיך אונטערגעצונדן.

איך בין די מאמע וואָס האָט אונטער עניים קשים ביז אין דער דאָר
אַריין, בנים מגדל געווען צו מעשים טובים.

אין בין די חסידישע טאָכטער וואָס האָט מיטן טאַטנס התלהבות
געטראָגן דאָס געשוירן קעפּל אין פאָלק אַריין.

איך בין די צווימען־ברעכערן וואָס האָט בָרויט און פרייהייט ̌ געטיילט
און די ליבע באַפרייט פון אונטער חופה־שטאַנגען.

איך בין דאָס פאַרצערטלט מיידל וואָס האָט זיך הינטערן אַקער
געשטעלט גרויען מדבר צו גרין לעבן באַצווינגען.

איך בין דאָס מיידל וואָס האָט אירע וויסע העגט באַפעלן
ציגל און שטיינער צו טראָגן צום אויפקום פון לעבן באַנייטן.

איך בין די ווערמעס פינגער שטייפן אַרום רידל אין לויער פון טריט
פון פּאָרוויסטער.

איך בין די וואָס טראָגט פאַרעקשנט אַרום אַן אלף־בית אַ מאָדנעם
און רוים אים אין קינדערשע אויערלעך אריין.

איך בין אָט די אַלע און נאָך אַ סך, אַ סך ניט דערמאָנטע.

און אומעטום,
און אַלעמאָל
בין איך
פרוי.

(1949, 106-107)

I Am Woman

I am the exulted Rachel whose love lit the road from Rabbi Akiba's.

I am the small, shy village girl who grew among tall poplars and blushed at the 'good morning' of brother's teacher.

I am the pious girl who paled as her mother's fingers trembled over her eyes at the candle blessing.

I am the obedient bride who humbly brought her head to the shears on the eve of her wedding.

I am the Woman of Valor who undertook bearing and nurturing for a little promised Paradise-light.

I am the refined daughter of a scholar who saved a Jewish city with her guarded body and then with her own hands set herself afire.

I am the mother who under inconceivable afflictions to the point of consumption, raised sons to good deeds.

I am the Hasidic daughter who with her father's ardor carried her shorn head into the people.

I am the bridle-breaker who shared 'bread and freedom' and freed love from under the *khupe* poles.

I am the fondled girl who behind the plow forced gray desert into green life.

I am the girl who ordered her white hands to carry bricks and stones to the raising of renewed life.

I am she whose fingers stiffen around the spade, lying in wait for the footsteps of the destroyer.

I am she who stubbornly carries around a strange alphabet and whispers it into the ears of children.

I am all these and yet many, many not mentioned.

And everywhere
And always
I am
Woman.

Through this catalog of women, Tussman enlarges these figures—conventionally valued, but not empowered—to establish a lineage of heroic predecessors for the speaker of the poem. When the individual women become larger than life as the speaker summons them, the reason for this summoning becomes apparent. That purpose emerges as a subtle defiance of the Nazi destruction of Diaspora Jewry. The poet has compiled this hagiography for the survival and perpetuation of her own Yiddish poetic voice.

What becomes even clearer in the poem, though, is that its "I" does not literally represent an individual person; rather, it signifies an identity transcending the self. Like the "I" of Walt Whitman's "Song of Myself," Tussman's "I" comes into being as it enters the experiences of many other individual Jewish women across the centuries. Tussman's "I" in this poem does not (like the Labor poets) claim to speak for inarticulate others. Rather, Tussman's "I," in its constant presence (repeated at the beginning of each of the fifteen verses of the poem) asserts a subjectivity made powerful by its extension into other selves. Like Whitman, Tussman's "I" does not become diffuse or "objective" by transcending the boundaries of the poet into others. Instead, this "I" becomes more concentrated, dense with the accumulation of multiple identities. Ever more subjective, ever more a representative of itself in the process of entering other selves, this "I" does not *represent* others; rather, the "I" *becomes* others, and through that transformation, defines its own boundaries.

By proclaiming "I am / Woman," the speaker seems to erase the boundaries of the individual self and assume a general identification with the female gender. She builds this generalized identity from the list of individual characters that she states herself to be. Since none of these characters writes a poem, the poet's literal "I" remains unarticulated. Yet, by saying that she is each of many other Jewish women who survive adversity, the speaker elaborately demonstrates her own identity as the writer of the poem. The very writing of this poem becomes a subversive act against the external forces of destruction, and by writing the poet survives. Although the "I" here is transcendent and inclusive, it is not confessional or transparent. It is as unrevealing of self as Yehudis's unanchored "I." But it is not an opaque persona, like Margolin's, nor a limited persona like Ulinover's. It is more like Dropkin's semitranslucent persona, for whom literary allusion mediates between the poem and the self.

Tussman's poem of 1949 differs so radically from two poems published in 1977 that one could imagine them written by different people. "*Aroys un arayn*" [Out Of and Back In] and "*Oys un vidervern*" [No-more and Becoming-again], the later poems, are short, lyrical, and introspective or private, whereas "I Am Woman" was long, expository, and narrative or public. These late poems probe the limits of the self and secure its delimited power. Their most salient detail is their evasion of the nominative personal pronoun. Yet despite the near absence of the pronoun, they offer a translucent poetic "I" that gives access to the self.

Unlike the glorified ingathering of many in the one in "I Am Woman," the poet in "Out of and Back In" describes a terrifying moment of transcending the self:

פֿון אינזיך
אַרויס,
פֿון זיך
אַוועק
ווּהין?

Out
Of the self,
Away
From oneself
Where to?

This departure is from "*inzikh*," from within the self, from the introspective, inwardness of self. Finding herself "*aroys*" and "*avek*"—out and away—from the containment of introspection, the poet seems lost, ques-

tioning where she will go. Then she discovers the roominess of being out
of confinement, away from containment. This discovery unfolds in the
metaphors of increasing physicality and movement:

קודם
אַרויס פֿון דער ענגשאַפֿט
אין חלל, אין שטח, און ברייטקייט
פֿאַרברייטן דעם שפּאַן,
פֿאַרלענגן דעם בליק,
צעווינן דעם גאַנצענעם גוף
אָט אַהער, אָט אַהין —

געראַם!

First
Away from the narrowness
Into void, into space, into expanse—
To broaden the stride,
To extend the glance,
To swing the whole body
From here to there—
Room!

The agreeableness of such liberation unfolds with these lines of the
poem: the terrifying "void," first entered, evolves into more neutral
"space" and then into an ample "expanse." In such expanse, the poet can
extend the limits of her physical movement—the broadening of stride
and the swinging of body—as well as her vision. She extends her glance
to the limits of limitlessness, from here to there, and perceives the
roominess of existence.

The general pleasures of boundlessness are then interrupted by a
located sensuosity. Suddenly the poet notices how her fingers are trembling and thereby making a demand:

די פֿינגער —
וואָס ציטערן אַזוי מײַנע פֿינגער
ווי קעצלעך מיט אײַנלעך נאָך בלינדע
פֿאַרוואָרלאָזט אין האַרבסטיקן פֿעלד?
וואָס מאָנען די שפּיריקע פֿינגער?

זיי בענקען:
מיט פֿינגערשע שפּיצן
באַרירן זיי ווילן
אין שפּאַן־אויף־אַ־שפּאַן
די היימישע ענגשאַפֿט
דערפֿילן.

(1977, 44)

My fingers—
Why do my fingers tremble
Like still-blind-eyed kittens
In an autumn field forsaken?
For what do my sensitive fingers clamour?

They are longing:
With tips of fingers
They want to be touching
In a space you can't turn in
The homey narrowness
To be sensing.[18]

As the poet's sensations move from her body to her fingertips, the pleasure in transcending limits turns into fear and longing. The fingertips are the outermost parts of the sensate body that contact the world beyond the self. In the limitless, self-less universe into which the poet has sprung, there is nothing to touch. Without the self, the fingers are like abandoned, newborn kittens with eyes still sealed shut. Such helpless creatures long for the now-absent limits of the introspective self, which seem in retrospect a *"heymishe engshaft,"* a homey or familiar narrowness that comforts rather than confines.

Tussman's poem "No More and Becoming Again" complements "Out of and Back In" by celebrating the return to this limited self:

אויס און ווידערווערן

ס׳טרעפט מיט מיר אַ וֶוערן־אויס׳:
פון וועלט ארויס,
פון זיך ארויס
אָן שרעק,
אָן פרייד,
אָן זיפץ, אָן טרער —
אויס.

פלוצלינג
ווי אַ נייַ־געבערן
קומט אַ וֶוידערווערן ׳,
קומט מיט פרומער פרייד
און טרערן
ווי כ׳וואַלט דעם שבת קודש
אין מיטן־וואָך
אין שטוב ביי זיך דערזען.

און איך בענטש דעם ווידערווערן.
ס׳איז אלע מאָל מיר ערשטיק־נייַ
און שטערענג

און רחמימדיק
און טוט רחמימדיק מיר ווײ.

(1977, 18)

No More and Becoming Again

A Becoming-no-more happens to me—
Out of the world
Out of self
No fear
No joy
No sigh, no tear—
Out.

Suddenly
Like a new birth
A Becoming-again
Comes with pious joy
And tears
As if in my house I beheld
The holy Sabbath
In the middle of the week.

And I bless the Becoming-again
Always as new as the first time,
As strict
And merciful—
And mercifully it hurts.[19]

The experience of being out of the self is characterized as the lack of all human emotions—fear, joy, sighs, tears. Earlier, in "Out of and Back In," the poet invented the simile of helpless newborn kittens to convey the sensation of abandonment when the self is transcended. Now, in "No More and Becoming Again," she develops a reverse simile, likening the equally sudden and unexplained return to self to a "*nay-gebern*" [a new birth]. This latter poem turns the simile of birth from literal imagery of the biological world into a figure of religious life; it links the rebirth to a miraculous interpenetration of holy time into mundane time, as the holiness of Sabbath might materialize on a weekday. This emphasis on rebirth affirms the tension inherent in the containment of self. "Out of and Back In," pivots on the paradoxical nature of freedom from self. In its last stanza, the poet blesses the return to self, which seems as new as the first awareness of self, not for its comfortable familiarity, but for the merciful pain it causes her. This pain brings the figure of rebirth back to a literal level, for the merciful pain is that of childbirth.

Only in the last two stanzas of "*No More and Becoming Again*," does the pronoun "*ikh*" appear directly, and then only sparingly. The near absence of an "I" in both poems, even though they explicitly address the problem of locating the self, may seem paradoxical, especially when compared with the overwhelming presence of the "I" in "*I Am Woman.*" The repeated "I" there marked the writing of poetry as an act appropriate to a Jewish woman seeking to link her effort with the subversively heroic acts of other Jewish women throughout history.

These two later poems depict a speaker isolated from all other people, lacking a collective context. She is a being in an unpopulated universe, in solipsistic relation to herself. The contrast between the expansive, social "I" of the 1949 poem and the limited self of the 1977 poems suggests a parallel development both of a woman aging and of the Yiddish poet's world diminishing. More important for this essay's concerns is the apparent shift from an assertion of the poet's individual womanhood through a collection of women to an examination of the existential self.

In conclusion, in this essay, I have attempted to trace a development of the poetic "I" in Yiddish poems by women in relation to the degree in which the poet reveals herself, by considering the transparency or opacity of first-person speakers that either reveal or obscure the poet. The analysis of the turn-of-the-century poet Yehudis reveals a forceful but unself-reflexive "I" which is shaped implicitly by poetic conventions. This poetic naiveté, though, does not necessarily lead to transparency. Despite the poet's energetic assertion of this "I," her limited language keeps the poem from unveiling the self. In an artful and deliberate concealment, the modernist Anna Margolin appropriates personae to obscure expression of the self. The two Margolin poems discussed are oriented self-referentially toward words and language—the very materials of poems. One of Margolin's contemporaries who is not Modernist per se, Miriam Ulinover, fashions a naive persona that effectively conveys the cultural Yiddish folk material valued by the poet. This apparently unmediated poetic "I" is unexpectedly *like* Margolin's polished personae, for it obscures the poet's self. For both Margolin and Ulinover, the poem is a medium by which culture is crafted, conveyed, modified, or invented, not a medium for self-revelation. The poems by Margolin and Ulinover exemplify a displacement of the self by the poetic "I."

The poem by Celia Dropkin takes up an aspect of a woman's personal experience that ought to be intimate, particular, and self-revelatory. Against such expectations, Dropkin appropriates and subverts the archetypal biblical narrative about human sexuality. The erotic "I" of this poem becomes an extended metaphor for all women—sexual but not procreative—who are excluded from the biblical story and ultimately from legitimate Jewish life. Dropkin's poetic "I" in this poem may reveal an aspect of the poet's self, empowered through her sensuality and at the same time disempowered by cultural conventions of sexuality. Thus, Dropkin's persona works both as a translucent inroad into her self and as a means of conveying the poem beyond the self into the sexual politics of its culture.

Tussman's 1949 poem reverses Dropkin's dynamic of the self as an example of a problem within the larger culture. This poem speaks with an "I" that transcends the poet's particular self to assume the identities of other, individual women whom the poetic "I" joins together to comprise a resistant, surviving cultural self. Recasting the collective in the "I" neither creates a transparent window into the poet's self nor drops an opaque mask over that self. In contrast, Tussman's poems of 1977 present the most direct correspondence between the poetic "I" and the revelation of the self—an ultimate translucence. They weave the gender identification of the speaker/self subtly into an extended metaphor of giving birth and of being born. Ironically, the most translucent poetic "I"—in Tussman's late poems—conveys the most intimate experience of dissociation from the self.

The interplay between "I" and "self" described here provides one example of the common strands joining Yiddish poems by women into a body of works. Furthermore, the differences between the internal counterpoint of self-definition in these poems and the external progress of individuation in poems by men even suggests a tradition of women's poetry. Such a tradition coexisted and sometimes converged with but did not conform to the mainstream of poems by men. When they allowed current assumptions about gender to blind them to the poems, Yiddish critics earlier in the century succumbed to the danger of grouping women poets together. Perhaps only now, late in the century and with the help of feminism's broadening perspectives, can we begin to see how complex the poems are and how intricate is a tradition of poems by women.

NOTES

1. For discussion of general problems of self in literature, see: Wood and Zurcher (1988). See also Layton and Schapiro, eds. (1986), especially Frederick Kirchhoff, "Reconstruction of the Self in Wordsworth's 'Ode: Intimations of Immortality from Recollections of Early Childhood,'" 116-129; Barbara Schapiro, "Thomas Hardy

and the 'Well-Beloved' Self," 130-147; and Ernest S. Wolf and Ina Wolf, "We Perished, Each Alone': A Psychoanalytic Commentary on Virginia Woolf's *To the Lighthouse*". Also see Laird (1988); Altieri (1980).

For studies of the self in literature with regard to gender, see: Celeste Schenk (1988). See also: Benstock, ed. (1988), especially Shari Benstock, "Authorizing the Autobiographical," 10-33; Susan Stanford Friedman, "Women's Autobiogrpahical Selves: Theory and Practice," 34-62; Elizabeth Fox-Genovese, "My Statue, My Self: Autobiographical Writings of Afro-American Women," 63-89; Patricia Meyer Spacks, "Female Rhetorics," 177-191. Also see Keller (1986)

For studies of the poetic "I," see: Muller (1979), and Williamson (1984).

For studies of women's poetics, see Donovan (1987). Also see Gilbert and Gubar, eds. (1979), especially Jeanne Kammer, "The Art of Silence and the Forms of Women's Poetry," and Barbara Charlesworth Gelpi, "A Common Language: The American Woman Poet."

On self and Yiddish literature see: Pratt (1983); Norich (1990); and Hadda (1988).

2. "Mainstream" is a metaphoric term that presents a problem when applied to Yiddish, because the literature itself has been marginalized for its entire 700-year history, first as a devotional literature written in *mameloshn* (mother tongue) rather than *loshnkoydesh* (sacred tongue), and more recently as a modern, secular literature. Nonetheless, I will use this term here, because (1) in the first half of the twentieth century, Yiddish anthologizers attempted to establish a Yiddish "classical" or normative canon self-consciously modeled on mainstream Western European poetry; and (2) the general orientation of much critical work on Yiddish literature has tacitly accepted the categories of "major" and "minor" writers, thus dividing it into a mainstream and its margins. See Hellerstein, (1991 and 1988); and Novershtern (1991).

3. On the *Yunge*, see Wisse (1988, 1-20; 45-73). On the tension between collective and individual voices in poems by Halpern and Mani Leyb, see Hellerstein (1987).

4. On the Introspectivists, see: Harshav (1986, 3-62); On Glatshteyn, see Hadda (1980).

5. See Adler (1980, 21-25).

6. Glants's assessment of what women had to offer Yiddish poetry echoes the Hebrew Revivalist Eliezer Ben-Yehuda's 1897 exhortation that "Only women are capable of reviving Hebrew—this old, forgotten, dry and hard language—by permeating it with emotion, tenderness, suppleness, and subtlety." (Feldman 1990, 495). This resemblance attests to how pervasive in Jewish culture were the stock assumptions about women as psychological beings able to alter the character of language with a direct transfer of their presumed personal qualities.

7. Resistance to self-disclosure also appears in modern Hebrew writing by women. This phenomenon as it occurs in fiction is discussed by Feldman (1990) and by Govrin (1988); and, as it occurs in poetry, by Miron (1990) and by Bar Yosef (1988). A comparative study of the resistance to self-disclosure in Yiddish and Hebrew poetry by women remains to be done.

8. All translations are by the author, unless otherwise noted.

9. Another poem by Yehudis, *"Tsum dikhter"* [To the (male) Poet] explicitly takes a generational stance—the young against the establishment and, perhaps implicitly, young women poets against established men poets. In *"Tsum dikhter,"*

there is no first person singular, but a collective first person plural. And yet other poems by Yehudis strike me as conventional mood poems, expressing the sorrowful lassitude that "*Breyte himlen*" overturns.

10. Novershtern assumes that the speaker of the second stanza is Caesar himself (1990, 440-441; 1991, 7-11). The main source for my reading here is a 1986 draft of the yet-unpublished typescript of my book, *A Question of Tradition: Women Poets in Yiddish*. For a brief treatment of this poem, see also Pratt (15). I am grateful to Avram Novershtern for letting me read the Yiddish typescript of "Precarious Balance."

11. *Royznkrants* not only means, literally, "garland of roses," but also "rosary." I believe that Margolin is deliberately playing with the irony of the word's metamorphosis into a Christian ritual object.

12. For a different reading of "*In kafe*," see Novershtern (1990, 443-444; 1991, 13-14).

13. On pen names in Yiddish prose, see Miron (1973,16-22; 155-158; 273-274).

14. See Hadda's essay on Dropkin's love poems in this volume.

15. A different version of the poem exists in Dropkin (1935, 51-52).

16. For a fuller discussion of this poem, see Hellerstein (1990, 145-149).

17. This is the legend of Rachel, daughter of the shepherd Kalba Shevua, whom Akiba secretly married against her father's wishes. Rachel urged Akiba to attend Beit Midrash for 12 years. When Akiba returned, he pardoned Rachel's father for his vindictive acts against the young couple. Perhaps Tussman reads this character as lighting the way to Rabbi Akiba's becoming a great scholar. See Bialik (1951). Thanks to David Stern.

18. Revised from my earlier translation in Harshav, eds. (1986, 612-613).

19. Revised from my earlier translation in Harshav, eds. (1986, 620-623.

WORKS CITED

Adler, Ruth. 1980. *Women of the Shtetl: Through the Eyes of Y. L. Peretz.* Cranbury, N. J.: Associated University Presses.

Altieri, Charles. 1984. *Self and Sensibility.* Cambridgeshire and New York: Cambridge Univ. Press.

Bar Yosef, Hamutal. 1988. ʿ*Al shirat Zelda* [On Zelda's Poetry]. Hakibbutz Hameuhad.

Benstock, Shari, ed. 1988. *The Private Self: Theory and Practice of Women's Autobiographical Writings.* Chapel Hill: Univ. of North Carolina Press.

Bialik, H. N. 1951. "*Sefer haʾagadah* "[The Book of Legends] In *Ketubot* 63: 179.

Donovan, Josephine. 1987. "Toward a Women's Poetics." In *Feminist Issues in Literary Scholarship*, ed. Shari Benstock, 98-109. Bloomington: Indiana Univ. Press.

Dropkin, Celia. 1935. *In heysn vint: lider* [In the Hot Wind: Poems]. New York: Posy-Shulson Press.

———. 1959. *In heysn vint: Poems, Stories, Pictures.* New York: Published by her children.

Feldman, Yael S. 1988. "Gender In/Difference in Contemporary Hebrew Fictional Autobiographies." *Biography* 11, 3 : 189-209.

———. 1990. "Feminism Under Siege: The Vicarious Selves of Israeli Women Writers." *Prooftexts* 10,3: 493-514.

Gilbert, Sandra M. and Susan Gubar, eds. 1979. *Shakespeare's Sisters: Feminist Essays on Women Poets*. Bloomington: Indiana Univ. Press.

Glants, A. 1915. "*Kultur un di froy*" [Culture and Woman]. *Di fraye arbeter shtime*, 30 October, 4-5.

Govrin, Nurith. 1988. *Hamahatsit harishonah: Devora Baron hayehah vitsiratah* [The First Half: Devorah Baron, Her Life and Work]. Jerusalem: Mossad Bialik.

Hadda, Janet. 1988. *Passionate Women, Passive Men: Suicide in Yiddish Literature*. Albany: SUNY Press.

———. 1980. *Jacob Glatshteyn*. Boston: Twayne.

Harshav, Benjamin and Barbara, eds. 1986. *American Yiddish Poetry: A Bilingual Anthology*. Los Angeles: Univ. of California Press.

Hellerstein, Kathryn. 1987. "The Demon Within: Moyshe-Leyb Halpern's Subversive Ballads." *Prooftexts*, 7,3: 225-248.

———. 1988. "A Question of Tradition: Women Poets in Yiddish." *Handbook of Jewish-American Literature: An Analytical Guide to Themes and Sources*, ed. Lewis Fried, 195-237. New York: Greenwood Press.

———. 1990. "Songs of Herself: A Lineage of Women Yiddish Poets." *Studies in American Jewish Literature* 10: 138-150.

———. 1991. "Canon and Gender: Women Poets in Two Modern Yiddish Anthologies." *Shofar* 9,4: 9-23.

Keller, Barbara. 1986. *Woman's Journey Toward Self*. New York: Peter Lang.

Kolatch, Alfred J. 1982. *The Name Dictionary: Modern English and Hebrew Names*. Middle Village, N. Y.: Jonathan David Publishers.

Laird, Holly A. 1988. *Self and Sequence: The Poetry of D. H. Lawrence*. Charlottesville: Univ. Press of Virginia.

Layton, Lynne and Barbara Ann Schapiro, eds. 1986. *Narcissism and the Text*. New York: New York Univ. Press.

Margolin, Anna [Roza Lebensboym]. 1929. *Lider* [Poems]. New York: no publisher.

Miron, Dan. 1973. *A Traveller Disguised: A Study in the Rise of Modern Yiddish Fiction in the Nineteenth Century*. New York: Schocken Books.

———. 1989 and 1990. "*Imahot meyasdot, ahayot horgot*" [Founding Mothers, Stepsisters]. *Alpayim* 1: 29-58 and *Alpayim* 2: 121-177.

Müller, Wolfgang. 1979. *Das Lyrische Ich: Erscheinungsformen gattungseigentümlicher Autor-Subjektivität in der englischen Lyrik*. [The Lyrical I: Presentations of Genre-Specific Author Subjectivity in the English Lyric]. Heidelberg: Carl Winter, Universitätsverlag.

Niger, Sh. 1928. *"Froyen lyrik"* [Women's Lyrics]. *Literarishe bleter* 5,46 (16 November): 909-910.

Norich, Anita. 1990. "The Family Singer and the Autobiographical Imagination." *Prooftexts* 10, 1: 91-107.

Novershtern, Avram. 1988. "Yiddish Poetry in a New Context." *Prooftexts* 8,3: 355-363.

———. 1990. "'Who Would Have Believed That a Bronze Statue Can Weep': The Poetry of Anna Margolin." Trans. Robert Wolf. *Prooftexts* 10, 3: 435-467.

———. 1991. "A Precarious Balance: The Poetry of Anna Margolin." Yiddish typescript introduction to *The Poems of Anna Margolin: Critical Edition*. Jerusalem: Hebrew University Press.

Pratt, Norma Fain. 1983. "Anna Margolin's *Lider*: A Study in Women's History, Autobiography, and Poetry." *Studies in American Jewish Literature* 3: 11-25.

Ravitsh, Melekh. 1927. *"Meydlekh, froyen, vayber—yidishe dikhterins"* [Girl's Women, Wives: Yiddish Women Poets]. *Literarishe bleter* 4 (27 May): 395-396.

Schenck, Celeste, 1988. "All of A Piece: Women's Poetry and Autobiography." In *Life/Lines: Theorizing Women's Autobiography*, eds. Bella Brodzki and Celeste Schenck, 281-306. Ithaca, N.Y.: Cornell Univ. Press.

Tussman, Malka Heifetz. 1949. *Lider* [Poems]. Los Angeles: Malka Heifetz Tussman Book Committee.

———. 1977. *Haynt iz eybik: lider* [Today is Eternal: Poems]. Tel Aviv: Yisroel Bukh.

———. 1986. *"Aroys un arayn"* [Out Of and Back In]. Trans. Kathryn Hellerstein. In *American Yiddish Poetry: A Bilingual Anthology*, eds. Benjamin and Barbara Harshav, 612-613. Los Angeles: Univ. of California Press.

Ulinover, Miriam. 1922. *Der bobes oytser* [Grandmother's Treasure]. Warsaw: Brothers Levin Epshteyn and Associates.

Weissler, Chava. 1987. "The Traditional Piety of Ashkenazic Women." In *Jewish Sprituality: From the Sixteenth-Century Revival to the Present*, ed. Arthur Green, 245-275. Philadelphia: Crossroad.

Williamson, Alan. 1984. *Introspection and Contemporary Poetry*. Cambridge, Mass.: Harvard Univ. Press.

Wisse, Ruth. 1988. *A Little Love in Big Manhattan: Two Yiddish Poets*. Cambridge Mass.: Harvard Univ. Press.

Wood, Michael R. and Louis A. Zurcher, Jr. 1988. *Development of a Postmodern Self*. New York: Greenwood Press.

Yehudis [Rokhl Bernshteyn]. 1928. *"Breyte himlen"* [Ample Heavens]. In *Yidishe dikhterins: antologye* [Yiddish Women Poets: an Anthology], ed. Ezra Korman, 63-64. Chicago: L. M. Stein.

The Influence of Decadence
on Bialik's Concept of Femininity

∽ HAMUTAL BAR YOSEF ∽

I.

Women and love play a central role in the writing of Hayyim Nahman Bialik, the figure known as the national poet of Hebrew literature and as one of the foremost voices of the Hebrew Revival (the period spanning the years 1890-1920). Criticism of Bialik during the first half of the twentieth century favored the public aspect of his poetry at the expense of works dealing with personal themes. The last forty years, in contrast, have shown growing interest in the personal side of Bialik's oeuvre. A number of prominent critics have even come to view it as the essence of Bialik's achievement. Generally, these critics have adopted a psychoanalytic approach to Bialik and, as they examine Bialik's attitudes toward love and sexuality, their interpretations emphasize a suppression or repression of eros, identifying sexual inhibition as a hallmark of Bialik's literary production.[1]

There can be no question that Bialik's poetry expresses authentic personal experiences and is open to psychoanalytic interpretation like any other literary work. We should nevertheless ask why Bialik's writing attracts more psychoanalytic readings than, for example, the literature of the Hebrew Enlightenment or the poetry of his contemporary, Saul Tschernihovsky. The answer is to be found in the connection between Bialik's writing and the atmosphere that prevailed in European literature at the turn of the century. I refer to the impact of Decadence and Symbolism. Freud's theories came into being against a background of sensitivity to the importance of repressed drives. The artistic representation of unconscious drives or instincts is one of the innovations of Decadent literature, and repressed sexuality and aggression are among its central themes.

Since the period of the Revival itself, the assumption has prevailed that Bialik is a Romantic poet (Miron 1987, 124-25; Aberbach 1988, 65-79). This idea, as it was first formulated by Yosef Klauzner, rested on the link between Romanticism and an ardent faith in national revival which is associated more with French and Russian Romanticism than with their English counterpart (Klauzner 1902, 545). Certainly, the presence of Romantic elements in Bialik's poetry, together with the centrality of the national experience, is undeniable. But Bialik's poetry should be seen as the junction of various contemporary literary influences. Prime among these is Decadence, which penetrated Russian literature and culture during the late 1890s and the early years of the twentieth century. Through this avenue Decadence exerted significant influence also on Hebrew writers (Bar Yosef 1990).

The experience of Decadence, as well as its basic assumptions—helplessness, pessimism, *ennui*, the stultification of emotion, addiction to sensual and aesthetic pleasure or to perverse impulses, alienation, the hopelessness of changing one's personal or social situation, indifference to social or national problems, amorality—all these stand in clear contradiction to the outlook and experience of the Hebrew national revival. Indeed, many Hebrew writers of the period are critical of Decadence. And yet, despite this general ideological rejection, the work of some writers of the period (particularly H.D. Nomberg, U.N. Gnessin, Yakov Steinberg, and David Fogel) shows evidence of attitudes, thought patterns, and formal elements originating in Decadent literature.[2] Early on there was some recognition of this phenomenon by Hebrew critics. In 1912 Yosef Hayyim Brenner observed elements of Decadence in Bialik's love poetry, and so located that poet's spiritual orientation in the artistic and cultural context of the *fin de siècle* (1985, 618). A closer look at Decadence and its premises can help show how the literary tradition operating during Bialik's period afforded him new modes of expression, ones which he adapted to his portrayals of women because they suited his own experiences.

Both the Decadent and Symbolist movements share the view that woman is more powerful than man and also that she is devoid of emotions. This contrasts with the Romantic view that femininity is identified with natural emotion. In other areas there are significant differences between the respective views of woman expressed by Decadence and Symbolism, particularly in the Russian context. The art and literature of Decadence may be characterized as having a misogynist, anti-Romantic orientation. Decadence, inspired by the philosophy and psychology of Schopenhauer and Eduard von Hartmann, discovered woman's primal physical character and portrayed her as aggressive and maliciously evil. The *femme fatale* constitutes a trap, love is merely an illusion. This view of woman was derived from a revolution in the view of humanity which occurred at this time, and which arose primarily from the discovery of unconscious drives and instincts as central determinants of human behavior (Dijkstra 1986, Bade 1979). In Symbolism, on the other hand, woman appears in a Neo-Romantic guise as ideal, spiritual, and pure. In Russian Symbolist poetry, which blended neo-Romantic principles and zealous nationalism, there are numerous manifestations of the mythological, mystical, yet highly contradictory figure of the "beautiful lady" (*prekrasnaya dama*) who symbolizes both the Russian nation and religious sanctity.

Elements of these beliefs enter into Bialik's corpus in a number of ways, for his poetry constitutes a kaleidoscopic reflection of major trends in contemporary Hebrew and European literature. Although Bialik's poetic treatment of women and love may be understood in the light of psychoanalytic investigation, there is always the danger, shared by any modern theoretical approach, that such an interpretative strategy might force a text written in quite another context into directions far distant from the world of the poet or the spirit of his times. To understand Bialik's love poetry and his treatment of female figures more fully, it is crucial to examine the stereotypes and conventionalized images of women prevalent in Bialik's literary milieu.[3]

II.

In Hebrew poetry written in Europe before the 1890s—the poetry of the Hebrew Enlightenment (circa 1860-1880) and of Hibbat Zion (Love of Zion, circa 1880-1895)—both woman, and man's relation to her, are almost devoid of sexuality. J. L. Gordon's long poem, "*Asnat Bat Potiferah*" (1865), is a rare exception of sexual expression in that period. Personal erotic love poems are even rarer in nineteenth-century Hebrew poetry. We should bear in mind that the very expression in Hebrew of love as physical attraction between a man and a woman, and especially the legitimation of such love, was viewed as perhaps the most dangerous of all assaults on the social order of Eastern European Jewry—which practiced a narrow system of arranged marriages, often at a young age. In the literature and journalism of the Hebrew Enlightenment one finds criticism of this practice (Gordon 1868; Lillienblum 1872); but, still, personal love poetry is rare in this period. Gordon's long poem "*Kotzo shel yod*" [The Point of a Yod] is one example of an attack on the institutions of marriage in Jewish society in Eastern Europe during the mid-nineteenth century.[4] The poem also contains an implicit recommendation that contact between men and women be spontaneously initiated—by the male, of course. In this poem, as elsewhere in Gordon's work, women are seen as modest paragons of virtue. In Hebrew Enlightenment literature, love coexists with other lofty spiritual, aesthetic, or moral emotions. These are unproblematically combined with wisdom, education, and practical skills. In essence, we are faced with a combination of Romantic and Positivist views, as are commonly found in Russian literature of the 1860s and 1870s.[5]

The scarcity of poems describing the personal experience of falling in love is due only in part to the social delegitimation of the subject, and in part to the remoteness of the possibility that a young Jewish man, however enlightened, would actually come to experience such love. It derived also from the limited contact between Hebrew literature written in Russia and European Romanticism. When the center of Hebrew Enlightenment literature shifted from Germany to Russia in the 1860s, the influence of Russian poetics—then dominated by anti-Romantic, Positivist approaches in the spirit of the "Natural School"—increased.

The few examples of personal love poetry in Hebrew Enlightenment and Hibbat Zion literature are to be found in the work of poets who absorbed the influence of German Romanticism, such as Micha Yosef Hacohen Lebenson (known as "Michal," 1828-1852), Mordechai Zvi Maneh (1859-1885), and Aba Konstantin Shapiro (1839-1900). Alongside poems describing courtly love, Lebenson writes powerful love poems which are not reticent in their description of physical arousal (Lebenson 1869: 26; 31; 37; 38). Yakov Fichman observes that even poets like M.Z. Maneh and A.K. Shapiro who wrote personal, lyric poetry and Romantic nature poetry, "almost never resorted to erotic poetry." He notes that when Shapiro did in fact write some "sharply erotic" poems, the poet suppressed their publication—which would, in any case, have been impossible during the period (Fichman 1946, 202; see also Kartun-Blum 1969, 27-28). In Hebrew Enlightenment and Hibbat Zion poetry we commonly find a female figure who symbolizes the Jewish nation. The poet expresses his love, longing, and feelings of tenderness for this abstract figure, variously portrayed as a sister (as in J.L. Gordon's "*Aḥoti Ruḥamah*" [My Merciful Sister]), or as a mother (as in "*Mishirei Tsion*" [From Songs of Zion] by Yehuda Leyb Levin).

As Miron has shown, Shalom Yakov Abramovitch (known as Moykhr Sforim or Mendele the Bookseller) was the first to break with the conventions governing the portrayal of women and love in Enlightenment literature (1979, 395-403). The physiological aspect of love plays a certain part in the subplot of *The Beggars' Book*, published in Yiddish as *Fishke der Krummer* in 1888 and in Hebrew as *Sefer hakabtsanim* in 1907-1909. Abramovitch's later works are influenced by Naturalism to some extent. In the same year that the Yiddish version of *The Beggars' Book* was published, Aryeh Leyb Mintz's excellent Hebrew translations of eleven of Heine's poems also appeared. Seven of them are poems of love and desire, including some which describe sexual fantasies. Despite the accepted tendency within Hebrew literature of the period to adapt such poems and censor them in accordance with readers' norms and tastes, Mintz does not hesitate to use such daring phrases as "*shadeihah*" (her breasts) or "*vateḥamemeini vateyaḥameini*" (and she warmed me and she rutted me). From the end of the 1880s and throughout the 1890s, interest in Heine grew. He was the object of numerous translations, pastiches, and publicist commentaries, and at the end of the 1890s the "epidemic" of interest in Heine inspired a vigorous polemic (Frishman 1895, Lillienblum 1898, Klauzner 1898, Bernfeld 1901). This polemic continued the argument arising in the wake of the publication of Y.L. Peretz's *Haʿugav* [The Organ] in 1894, a work devoted mainly to love poetry in the style of Heine, including poems emphasizing the physiological and nonemotional aspects of man's desire for women.

III.

The development of the concept of femininity in Bialik's poetry reflects the general development of his poetics. In his early poetry we can find traces of Enlightenment and Hibbat Zion poetry, but toward the end of the first decade of his literary career elements of Decadence and Symbolism become more and more prominent.

In Bialik's early poems (many of which have not been canonized), the portrayal of woman is dominated by the conventions of allegorical characterization in Hibbat Zion poetry (Miron 1986, 204-207). The epic poem "*Malkat Shevʾa*" [The Queen of Sheba] (1890-1891; in Miron 1983, 107), depicts a woman devoid of sexuality—the embodiment of the human ideal of wisdom and spiritual purity. "*Hakayits*" [The Summer] (1891;

ibid., 119) describes a pastoral love affair between a shepherd and a drawer of water, while the erotic encounter between the forces of nature is conveyed through the imagery of the Dinur River: "a melting pot for purifying the evils of human existence." "Lekhi dodah" [Go, Beloved] (1892, ibid., 186) is a clear example of the allegorical representation of Hebrew nationhood. "Dim*ot eim" [A Mother's Tears] (1892, ibid., 186) was written under the unmistakable influence of "Legenda o chashe" [The Legend of the Goblet] by the Jewish-Russian poet Simon Frug, whose model of nationalist poetry Bialik tried to imitate for a while. The image of the weeping mother continues the sentimental tradition of Hibbat Zion poetry. (This is a figure which Bialik frequently evokes in many of his later poems, as well; but as he develops as a writer Bialik distances himself from allegorical characterizations and adopts more modern techniques.)

Accepted wisdom aside, few of Bialik's poems, or love poems for that matter, are quintessentially Romantic. The Romantic experience is generally conveyed in his poetry with full consciousness of its distance from the actual realities of life, as an expression of childhood dreams or personal and poetic longing mediated through the poet's scepticism, guilt, or self-irony. Even an apparently Romantic love poem like "Mikhtav katan li katavah" [She Wrote Me a Short Letter] (1897) ends with the separation of the Romantic experience from actual life. This poem takes the form of a love letter, which a woman addresses to the speaker/poet. She longs for a relationship and proposes a Romantic ideal of spiritual love, a love which is "the source of life, the desire and faith of the soul." After reading the letter, the narrator/addressee concludes: "You are too pure to be my companion / Too holy to live with me / Be my goddess and angel / I will pray to you and serve you." While Bialik accepts the Romantic view of woman, he is aware that such a figure cannot be a flesh-and-blood partner, but only a disembodied entity and source of inspiration.[6]

Bialik's reservations about Romantic love are even more evident in "*Im dimdumei hahamah" [With Twilight] (1902). The image of the lovers that appears at the beginning of the poem takes the Romantic idea of love to its extreme. Standing by the window looking out at the limitless distances, the man and woman are merged into one entity, united in their longing for the "golden isles" which represent dreams and ideals. But the lyrical I/lover says that those isles "made us proselytes under any skies / and transformed our lives into hell." Social disconnection and *ennui* are the fate of those who devote their lives to such Romantic love. Here Bialik depicts love as a total physical and spiritual fusion, yet he finds in this experience a key not to heaven, but rather to a barren hell.

Romantic love does not appear even in Bialik's folk poetry, a body of work comprising thoroughly artistic poems produced according to the stylistic dictates of the folk genre, which was popular in German and Russian Romantic poetry. Most of the folk poems are monologues of a woman longing for a groom. Three qualities demonstrate the non-Romantic nature of these poems: first, the poet's awareness of the repressed sexual needs of women; second, a humorous and deflating attitude to unrequited love and enforced loneliness; and last, the ironic gap between the limited consciousness of the woman living in a world of legends and illusions on the one hand, and the impoverished reality implied in the poems on the other.

The young Bialik, who admired J.L. Gordon, did not inherit the latter's interest in the social fate of the Jewish woman or her need to fight for her rights. The poem "Reḥov haYehudim" [The Street of the Jews] (1894; in Miron 1983, 270), which includes explicit allusion to Gordon's "Kotzo shel yod," is exceptional in Bialik's oeuvre for its protest at the lot of women. Bialik will return to the issue of woman's social fate only in his later years, in the framework of his cycle of long poems "Yatmut" [Orphanhood] (1934), and particularly, "Almenut" [Widowhood] (1934). There, however, in contrast to Gordon, Bialik does not criticize any social or religious institution. With naturalistic precision, Bialik portrays the dehumanization of the individual woman, and depicts the collective existence of a whole social grouping of women living in a manner which makes them "more angry than scavenging she-cats summoned to a cruel skirmish." In this depiction the fate of the mother and of her counterparts is the result of an inevitable battle for survival.

Two of Bialik's early poems represent sexuality via the symbol of the snake, a symbol originating in the biblical narrative and one whose negative sexual import was developed in the Midrash and Kabalah. "Ḥavah vehanaḥash" [Eve and the Serpent] (1891-92; Miron 1983, 102) reconstructs the biblical story in the form of a dialogue between Eve and the snake. It is a lighthearted, rhyming feuilleton with which Bialik might have sought to amuse his fellow students during the sexual crisis of adolescence. Those who seek evidence of misogyny in Bialik, the young religious scholar, may find it in this poem. The other early poem which turns to the snake as a symbol, "ʿEinehah" [Her Eyes] (1892), adopts a frankly erotic tone. This openness about sexuality offended contemporary readers and editors (Miron 1983, 196), and so the publication of the poem met with a number of obstacles.7 Indeed, judged by the standards of that time, "Her Eyes" is a thoroughly daring poem, if only because it describes a personal encounter between a man and a woman who are sexually attracted to one another. Furthermore, it bestows initiative on the woman. She looks at the man with dangerous intent, casting him a glance which the poet describes this way: "Two adders, black cobras / I saw forking, bursting forth / From her eyes into my heart / They descended and struck."

And yet, despite the thematic daring of the poem, despite its description of sexual arousal, and despite the insidious look of the woman, "Her Eyes" is nevertheless remote from the Decadent view of woman. The woman it describes is not a physiological entity. Her eyes, and no other organs, transmit her erotic address to the man she confronts. For his part, he does not perceive the woman as a sexual object. Rather, he senses the duality of an experience that combines exalted mysticism and powerful demonic attraction. Reacting to her stinging look with fear, he invokes the magic formula usually reserved for exorcising an evil spirit or frightening off the devil. Finally, in contrast to the emotional frigidity which characterizes Decadence, the emotional power of the particular experience this poem describes is enormous. In the last stanza the poet testifies that, although the woman herself has disappeared, the impression and effects of her glance remain with him. It is not here, but only later that Bialik's poetry displays clear affinities with Decadence.

IV.

The poem *"Noshanot"* [Obsolescence] (1894-97) represents one of the earliest points of genuine confluence between Bialik and the Decadent view of woman. Heine's influence on "Obsolescence" is clear. Romantic in situation and material, its tone is light and pleasant. But from the outset, its Romanticism is too cloying, and hence subject to suspicion. Gradually the Romantic experience represented by the female figure is depleted and loses credibility since it is not shared by the male participant. He is not interested in the pure beauty of the clouds, the moon, the wind, and the nightingale's song, but in the physical beauty of the woman. "Her grace" at night, he states, not nature, inspires his poetry. The last stanza of the poem, which Bialik added only in 1897, gives the poem its bitingly sarcastic conclusion à la Heine. The conclusion is profoundly anti-Romantic in that it robs love of its emotional content and revitalizing force. It also identifies love with obsolescence, i.e., with cyclical natural and social processes that repeat themselves with barren monotony—a typically Decadent motif. It is a small step from this kind of mockery of love inspired by Heine to the desolate sexual encounters described by Baudelaire.[8]

The enthusiastic reception of Heine in Hebrew literature of the 1890s is one indication of that literature's interest in the type of Western European belles-lettres then considered Decadent in Russia.[9] During this period a shift occurred in the way Heine was viewed. Although he had been seen exclusively as a fighter for justice and liberal ideas who deep-down always remained faithful to his Jewishness (Shulman 1875), Heine began to be perceived as an intellectual and a hedonist, an egoistic pessimist without moral idealism or national affiliation. Despite this he was still perceived as a "distant brother" (Bernfeld 1898) and an admirable artist all the same.

The earliest undeniable example of the Decadent influence on Bialik's view of woman is to be found in *"Haʿeinayim hareʿeivot"* [Those Hungry Eyes], one of Bialik's most impressive poems. This poem was first printed in the *Tushiya* edition of Bialik's poems (1902), where it was not dated. Bialik never published it in a Hebrew periodical. "He probably assumed that its powerful and open eroticism would diminish its chances of publication in a periodical," writes Miron (1983, 334). The poem is included in the copybook manuscript Bialik assembled in 1897 in an attempt to publish his first book. This indicates that the poem itself was written no later than 1897.

The first major inroads Decadence made into Bialik's poetry occurred during the mid-1890s. The Decadent influence reached its culmination in the poem *"Beit ʿolam"* [The Cemetery] (1901). This period saw the appearance of *"Hokhrei hadaʿat hamelumadim"* [The Learned Pedants] (1894), *"Baʿarov hayom"* [At Twilight] (1895), *"Mishirei hakayits"* [From the Songs of Summer] (1897), *"Bitshuvati"* [On My Return] (1896) and *"ʿAl levavkhem sheshameim"* [On the Ruins of Your Heart] (1898), all of which bear traces of Decadent *ennui*, as well as other hallmarks of the Decadent tradition. Here, then, is "Those Hungry Eyes," the first important example of this development:

הָעֵינַיִם הָרְעֵבוֹת הָאֵלֶּה שֶׁכָּכָה תִּתְחַבֵּעְנָה,
הַשְּׂפָתַיִם הַצְּמֵאוֹת הָאֵל הַשְּׁאֵלוֹת: נַשְּׁקֵנוּ!
הָעֳפָרִים הָעוֹרְגִים הָאֵלֶּה הַקּוֹרְאִים: תָּפְשֵׂנוּ!
חֲמוּדוֹתַיִךְ הַצְּפוּנוֹת שֶׁשָּׂבְעָה כִשְׁאוֹל לֹא־תֵדַעְנָה;

כָּל־עֲטֶרֶת הַגְּוִיָּה הַזֹּאת שֶׁפְעַת חֶמְדָּה מְלֵאָה,
כָּל־הַשְּׁאֵר הַלָּזֶה, כָּל־הַבְּשָׂרִים הָאֵלֶּה שֶׁכָּכָה
הִלְעִיטוּנִי מִמְּקוֹר תַּעֲנוּגִים, מִמַּעְיַן הַבְּרָכָה —
לוּ יָדַעַתְּ, יָפָתִי, מַה־קָּצָה בָם נַפְשִׁי הַשְּׂבֵעָה.

זַךְ הָיִיתִי, לֹא־דָלַח הַסַּעַר רִגְשׁוֹתַי הַזַּכִּים
עַד שֶׁבָּאת, יְפֵה־פִיָּה, וּבְרוּחֵךְ נָשַׁפְתְּ וְנִדְלַחְתִּי.
וַאֲנִי, נַעַר פֹּתֶה, לְרַגְלַיִךְ בְּלִי־חֶמְלָה הִשְׁלַכְתִּי
תֹּם לְבָבִי, בֹּר רוּחִי, כָּל־פִּרְחֵי נְעוּרַי הָרַכִּים.

רֶגַע קָטָן מְאֻשָּׁר הָיִיתִי בְּלִי־חֹק, וָאֲבָרֵךְ
אֶת־הַיָּד הַחֹלֶקֶת לִי מַכְאוֹב הָעֹנֶג הָעָרֵב;
וּבְרֶגַע קָטָן שֶׁל־תַּעֲנוּג, שֶׁל־אֹשֶׁר וָגִיל, עֲלֵי חָרֵב
עוֹלָם מָלֵא — מַה־נָּדוֹל הַמְּחִיר שֶׁנָּתַתִּי בִּבְשָׂרֵךְ!

(1966, 126)

Those hungry eyes, so beseeching,
Those thirsty lips, asking: kiss us!
Those twin fawns calling: catch us!
Your hidden enchantments endlessly voracious as the pit of Hell.

All the plenty of this body, the full abundance of loveliness,
All this flesh, all these limbs that so
Filled me from a fountain of pleasures, a spring of blessing,
If only you knew, my lovely, how my sated soul is tired of them.

Innocent I was, no storm had muddied my pure feelings
Till you came, pretty one, a wind blowing fiercely and I was muddied.
And I, a foolish lad, without remorse threw down at your feet
My innocence, my pure spirit, all the flowers of my tender youth.

For a short moment I knew boundless joy and I blessed
The hand that bestowed on me that sweet pain of pleasure
And in a short moment of delight, of happiness and joy
My entire world was destroyed—how high was the price I paid for your flesh.[10]

The first stanza lists only the woman's physiological attributes. Until
the speaker addresses her as "my lovely" at the end of the second stanza,
she exists only as flesh, as a series of limbs combined in "the plenty of
this body." The detailing of the woman's demanding limbs in the first
stanza proceeds up the scale of sexuality from eyes, to lips, breasts, and

finally to those more "hidden enchantments." The poet not only dismembers the woman's body, emphasizing his treatment of her as a sexual object, he also transforms the woman and her limbs—all of which appear in the plural in the Hebrew text—into a veritable gang lying in ambush to ensnare him.

The second stanza concentrates on a state of excessive sexual plenitude where satiety borders on nausea. At the end of this stanza, the speaker addresses the woman in a tone replete with weariness and disgust. Calling her "my lovely" only emphasizes the indifference of the man who suffers from sexual overindulgence. This stanza is also progressive in its expression of the increasingly negative emotions of the speaker. Words with positive connotations still appear in line one, such as "plenty" ('*ateret*) and "loveliness"(*hemdah*). The word used for body (*geviyah*) has resonances of the word for corpse, although a more neutral reading is also supported by such intertexts as Dan. 10:6.[11]

The appearance of the word "*she'er*" (flesh) in the next line militates against such a neutral reading of "*geviyah*" (body). Bialik uses this word to translate the French word *chair*. Thus he is able to invest this biblical word with a new meaning. According to Klauzner, Bialik adopts Taviov's translation of the French word (1898, 63). The word "*she'er*" evokes all the simultaneously attractive/repulsive associations it has in Baudelaire's poetry and in its Russian Decadent offshoots. The Russian translation of this word [*plot'*] is typical of the lexicon of Bryusov, the most prominent exponent of Russian Decadence (Donchin 1958, 165). The addition of the deictic "*halazeh*" (literally "that one"—a term alluding, however, to the phrase uttered by Joseph's brothers in Gen. 37:19, "Behold this dreamer cometh") reinforces the sense of the speaker's alienation from, and hostility toward, the woman's flesh. In the same line, the woman's body is referred to in the plural (*besarim*) in a form reminiscent of the Hebrew idiom for "the desires of the flesh" (*ta'avot besarim*). Used in isolation, "*besarim*" converts the woman's body into a kind of shelf for the display of various types of meat. Sexual delights are conveyed using a metaphor which transforms the man into an animal who is force-fed against his will. As was the case in the first stanza, only the last line—and not the preceding three—contains an explicit expression of repulsion and disgust. The phrase "sweet pain of pleasure" (stanza 4) reflects a view of the sexual act as both pleasurable and painful, and bears some affinity to the Decadent tendency to describe perverted sensual experiences.

The desolation brought about by a surfeit of pleasure is a central motif in the work of Baudelaire, as well as in Huysman's *À rebours* (1884)—two of the major sources of European Decadence. Its philosophical under-pinnings are to be found in Schopenhauer's *Parerga und Paralipomena* (1851)—his most widely disseminated and most popular work (Schopenhauer 1972 I: 328-332). The world of the dandy, bathed in lux-ury, surrounded by women of whom he has already grown tired, is totally foreign to the Jewish lifestyle with which Bialik was familiar. Biographical evidence does suggest that Bialik yearned for a great and passionate love, but did not at all aspire to be a Don Juan (Shva 1990, 71). In fact, he treated with disdain pride in amassing sexual conquests. So how does this theme of surfeit and overindulgence permeate an essen-tially erotic poem, despite its distance from the reality actually experi-enced by Bialik? It seems to me that the answer lies not only in the expo-sure of Bialik's subconscious male ego but also in his awareness of the cultural importance of the theme, and in his habit of using his poetry to express the collective tendencies he perceived in his environment. Nevertheless, it is important to emphasize that Bialik's reaction to such Decadent patterns of thought is not identification, but repulsion and conflict.

This is evident in the last half of the poem. In the third and fourth stanzas the character of the speaker changes. Here we find a man whose very being rebels against the identification of love with mere sex, a man unable to internalize the image of a bored and disgusted hedonist. The male figure in the second half of the poem has not renounced his basic self-image as a person with a pure soul, and he blames the woman, with whom he has had a sexual encounter, for corrupting his "innocence." The poet laments the fact that momentary subordination to sexual delights, without thought of love or procreation, has compromised his moral and spiritual purity. This is probably the first time in modern Hebrew literature that the woman is portrayed as more passionate than the man, and is seen as responsible for satisfying her sexuality. In this sense, too, we confront a Decadent poem. But one of the obvious differ-ences between Bialik and the Decadent poets is his "obsolete" belief in moral purity as a characteristic of the poet and as an ideal characteristic of all human beings. Laments over lost purity, it should be noted, are wholly absent from French and Russian Decadent poetry. The poem is typical of the manner in which Bialik absorbs Decadence and, to this extent, it is representative of the literature of the Hebrew Revival as a whole. Decadent influences, while evoking resistance and self-loathing, are seen as irreversible and inevitable impositions.

"Those Hungry Eyes" is one of the two poems Brenner cites as representing the "decadent content" of Bialik's love poetry. This observation occurs in an article on Tschernihovsky, whose poems Brenner sees as expressing a "healthy" attitude to love. His examples from Tschernihovsky all clearly portray love as a sexual act. In Bialik, on the other hand, says Brenner: "There is no healthy, whole, synthetic treatment of the fundamental principle of human life" (618). Brenner is correct in identifying traits stemming from Decadence in Bialik's expressions of repulsion or fatigue at the female body and at female sexuality. But Brenner fails to account for the anti-Decadent self-image revealed in the course of the poem. He also ignores the poem *"Beshel tapuah"* [Because of an Apple] (1898) and the story *"Me'ahorei hagader"* [Beyond the Fence], unequivocal examples of healthy love in Bialik's work.

V.

The Decadent orientation toward woman is prominent, too, in the poem *"Rak kav shemesh ehad"* [Just One Ray of Sun] (1901). Ziva Shamir writes that this poem is the product of the "climate of the generation." She also points to the similarity between Bialik's poem and Baudelaire's *"Une charogne"* [The Carrion] (Shamir 1987, 234-35). The last word of the poem—*"nivlatekh"* (your corpse or carrion)—is the main source of their similarity. But even in this poem Bialik's spiritual position differs from that of Baudelaire and the Decadent poets, as we shall shortly see.

רַק קַו־שֶׁמֶשׁ אֶחָד עָבְרֵךְ,
וּפִתְאֹם רוֹמַמְתְּ וְנָדַלְתְּ;
וַיִּפַּתַח חֶמְדָּתֵךְ וּבְשָׂרֵךְ,
וּכְגֶפֶן פֹּרִיָּה בָּשָׁלְתְּ.

וְרַק סַעַר לֵיל אֶחָד עָבְרֵךְ,
וַיַּחְמֹס אֶת־בִּסְרֵךְ, נִצָּתֵךְ;
וּכְלָבִים נְבָלִים בַּחֲדָרֵךְ
יָרִיחוּ מֵרָחוֹק נִבְלָתֵךְ —

(1966, 128)

Just one ray of sun passed over you
And suddenly you rose and grew
It unfurled your loveliness and your flesh,
And like a fruitful vine you ripened.

Just one nocturnal storm passed over you
And destroyed your unripe fruit, your bud,
And vile dogs sniff, from afar,
Within your beauty—a corpse.[12]

To depict the woman the poem uses two interfused metaphors: that of the vine from the biblical verse "Thy wife shall be a fruitful vine by the sides of thy house" (Ps. 128:3), and that of the proud woman sniffed at by dogs, which is reminiscent of the story of Jezebel (2 Kings 9:10). The first image is more prominent in the first stanza, where it is formulated using the simile, "like a fruitful vine you ripened." But even here the second picture is implied in the line "It unfurled your loveliness and your flesh." The second stanza develops the image of the vine, but uses the word "*bisreikh*" (unripened fruit) which is a near homophone of the word for "flesh" ("*besarekh*") in the first stanza. Shamir writes that the poem "merges descriptions of rot and blossoming, and vice versa" (ibid.). In fact, the poem describes a process whereby the picture of the rotting flesh gradually absorbs that of the blossoming vine. The construction and development of the metaphor—the passage from viewing the woman in terms of light, splendid beauty and fertility to a perception of the stench of her rotting flesh—dramatizes the passage from the biblical to the Baudelairean-Decadent conception. The first presents fertility as the chief characteristic of the married woman; the second sees the woman essentially as flesh capable of evoking both attraction and repulsion.

In Baudelaire's poem, however, the speaker expresses neither admiration of, nor sympathy for the woman. On the contrary, he shows her the corpse of a horse out of a somewhat sadistic impulse. Bialik, on the other hand, describes a mature woman who, at the height of her beauty and fertility, falls prey to a "storm" which robs her of her delicate and as yet unripe fertility. Following the injury inflicted by the storm, "vile dogs" appear and smell "from afar" her stench of carrion. The words "from afar" hint at both a physical and temporal distance. The woman is still at the height of her glory, but in the eyes of the dogs (and not necessarily in the poet's view!) she is already a corpse. The dogs are attracted to her not because she has become, as Zemah would have it, a bitch in heat (330), but because vile and scavenging dogs habitually seek out carrion. The word "*nivlatekh*" (your carrion) echoes the word "*nevalim*" [vile], and it is possible to construe it as indicative of the dogs' perspective on the woman. The poem's conclusion expresses disgust at the dogs, as much as at the woman. According to Zemah, the sound "*ekh*," which appears in the paired rhymes of the first stanza and which concludes line-endings throughout the second stanza, conveys the poet's disgust at the woman. But it may also be read as evoking a sense of monotony, or even as echoing the sighs or anger of the poet at the evil inflicted on the woman. Even if the sound pattern does convey disgust, it is, as stated, directed at the dogs as well as at the woman.

The expression "*sa͑ar leil*" (a nocturnal storm) is generally interpreted as allusive to a sexual encounter. Such an interpretation poses the question of how it is possible to reconcile the vine's initial maturity with the woman's seduction—and deflowering—at the hands of the man. Does she bloom after having borne fruit? One resolution lies in viewing the poem as describing the illusion of fertility which is cruelly withdrawn. Thus the storm does not represent intercourse but the miscarriage of a fetus—the bud of the fertile vine—whose death condemns the woman to infertility. The woman hereby retains her glory, but the life she is destined to live will be one of decay rather than of growth. Bialik might be drawing here on family experience, but even so, the meaning of the poem is not exhausted by such a reading. Instead, positing a miscarriage enables the poem to be invested with symbolic meaning both at the poetic level (Shamir, 223) and at the national level, where it conveys Bialik's mistrust of temporary, and ultimately unproductive, enthusiasms—a theme expressed in his long poem "*Metei midbar*"[The Dead of the Desert] (1902), as well as in various other poems and utterances. Bialik's criticism of rapid processes which bring no lasting gain reflects his adherence to the views of Ahad Ha͑am. This is not to say that the present poem is a nationalist one, but that despite its Decadent characteristics, "Just One Ray of Sun" does express Bialik's fundamental moral and spiritual stance.

VI.

A Decadent orientation towards femininity also emerges in some of Bialik's nature poems. Various feminist theorists have pointed to the connection between nature and femininity in European art and literature, especially in Romanticism (Macmillan 1982; Dijkstra). This is one of the most deep-seated stereotypes of male thought and culture in the West. The link is also strongly present in Decadence, but here the drastically revised view of nature goes hand in hand with a new orientation towards woman. In Decadence, both woman and nature are subordinated to the principle of evil camouflaged as refined and tempting beauty. Both woman and nature are dangerous illusions, tempting death traps.

This view is echoed in Bialik's poem, "*Beit ʿolam*" [The Cemetery] (1901). Here nature is represented by the image of terebinth trees. The choice of a tree that is not indigenous to Eastern Europe underscores its symbolism: nature is a pagan force possessing mythological powers. Nor is the choice of a tree whose name is in the feminine (*elah*) coincidental. These terebinths engage in a monologue which is gradually revealed as malicious and devouring, a form of temptation enticing the poet into a trap of decay and death. This is the trap constituted by nature, but it is also the trap of femininity. It is significant, too, that this poem's last verse, "The tombstones also pitied me," connects the terebinths with tombstones, thus equating nature and death—two collectively female entities in the Hebrew text. Additionally, feminine pity is perceived as part of the dangerous temptation to rest in the arms of death.

In "*Levadi*" [Alone] (1902), we find the same fear of the suffocating embrace of the merciful woman who is simultaneously in need of mercy. The female figure in this poem is a reincarnation of the merciful and suffering mother who symbolizes the spirit of the Jewish nation in Hibbat Zion poetry. The "I" or speaker of the poem declares his loyalty to her. He remains "under her wing" (a Hebrew expression reminiscent of the traditional liturgy for the dead) (Zemah, 169), even when her embrace has become too narrow for him. In contrast to the prevailing tradition of Hibbat Zion poetry, the poet's identification with the nation's unfortunate lot is not presented as a conscious and just act of volition, but as a regressive and irrational attraction to darkness and death.

"*Givʿolei eshtakeid*" [Last Year's Stalks] (1903; see Lachover 1950, 469) is a poem describing the transition from the old to the new. It takes the form of a monologue. A man addresses a woman in a garden in spring and describes how the gardener's daughter—"a beautiful and innocent girl"—collects last year's withered stalks for burning. In the edition of his works published in 1908, where poems are arranged according to subject matter, Bialik himself placed this poem in the section on nature. The poem's critics have also viewed it as describing a love which has passed (Fichman, 50; Perry 1977, 184-86). Still other critics view it as a nationalist poem (Lachover, 469-70), or even as an *ars poetica* (Shamir, 192-98). Indeed, the poem encourages diverse interpretations, whether directed at the private or public sphere, and in this respect it bears an affinity with the tradition of Russian Symbolism.

The poem's description of natural processes, as well as its description of the relationship between the man and the woman, places in the foreground the principle of cruelty. Unlike "*Paʿamei aviv*" [The Footsteps of

Spring] (1900), this spring poem lacks descriptions of sunrise and blossoming plants. Instead, it focuses on the process of pruning and of burning the withered stalks. Man and woman are coupled in a cruel relationship, too. The man uses the processes occurring in the garden as emblematic of the relationship between the sexes, which is similarly governed by the principle of painful substitutions and the replacement of the old by the new. The gardener's daughter represents a radicalization of the destructive processes of spring, governed by hoe and pruning shears.

The two female figures of the poem, the addressee and the gardener's daughter, are described against a backdrop of growth: long, frail branches knock at the "heart's walls" of one of them while the second bears dry branches to the bonfire. One figure represents helplessness, aridity, passivity, and lack of emotional response; the other, unconscious cruelty veiled by beauty and innocence. Both of them participate in the determinist process of decay and renewal to which nature is subject in spring. The first woman signifies the stage of delicate destruction; the second, the inevitable cruelty which is a prerequisite of renewal and vitality. Both female figures represent natural laws and processes: the inevitable degeneration of the old, destruction as the price of growth.

Nevertheless, it is clear that the poem cannot be considered quintessentially Decadent, because its very faith in the possibility of growth represents a denial of the Decadent worldview. The link between cultural growth and cruelty is one that Bialik probably assimilated in a Nietzschean context. It was widespread in Russia at the turn of the century and has been identified as one of the chief characteristics of Russian Symbolism (Glazer-Rosenthal 1986). The fact that the stalks are collected for burning by a beautiful and innocent girl, however, returns us to the Decadent orientation toward femininity.

Like "The Cemetery," "*Hayah ʿerev hakayits*" [One Summer Evening] (1908) depicts nature as ruled by mythological female figures:

וּבְנוֹת לִילִיּוֹת זַכּוֹת שׁוֹזְרוֹת מוֹזְרוֹת בַּלְּבָנָה
חוּטֵי כֶסֶף מַזְהִירִים,
וְהֵן אֹרְגוֹת כְּסוּת אַחַת לְכֹהֲנִים גְּדוֹלִים
וְלִמְנַדְּלֵי חֲזִירִים.

(1966, 197)

Lilith's daughters weave in the moonlight, spinning
Threads with a silvery shine,
Sewing a single cloth for the high priests
And for those who herd the swine.[13]

Lilith is a female Satan, as is well known in Jewish folklore. Nevertheless, in the first two lines, the daughters are subject to the illusion of Romantic purity, thanks to the presence of such words as "*zakot*" (pure) and "*mazhirim*" (shining)—a word derived from the same root as the word "*zohar*" with its mystic connotations. The repetition of the letter "*z*" is perceived as a musical or onomatopoeic imitation of the sound of the loom. But in the next two lines the daughters of Lilith are an amoral influence. The subtle beauty of nature becomes a cover, and also a deceptive camouflage which does not differentiate between the pure and the defiled.[14] Retrospectively, the spinning daughters are reminiscent of the spider-woman weaving a trap for men: a typical motif in Decadent art. The very same motif recurs in the second stanza of "*Bitshuvati*" [On My Return] (1891-92):

שׁוּב לְפָנַי: זְקֵנָה בָלָה,
אֹרְגָה, סֹרְגָה פֻזְמְקָאוֹת,
פִּיהָ מָלֵא אָלָה, קְלָלָה,
וּשְׂפָתֶיהָ תָּמִיד נָעוֹת.

(1966, 14)

Again, before me: a wizened old woman
Weaving and knitting stockings.
Her mouth is filled with curses and oaths,
Her lips forever moving.[15]

Additionally, the picture of dead flies lying bloated in a spiderweb in the fourth stanza of the latter poem represents a significant analogy to the old woman. In "One Summer Evening," nature is forced to participate in human corruption, a process which culminates in the transformation of the "flesh" (*she'er*) into a mythological figure: "He rolls, demented in his spew, and wallows in fleshly pleasure sunken." It is difficult to find a more pointed repugnance for sexuality in Bialik's poetry. Throughout the poem, nature is feminine. This is especially marked in the fifth stanza: "And passion stirs even in blades of grass / In stones beside the road." The irregular change of grammatical gender in the word "grass" (from *isvei*—masculine, to *isvot*—feminine), a change not determined by prosodic constraints, is in line with the (highly negative) characterization of nature as female.

VII.

"*Ayeikh?*" [Where Are You?] and "*Tsiporet*" [Butterfly], both written in 1904, describe a powerful experience of elevated love unmarred by nausea or disgust, and free of the demonization of the *femme fatale*. Even so, both poems constitute subtle, almost imperceptible variants on the Decadent model of male-female relationships. In a letter to S. Ben-Tsion (written on November 6, 1904), Bialik claims that both poems were written under the impression of a short love affair which the poet had had at that time in the summer resort Mrozy (Bialik 1938, I: 254-255).

"Where Are You?" is symmetrically divided into two stanzas of twelve lines each, separated by a single line containing the lone word "*ayeikh?*" The first stanza describes with increasing intensity the speaker's anguish and physical passion. The woman is initially described as a spiritual entity: "*yeḥidat ḥayai ushekhinat maʿavaiai*"([Soul of my life. . .of my desire). This formulation relies on words that carry religious connotations, *yeḥidah* and *shekhinah*. However, this figure immediately assumes a more active manifestation as well. Both the man and the woman are in hiding, but the speaker expects the woman to come out from her hiding place and enter "my refuge" in order to save him and to rule over his life ("Queen of my fate"). The woman, ruler and savior though she be, is also lethal. Here the relationship assumes overtones of the mating rituals of insects, in the course of which the woman kills and devours the male. This is a common phenomenon among spiders, while the male butterfly, for his part, dies after mating for the first time. These metaphors—which were widespread in Decadent art and literature—hover over the last lines of the first stanza:

וּבֵין שָׁדַיִךְ יוֹמִי אוֹצִיא,
כִּגְוֹעַ בָּעֶרֶב הַיּוֹם בֵּין פִּרְחֵי בְשָׂמִים
צִפֹּרֶת כְּרָמִים.

(1966, 170)

"I will end my days between your breasts
Just as, at twilight, among fragrant flowers,
A vineyard butterfly expires.[16]

Bialik uses the rare feminine word "*tsiporet*" for butterfly (instead of the usual masculine word, "*parpar*") as a means of emphasizing the feminine, passive, and fragile nature of the male partner. The use of this unusual word also emphasizes the feminine identity of the poet-lover. The death of the man-butterfly between the woman's breasts, after inter-

course has taken place, evokes the scent of "fragrant flowers," a component of the erotic experience which links the concluding lines of the first
stanza with various other elements in the poem and with components of
the Decadent tradition such as the emphasis on physical sexuality; the
motif of the ruling and lethal woman; the metaphorical mediation of
intercourse through the image of the mating rituals of insects; and the
portrayal of the woman as spider. Although these allusions are muted
and subtle, their source is unquestionable.

The poem in its entirety polarizes the woman in the sense that Zemah
discerns (34-36): the woman is at one and the same time a sacred spiritual
entity and the powerful stimulus of dangerous sexual attraction. This
contradictory view of woman, and the poem's rejection both of naturalistic elements and of an attitude of revulsion towards female sexuality,
make "Where Are You?" a Symbolist rather than a quintessentially
Decadent text. A similar view of woman is presented in "*Megilat haʾeish*"
[The Scroll of Fire] (1905), where the fictive reality is clearly structured
around pairs of symbolic opposites.

In "Butterfly" the image of the man as a butterfly recurs, this time as a
butterfly caught in the woman's net. The context is a highly romantic
situation which almost totally diffuses the Decadent residue of the
metaphor. The man and the woman stroll in the peaceful and flowering
fields. Nature flowers and flourishes, and an atmosphere of purity and
mystery pervades all. Suddenly white butterflies rise out of the field, and
one lands on the woman's braids. The butterfly, again designated
"*tsiporet*," has an implied message for the speaker: "And he seemed to
tell me: Get up and kiss her and resemble me, the butterfly." In response,
the speaker asks: "But you—did you sense the butterfly or me? / Do you
realize that my soul is also held captive, and hovers suspended, waiting
for redemption / in your plaited braid?" In the passage from symbol (the
butterfly) to that which is symbolized (the speaker), the picture is transformed: the butterfly rests on the woman's plait and seems to kiss her, a
suggestion he offers the speaker, but the speaker perceives the young
woman's plait as a trap within which he flutters captive, or as a noose:
"suspended [from] your plaited braid." It is no accident that the word for
suspended, "*teluʾah*," (not the regular *teluyah*), and that for plaited,
"*keluʿah*," rhyme.

In the poem's last stanza the woman's eyes and her braid evoke contradictory meanings: the eyes express chastity while the braid seems to
solicit a transgression: "your braid. . .says 'Yes'." The speaker accepts the
invitation and remonstrates with the woman in a manner which both

reveals and conceals his intentions: "Hurry, hurry sister, let's reach the wood / underneath the canopy of its happiness I will devote all my soul to you / and all my love suspended by a hair / we will slay with a kiss." The expression "my love suspended by a hair" (allusive of the mishnaic "mountains suspended by a hair," *Hagiga* 1:8) serves on the one hand to develop the previous metaphor which describes the strength of the man's passion, while on the other hand its idiomatic overtones comically undermine the weight and force of these mountains of love. The conclusion of the poem explicitly suggests that this is the sort of love that will be extinguished after the first kiss. Here—as in "Where Are You?"—the physical realization of love is linked to death. But here it is a question not of Romantic *Liebestod*, but rather of light irony in the manner of Heine.

VIII.

When Brenner speaks of the decadent Bialik, he cites not only "Her Eyes" but also *"Hakhnisini"* [Take Me Under Your Wing] and "She Wrote Me a Short Letter" in support of the contention that Bialik is wary of healthy relationships and flees them. This means that Brenner fails to distinguish carefully between Decadence and Symbolism. He includes in his concept of Decadent love the spiritual worship of woman, characteristic of Russian Symbolism. Although it is not always easy to differentiate these modernist movements, it is important not to overlook their differences—particularly regarding their respective relationships to woman and to love.

Decadence discovered woman's primal and cruel nature embodied in the *femme fatale*: sensual and impassive, she entraps man in her delicate glistening net, there to suck his marrow. Decadent art described love as a bestial and physiological phenomenon that places power and initiative in the hands of the woman, while the sensitive and helpless man is condemned to be sated with cloying female passion. Symbolism, on the other hand, restores the spirituality and sanctity accruing to woman in Romanticism, but neither her vital, natural, earthy aspect, nor her emotional warmth. Woman in Symbolism is an incorporeal entity, a two-faced deity, a paradox of purity and corruption.

Using such differentiations, we can see clearly that the quintessentially Decadent portrait of woman is present in only two of Bialik's poems—"Those Hungry Eyes" and "Just One Ray of Light"—and even here the poet's attitude is not purely Decadent. In the other poems analyzed here, poems written between the years 1897-1908, Decadent influences consist of the treatment and pictorial realization of femininity, together with the link between female characteristics and natural processes. In various other poems of Bialik, and in the epic, "The Scroll of Fire," his orientation towards woman and love is closer to Symbolism. The assumption that Bialik's poetry in general, and his love poetry in particular, is Romantic came into being through the accepted but inaccurate linking of Decadence with Symbolism on the one hand, and early nineteenth-century Romanticism with *fin de siècle* Neo-Romanticism on the other. Reestablishing distinctions between these phenomena can reveal more subtle nuances, as well as interesting conflicts in Bialik's poetry.

Such a view of Bialik's poems also demonstrates the more general principle I have argued here: i.e., that the explanation of Bialik's concept of love and femininity—which today might seem bizarre, perverse, or even misogynist—should take into consideration not only biographical facts and psychoanalytic speculation but also the aesthetic and cultural conventions and stereotypes of Bialik's time. Sensitivity to the role which cultural stereotypes play in creating the artistic image is one of the most important contributions of feminist criticism to the understanding of literature and of ourselves. This tool is indispensable as a complement and a corrective to current psychoanalytic readings of Bialik.

— Translation from the Hebrew by Louise Shabat Bethlehem

NOTES

1. In his three short essays written in 1933 and 1949, Dov Sadan took a psychoanalytic appraoch to Bialik's poetry as a whole (1951). As early as the late fifties, Dan Miron dealt with the symbolism of sensual love in Bialik's poetry (1958, *"Toldot hataltal"*). In a series of interpretations of Bialik's poetry written mainly at the end of the fifties, Eddy Zemah places the conflict between pure and earthly love, and the suppression of eros, at the center of Bialik's experiential world (1976). Miron recently has returned to the question of the young Bialik's sexual identity (1986, *Haperidah min haʾani heʿani*). He finds in Bialik's early love poetry an implied declaration of the poet's right to indulge in his own solipsistic world, without being bothered socially or sexually. Miron finds Bialik's early sexual inhibitions as stemming from an undeveloped ego identity and childhood trauma.

2. A similar critical stance, strongly inspired by Nietzsche, was also present in Russian Symbolism, which greatly influenced both Hebrew literature and the work of Bialik at the beginning of the century. In contrast to Western European Symbolism, Russian Symbolism shows a marked resistance to Decadence (Maksimova 1972; Dolgopolov 1976; Poggioli 1960; Bristol 1980, 1985).

3. Feminist research into Hebrew literature has virtually ignored Bialik and his representation of women, despite the fact that his works form part of the basic

cultural baggage of anyone educated in Israel. Nehama Aschkenasy's *Eve's Journey: Feminine Images in Hebraic Literary Tradition* (1988, 94-96) devotes a few pages to two of Bialik's poems.

4. For discussion of this poem, see Aschkenasy (1988, 19-21).

5. Nikolai Chernyshevski's novel *Chto Delat? [What Is To Be Done?]* (1862) may be seen as prototypical of such a combination, as may some of the poems of Nikolai Nekrasov, the poet whom Gordon considered exemplary.

6. A more overtly Romantic poem is the uncanonical *"Bamanginah"* [In the Melody] written in 1893 following the poet's engagement. This is a superficial, even clichéd formulation of spiritual love in the conventional Romantic sense, a love which exalts and saves the soul. Small wonder that Bialik suppressed the publication of this particular poem. See Miron (1983, 205).

7. After writing "Her Eyes" in 1892, Bialik submitted it to *Luaḥ Aḥiʾasaf*, which was edited by Ben-Avigdor. Even after Bialik had corrected the poem according to the editor's recommendation, Ben-Avigdor would not publish it. Then Bialik sent it, together with some other poems that had been refused by various journals, to the *Talpiyot* supplement, where it was published in 1895.

8. It is worth noting that Heine was himself admired not only by Tyutchev and Balzac but also by Baudelaire and Nietzsche (Kopp 1988).

9. On this epidemic of interest in Heine, and the articles, translations, and imitations he inspired, see Lillienblum (1898).

10. This literal translation of the poem is by Naomi Sokoloff.

11. The Hebrew preserves an allusion to the "abundance of peace and truth" of Jer. 33:6, and to the "desire of women" mentioned in Dan. 11:37.

12. Translation by Naomi B. Sokoloff.

13. Translation by Naomi B. Sokoloff.

14. See Gen. 20:16, "he is to thee a covering of the eyes."

15. Translation by Naomi B. Sokoloff.

16. Translation by Naomi B. Sokoloff

WORKS CITED

Aschkenasy, Nehama. 1988. *Eve's Journey—Feminine Images in Hebraic Literary Tradition*. Philadelphia: Univ. of Pennsylvania Press.

Aberbach, David. 1988. *Bialik*. London: Grove Press.

Baer, J. Arthur. 1980. *Schopenhauer und die Russische Literatur des später 19. und frühen 20.* [Schopenhauer and Russian Literature of the Late Nineteenth and Early Twentieth Centuries]. Slavische Beiträge, Munich: Sagner.

Bade, Patrick. 1979. *Femme Fatale: Images of Evil and Fascinating Women*. New York: Mayflower Books.

Bar Yosef, Hamutal. 1990. "Bialik and Russian Poetry," *Ariel* 82: 47-63.

Bernfeld, Shimon. 1898. *"Aḥ raḥok"* [A Distant Brother]. *Hashiloaḥ* 3: 117-124; 216-223; 310-320.

———. 1901. *"Melekhet maḥshevet—Teḥiyat haʾuma"* [A Work of Art—The Revival of the Nation]. *Hador* 1 (14): 10-12.

Bialik, Hayyim Nahman. 1938. *Igrot* [Letters]. Ed. Fishel Lachover. 4 vols. Tel Aviv: Dvir.

―――. 1966. *Kol shirei Ḥ.N. Bialik* [Collected Poems of H.N. Bialik]. Tel Aviv: Dvir.

Brenner, Yosef Hayyim. 1985. *Y.H. Brenner—Kol kitvei* [Y.H. Brenner—Collected Works]. Ed. I Kafkafi. Tel Aviv: Hakibbutz Hameuhad and Sifriat Poalim.

Bristol, Evelyn. 1980. "Idealism and Decadence in Russian Symbolist Poetry." *Slavic Review* 39: 269-80.

―――. 1985. "Decadence"; "Symbolism". In *Handbook of Russian Literature*, ed. Victor Terras, 94; 460-64. New Haven, Conn.: Yale Univ. Press.

Dolgopolov, L. 1976. *"Enskaya literatura kontsa, XIX nachala xx veka kak etap v literaturnom razvitii"* [Russian Literature at the Turn of the Century as a Stage of Literary Development]. *Russkaya Literatura* T. 1: 93-109.

Donchin, Georgette. 1958. *The Influence of French Symbolism on Russian Poetry.* The Hague: Mouton.

Dijkstra, Bram. 1986. *Idols of Perversity: Fantasies of Feminine Evil in Fin de Siècle Culture.* London and New York: Oxford Univ. Press, 1986.

Fichman, Yakov. 1946. *Shirat Bialik* [Bialik's Poetry]. Jerusalem: Mossad Bialik.

―――. 1951. *Beit hayotser* [The Workshop]. Tel Aviv: Hakibbutz Hameuhad.

Frishman, David. 1895. *Mikhtavim ᶜal devar hasifrut* [Letters on Literature]. Warsaw: Achiasaf.

Glazer-Rosenthal, Bernice, ed. 1986. *Nietzsche in Russia.* Princeton, N.J.: Princeton Univ. Press, 1986.

Gordon, D. *"Darkhei harefuʾah"* [The Ways of Medicine]. *Hamagid.* 12(9): 11.

Kartun-Blum, Ruth, ed. 1969. *Hashirah haᶜivrit bitkufat Ḥibbat Tsion* [Hebrew Poetry in the Hibbat Zion Period]. Jerusalem: Mossad Bialik.

Klauzner, Yosef. 1898. *"Shirei ahavah"* [Love Poems]. *Haʾeshkol* 1: 54-71.

―――. 1902. *"Sifrutenu"* [Our Literature]. *Hashiloaḥ* 10: 423-52.

Kopp, Robert. 1988. *"Nietzsche, Baudelaire, Wagner - a propos d'une définition de la decadence."* *Travaux de la littérature Boulogne* 1: 203-16.

Lachover, Fishel. 1950. *Bialik—ḥayav vitsirato* [Bialik—His Life and Work]. Jerusalem: Mossad Bialik.

Lebenson, Micha Yosef Hacohen (Michal). 1869. *Shirei Bat-Tsion* [Songs of the Daughter of Zion]. Vilna: Reuven Rom.

Lillienblum, Moshe Leyb. 1872. *"Mikhtav el hamol"* [Letter to the Publisher]. *Hamelits* 12(9): 65-66.

―――. 1898. *"Divrei zemer"* [Songs]. *Luah Aḥiʾasaf* 5: 19-20.

Macmillan, Carol. 1982. *Women, Reason and Nature.* Princeton, N.J.: Princeton Univ. Press, 1982.

Maksimova, V.A. 1972. *Russkaya literatura kontsa XIX nachala XX veka* [Russian Literature at the Turn of the Century]. Moscow, T. 11.

Mintz, Aryeh Leyb. 1888. *"Mishirei Heine"* [From the Poems of Heine]. *Knesset Israel* 3: 392-96.

Miron, Dan. 1958. *"Toldot hataltal"* [The History of the Curl]. *Massa (Lamerhav)*, 1 March.

———. 1979. *Bein hazon le'emet* [From Romance to the Novel]. Jerusalem: Mossad Bialik.

———. 1986. *Haperida min ha'ani he'ani* [Taking Leave of the Impoverished Self]. Tel Aviv: Ha'universitah hapetuhah.

———. 1987. *Bo'ah Laylah* [Come, Night]. Tel Aviv: Dvir.

Miron, Dan et al., eds. 1983. *Hayim Nahman Bialik—shirim 1890-1898* [Hayyim Nahman Bialik—Poems, 1890-1898]. Tel Aviv: Dvir and the Katz Institute, Tel Aviv Univ.

Peretz, Yehuda Leybush. 1894. *Ha'ugav* [The Organ]. Warsaw: Halter & Eizeshtat.

Perry, Menachem. 1977. *Hamivneh hasemanti shel shirei Bialik* [The Semantic Structure of Bialik's Poems]. Tel Aviv: Tel Aviv Univ.

Pogglioli, Renato. 1960. *Poets of Russia*. Cambridge, Mass.: Harvard Univ. Press.

Sadan, Dov. 1951. *"Ba'afeilat hasetirah"* [In the Darkness of Paradox] (1933); *"Le'or hameziga"* [In the Light of Mélange] (1951); *"Hameshulash"* [The Triangle] (1951). *Avnei bohan* [Touchstones]. Tel Aviv: Mahberot lesifrut.

Schopenhauer, Arthur. 1972. *Parerga and Paralipomene*. 2 vols. Oxford: Clarendon Press.

Shamir, Ziva. 1987. *Hashirah me'ayin timatseh—ars poetica bitsirato shel Bialik* [Where is Poetry? Bialik's *ars poetica*]. Tel Aviv: Papyrus.

Shulman, Eliezer. 1875. *"Mimekor Yisrael—toldot Heinrich Heine veLudvig Berne"* [From the Jewish Tradition: Heinrich Heine and Ludwig Berne]. *Hashahar* 7,2: 1-8.

Shva, Shlomo. 1990. *Hozeh lekh berah—sipur hayav shel Hayim Nahman Bialik* [Seer, Go!]. Tel Aviv: Dvir.

Zemah, Eddy. 1976. *Halavi hamistater* [The Lion in Hiding]. 3rd ed. Jerusalem: Kiryat Sefer.

Tzili: Female Adolescence and the Holocaust in the Fiction of Ahron Appelfeld

∽ NAOMI B. SOKOLOFF ∽

"Each time I have a period—and that has only been three times—I have the feeling that in spite of all the pain, unpleas-antness and nastiness, I have a sweet secret, and that is why, although it is nothing but a nuisance to me in a way, I always long for the time that I shall feel that secret within me again."—Anne Frank, age 14 1/2

"How good it was to lie curled up, with a blanket over her head, to feel the pulsing of her body and to listen to its sweet murmurings. She longed to tell Maria this sweet secret. . . ."— "Kitty," by Ahron Appelfeld

"Without parents, wandering in strange fields. . .we felt the secret of our Jewishness. It was a sweet secret. . . .We knew, because of that secret, we were fair game for every axe and rifle, but without it our existence would have been even less."—"Holocaust Writing: Personal Reflections," by Ahron Appelfeld

The fiction of Ahron Appelfeld is known equally for its obsessive concern with the Holocaust and for its indirectness in referring to the Holocaust. Time and again, his narratives recount incidents that take place before the war or after. The novella *Tzili*, however, records events of the Shoah period itself. This fiction follows the misadventures and suffering of a young girl who, at age 12, finds herself abandoned by her family when they flee the Gestapo. She manages to live through the war by wandering for several years, hiding in the forest, taking refuge here and there with peasants, partisans, or other Jews on the run. Of all

Appelfeld's fiction, *Tzili* most closely approaches Appelfeld's own history of uprooted childhood and wartime wanderings.[1] It is striking that precisely here the author has chosen to focus not on a male protagonist, but on a female one.

What are the implications of this choice?

To ask the question is to broach several issues of interest to recent feminist debate. First, feminist criticism has accorded new visibility to portrayals of female adolescence in imaginative writing. Previously, studies of the *Bildungsroman*, or the novel of youth, most often concentrated on texts populated by male protagonists, and so took the experience of the boy as a general human norm. New studies, in contrast, have drawn attention to patterns of development common to young girls and female characters. They have noted psychoanalytic factors as well as social mores and expectations which frequently endow coming of age and sexual maturation with distinct implications for the two sexes. A second area of thematic issues which has lately come under scrutiny is that of women in the Holocaust. While much discussion has emphasized the mass dehumanization wrought by the Shoah, feminist studies have tried to discern what was distinct about women's circumstances under the persecutions of the Nazi regime. Such inquiry has attempted to identify differences between men and women regarding strategies of survival, resistance, and, for those who escaped death, emotional adjustment in the aftermath of the trauma.[2] Literary interpretation along these lines has asked how belletristic texts have portrayed women's lives in relation to the Nazi era.

These questions clearly call for a rereading of *Tzili,* as concerns with female adolescence and the Holocaust converge in that novella.[3] The point of departure for my own discussion of this text is a conviction that Appelfeld's decision to feature a girl character, marking this fiction with sexual difference, makes a significant difference in various ways. The focus on Tzili constitutes an act of authorial distancing from fictional character which serves, among other things, as a kind of defense; it is aimed at offsetting the uncharacteristic proximity to autobiography and helps the novel to avoid sentimentality.[4] In addition, the text gains advantages in terms of plot possibilities, and, most important, it creates a resonant set of symbols.

To assess these matters it is useful to look at the novella's treatment of a topic that has been a prime preoccupation of feminist criticism: the silencing and sounding of female voice.[5] It has often been argued that literary traditions dominated by men have suppressed women's voices and disregarded women's perspectives. Female figures have appeared mostly through the filter of male perceptions, particularly as those characters lack their own self-expression and as little attention is paid to their inner lives. At an extreme, this disregard fosters a tendency (among readers and writers) to view woman as blank—intellectually and spiritually empty. Tzili, a dullwitted, semi-mute protagonist, has elicited rancor for just such reasons. She has been seen as yet another instance of the mindlessness often imputed to women characters in texts by men.[6] It is imperative to point out, though, that while her lack of language is central to the text, so is her struggle to achieve voice. It is this latter phenomenon, I will argue, which is integrally linked with her female identity and also, specifically, with her adolescence.

This current paper proposes to reexamine Tzili's blankness by considering her silence in relation to her interiority or lack of it, her capacity for external expression, and the extent to which these both relate to her strength of will and her powerlessness. Such matters tie in with her passage from girlhood to womanhood, since Tzili is a youngster who for the first time deals with menstruation, intercourse, and pregnancy. As her sexual maturation brings her to an awareness of inner regions of her self, she enters into dialogue with her memories and attains a new sense of attachment to others. Her physical developments foster in her also a new degree of volition and outspoken self-assurance. Continuing tensions between speech and silence, as they emerge in this process, prove indispensable to an understanding of the novella, for they contribute to one of the fundamental aspects of Appelfeld's art; throughout his oeuvre the author's treatment of the Holocaust revolves about the difficulties entailed in speaking of trauma, and Tzili's tentative, painful relation to language puts into relief Appelfeld's struggle with the sayable and the unsayable.

As Tzili animates many of Appelfeld's artistic principles and recalls many of the ideas he has voiced elsewhere on the fate of the Jews in the Shoah, this novella invites discussion in terms of one of the basic, knotty problems of feminist criticism: to what extent is the particularity of woman's experience recognized as a valid literary topic? In Western literature, writing which deals with women has been dismissed commonly as overly narrow or thematically trivial. (Both the themes of such writing and the reactions to them have reflected the fact that women often have been left out of public activity and restricted to domestic life.) Appelfeld's narrative poses this question: Is Tzili's a story of female predicaments, or is she used, as many female figures have been in Hebrew writing, as a symbol of collective issues? Does her being a woman make her distinct, or is she an emblem for the plight of the Jews in general?

Tzili begins as a nearly dumb figure, virtually without language. Devoid of inwardness, she is more an absence than a presence, and initially she is referred to as something not quite human, a *"yitsor shaket,"* or mute creature (6). She is acted upon by others, defined through their perceptions more than through her own, and so she is predictably vulnerable to victimization. Dangers come to her, moreover, especially because she is female. As she wanders through the countryside she seeks shelter from a prostitute who schemes to sell her body; in the fields an old man tries to rape her; later she finds herself in the home of a peasant couple where the husband lusts for her while the wife, ever watchful, blames Tzili for this domestic misfortune. Tzili's situation changes with the development of her own sexuality, particularly as she meets up with a man named Mark. He has escaped from a camp and devises a makeshift home for them in a bunker. Here she experiences her first sexual intimacy, she becomes pregnant, he disappears, and in the course of these events she reaches a new interiority. Gaining emotional depth, she achieves a previously unattained facility with language, acquires a richer consciousness, and engages for the first time in extended thought and conversation with others.

The turning of the narrative focus to life within coincides with Tzili's physical development, itself a process of increasing inwardness. The narrator underscores this growth inside and grants it positive value when he remarks on the transformation of her pubertal body: "her femininity blossomed within her, blind and sweet" (96; *"nashiyutah parhah bah bimtikut zarah,"* 46). This description recalls descriptions of Kitty, the pubescent protagonist from Appelfeld's story of that same name. Kitty lies in bed listening to the stirrings and rustlings of her growing body, thrilling to "the sweet secret" (235, *"hasod hamatok,"* 51) within: Emphasis on inwardness again converges with sweetness when Mark takes advantage of Tzili's flowering. His penetration of her yields a turning in of her awareness and initiates a relatively joyous time in her life. In this text, as in others by Appelfeld, hiding becomes a world unto itself, with its own peculiar comforts and emotional rewards.[7]

It is when Mark leaves that Tzili gains a depth which is also verbal. First she imagines that he speaks to her: "Mark's voice came to her and she heard, 'A man is not an insect. Death isn't as terrible as it seems'"

(106). This familiar remark gives her new confidence, and she begins to perceive her lost companion as an almost palpable presence: "He would surprise her at every turn, especially his voice. It seemed to her that he was hovering nearby, unchanged but thinner and unable to emerge from his hiding place" (114). This internalization of the other, the coming of memory, is allied with the physical bond they once shared. Indeed, the narrative makes the connection between body and spirit more explicit by stating, "it did not take long for her to understand: Mark was inside her." Several paragraphs later it is spelled out that this situation has a literal dimension. Tzili is pregnant; Mark's seed has entered her. Subsequently, her sense of communion grows, and she begins to converse with him freely, "simply, as if chattering to a companion while she worked" (116). Finally she also makes more extended comments and thus, as her belly expands, so does her eloquence. Altogether, the protagonist's blankness has been fundamentally altered, in two senses. First, as her mental and physical emptiness has begun to fill, imbecility is replaced by a richer, more substantial inner life. Second, responding to this growth of mind, the text invests more detail in representation of her consciousness and self-expression.

It is possible to trace the evolution of Tzili's experiences through textual changes in the representation of her voice. Her words serve as a particularly useful gauge of her innerness and its transformations, and so this character neatly illustrates the feminist theoretical model that links capacity as a speaking agent with inwardness and recognition of inwardness. In many texts, what characters say may be at odds with the workings of their inner thoughts or subconscious, thus complicating the concepts of voice and self. Other characters may have a rich mental life but remain outwardly silent. Tzili's speech, though, is a direct index of her emptiness or fullness.

Early on, Tzili makes herself known through a series of truncated conversations. She does not initiate talk; she merely responds to inquiries—often with a single word, usually uncomprehending. As such she is an avatar of the myth of Echo and Narcissus. This archetype has received new attention and privileged status in feminist criticism, because it provides an occasion to protest the quelling of female voices.[8] At issue is the woman who offers but an ethereal reaction to the words of others and who therefore is often victim to their self-centered disregard of her needs. Tzili fits this pattern at the opening stages of the narrative, for she takes her cue from others and yields to their demands, offering

statements which consist largely of repetition. Take, for instance, the
following exchange with Mark:

"למה לא תלכי לכפר להביא לנו משהו לאכול.
אין לנו מה לאכול. את המעט שהיה כבר חיסלנו".
"אלך", אמרה.
"ולא תשכחי לשוב", הטיל ספק בכוונתה.
"לא אשכח", אמרה צילי ופניה כוסו סומק.
מיד תיקן ואמר: את יכולה לקנות מה שאת רוצה. אין זה
חשוב, רק משהו למלא את הבטן. הייתי הולך ברצון אבל
אותי יזהו. חבל שאין לי בגדים אחרים. את מבינה".
"אני מבינה", אמרה צילי בהכנעה (35).

"Why don't you go down to the village and bring us
something to eat? We have nothing to eat. The little we had is
gone."

"All right, I'll go," she said.

"And you won't forget to come back."

"I won't forget," she said, blushing.

Immediately he corrected himself and said: "You can buy
whatever you want, it doesn't matter, as long as it's something
to fill our bellies. I'd go myself and willingly, but I'd be found
out. It's a pity I haven't got any other clothes. You
understand."

"I understand," said Tzili submissively (68).

Tzili's speechlessness undergoes significant change when, from the
slight and demeaned status of the echo, she becomes a kind of echo
chamber: a vessel or space in which the voice of absent others remain
and take on greater resonance. When those close to her become even
more shadowy than she, whose name means "my shadow," their unsub-
stantial but haunting selves come floating to the surface. Her semicapac-
ity to address them and so grant them recognition makes those others felt
as spectral but keenly dynamic forces. Mark's phrases—in particular,
"man is not an insect, death is not so terrible"—become an oft-repeated
refrain that, in her mouth, signify a gain in self-respect and forcefulness.
Tzili never achieves a highly individual or original voice, and this, to be
sure, is a limitation (to be a vessel, to contain and sustain the accomplishments of others, is hardly a flattering position in feminist reckoning). All the same, for Tzili this advance is a genuine step forward from
the vacuity of her beginnings. She then makes a further move toward
dignity and self-respect by learning to speak up for herself. When some

peasants beat her, she says, "No you won't. I'm not an animal, I'm a woman" (116). Finally she engages in monologues which, though brief (ten lines, at most) do express her perspectives. In one speech she beseeches the absent Mark to return to their mountain home; in another she thanks Maria the prostitute for having sheltered her and so for helping to save her life. At this point Tzili is surprised by the abundance of words that come from her mouth: "All the years of the war she had not thought. Now the thoughts came floating to the surface of her mind" (131).

Sadly, Tzili's newly expressive discourse does not triumph. As the war ends and the refugees emerge from the camps and bunkers, the voices she has carried within her begin to fade. After the catastrophe all comment seems misguided and inadequate. Accordingly, one of Tzili's traveling companions declares a "cease words" (182). This woman, a cabaret singer named Linda, insists that now is a time for silence. In this context the insights Tzili has gathered during the war also come to seem at best tentative and elusive. Reinforcing the impression of culminating defeat, her child—like her message of newfound strength—is stillborn. Significantly, too, Tzili does not have the last word, nor even the narrator's attention at the conclusion of the novella. Instead, the final lines turn to Linda, as she sings old Hungarian lullabies. This ending stalls any forward progression in Tzili's quest for voice. In a reversion to a previous state of affairs, the main character is left to the side, exhausted and silent once again. Figured here as a kind of baby, sung to by an inadequate, partly pathetic and partly grotesque, substitute mother, Tzili fades away into helplessness. In other words, she remains submerged in her continuing need for a childhood never fully lived and now unrecoverable. Adolescence has enacted for Tzili only an illusory or incomplete passage to maturity, leaving her an almost wordless creature. She is but a chimera hovering between speech and silence.

A number of stylistic indicators signal those changes in Tzili's voice which, in the latter part of the text, suggest her discouragement and contribute, too, to a collective failure of speech and words. In the aftermath of the war there no longer appear any relatively sustained declarations such as she once directed to Mark and Maria. Instead, conversations of the old sort resume. Again she meets a string of characters and their encounters are conveyed via short questions or curt dramas of silence which suggest little mutual understanding. Here, though, brevity indicates not so much simple emptiness as a sense of loss, a void where something used to be. Take the following scene where she comes across three men in a bunker:

עיניהם הדלוקות בצבצו מתוך הסמרטוטים ערות
ועליזות משהו.
"מי את".
"שמי צילי".
"אם כן משלנו את, היכן השארת את כולם".
"אני", אמרה צילי, "איבדתי את כולם".
"אם כך בואי אלינו. מה יש לך בתרמיל".
"בגדים".
"ולחם אין לך". קולו נשמע לא נעים.
"מי אתם", שאלה.
"אינך רואה, אנחנו פרטיזנים. אין לך לחם בתרמיל".
"אין לי", אמרה וביקשה ללכת.
"לאן את הולכת".
"אני הולכת אל מארק".
"אנחנו מכירים את האיזור היטב, אין כאן איש. מוטב
שתשבי עמנו.
אנחנו נשעשע אותך".
"אני", אמרה צילי, בידרה את מעילה המרופט, "אשה
בהריון" (55).

Their bloodshot eyes peeped through their rags, alert and somehow gleeful.

"Who are you?"

"My name is Tzili."

"So you are one of us. Where have you left everyone?"

"I," said Tzili, "have lost everyone."

"In that case why don't you come with us? What have you got in that haversack?"

"Clothes."

"And haven't you got any bread?" one of them said in an unpleasant voice.

"Who are you?" she asked.

"Can't you see. We're partisans. Haven't you got any bread in that haversack?"

"No, I haven't," she said and turned to go.

"Where are you going?"

"I'm going to Mark."

"We know the whole area. There's no one here. You'd better stay with us. We'll keep you amused."

"I," said Tzili opening her coat, "am a pregnant woman" (119-120).

Much is going on under the surface: delicate negotiations of trust and hostility, tempered by memories of similar encounters in the past, lead to an oscillation between the self-effacement of the one-word answer and new self-assertion. Nonetheless, the richness of interaction is camouflaged in large part because there are few authorial explanations about what the represented speech acts accomplish. That is, the sentences require the reader to infer a good deal in order to divine the illocutionary force of the statements made. It is as if the reader must supply the correct verb tag, such as: complained, argued, pleaded, admitted, opined, reprimanded, congratulated, promised, thanked, and so on. Such markers are minimized here and so the text renders the characters' comments more difficult to understand. It is as if these events were reported across a great cultural divide.

In the example given, for instance, Tzili's statement that she is pregnant may be a defiant protest, a serene assertion of her dignity, or else just stupid reiteration of self-evident fact. True intents remain muffled. Interpretation depends on assumptions about speech acts, and these must be based on shared expectations about human behavior, that is, on ordinary codes of knowledge about how the world works. This element is precisely what remains strikingly absent from Appelfeld texts. A lot must be known about the circumstances in which the words take place in order to appreciate Tzili's conversation, but the author evades filling in such background. Indeed, Appelfeld shies away from representing the Holocaust in documentary detail, maintaining that the period and its events are unexplainable to those who were not there, incomprehensible even for those who were.

This writing, therefore, recalls the experience Appelfeld's audiences have on listening to the author lecture. As much is conveyed by facial expression, intonations, silences, and glances at the crowd as by words. For the reader who has heard this writer in person or who is familiar with his fiction as a whole, the texts themselves come alive with potential;[9] for others the *sotto voce* effect may have less force. Seymour Chatman, writing of formalistically similar exchange in Hemingway's prose, notes that that author's dialogues are pregnant with meaning (1979, 161-66; 176-77). The phrase would apply aptly to a description of Tzili, for her pregnancy is so closely allied with her verbal skills. Her experience of fullness and then stillborn emptiness is presented as part of her developing interiority and her attempts at exterior expression. Her child, which is her burden but also her only hope, is an extension of her struggle to achieve discourse. Consequently, her words, on the surface banal, are perhaps full of meaningful emotion and perhaps not. That Tzili's taciturnity is not simply idiosyncratic but part of a general phe-nomenon is evident in the speech of the men in this passage. It is hard to ascertain to what degree the men are welcoming, threatening, or solici-tous of Tzili's welfare. It is clear that the meeting is in part unpleasant, but, then, is the "*ʿalizut*" of the partisans vicious? Is their glee a some-what more benign matter of sardonic amusement? Perhaps it is the kind of genuine festivity, the oddly macabre merriment amidst catastrophe that has marked other writing by Appelfeld (e.g., his novella *Badenheim 1939,* and his essays depicting the carnivalesque life of refugees on the beaches of Italy at the war's end).

It should be noted that the elusive quality of this prose stems too from the peculiarities of Hebrew as an artistic medium. A language adopted by the author during his own adolescence, it is not part of the milieu depicted in the narrated events. For this reason it serves as a vehicle to a world in which it was never spoken. Lacking in colloquialism and speci-ficity, Appelfeld's prose has been described as an intractable medium of return to the past.[10] It aims for a kind of universalism and yields a verbal limbo, a creative region proper only to the memory and the imagination. In *Tzili* the writer's language has already become much more natural than it was in earlier works, yet it is still devoid of the mimetic particu-larity that would convey the characters' speech as part of an identifiable, familiar social context.[11]

Altogether, Tzili's vacillations between speech and speechlessness link her with major generating tensions that define Appelfeld's fiction. In his essays Appelfeld has remarked that a contradictory impulse toward articulation and silence constitutes the very soul of the survivor (1979).[12] This individual, he writes, feels a pressing need to attain distance from the horror of the Shoah, but this same individual is also motivated by a desire to bear witness. Tzili's is a partial silence which becomes a natural form of expression in this context. She speaks in oddly appropriate half-measures about a catastrophe too great to be spoken of more directly, and so her relation to language enhances Appelfeld's aesthetic. Her ini-tial incomprehension, as a filter of events, helps deflect attention away from atrocity. Bringing dramatic justification to Appelfeld's well-known indirectness in referring to the Holocaust, her limited understandings also bring to the fore a sense of incomprehensibility and unexpectedness in the catastrophe.[13] Later, her reversion to half-silences buttresses the author's well-known penchant for understatement. Tzili's hushed voice, together with the author's idiosyncratically minimalizing descriptions, produces ambiguities fundamental to an art which aims at once to reveal and conceal.

Tzili's feeblemindedness and lack of education also enhance Appelfeld's art as they add to plot possibilities. Though serving as a prototype of mute victimhood, Tzili can increase her chances for survival through her silence. Because she departs from the stereotype of the clever Jew, this character can pass more easily as a Gentile. All told, she dramatizes especially well the precariousness of a life spent in hiding and wandering. She is at one and the same time more helpless, and more likely to protect her safety.

It should be noted that her being female works in tandem with these aspects of her silence. As a young woman Tzili is more vulnerable, because she is more susceptible to sexual attack (in accounts given of the Shoah, women survivors typically mention abuse and degradations of a sexual nature). At the same time, as a woman, Tzili is less readily identifiable as a Jew. During the war males could pass less easily as Aryans, because circumcision often gave them away. That women were not so readily suspected of being resistance leaders also made escape through disguise more of a viable option for them than for men. In these regards Appelfeld's novella reinforces ideas stated elsewhere about women during the Nazi era, and in these respects the text relies on parallels between women's powerlessness (or relative power) and silence (or stunted speech).

In the middle portions of the narrative, however, when Tzili becomes a speaking subject, her language is not just parallel to but also directly associated with her femaleness. Here her patterns of development suggest a message of inspiration that is not so much part of Appelfeld's stylistics as part of his motivation and his vision as an artist. Appelfeld has written that, throughout his wartime wanderings as a child, knowledge of his Jewish identity brought him a necessarily hidden, stifled, but prevailing sense of strength. His consciousness of Jewishness within allowed for a sustained sense of self, and this sense of self eventually gave rise to the author's artistic expression, much as Tzili's femininity fosters for her an inner voice that leads to proud self-assertion. Appelfeld has left explicit hints of this parallel. In a comment that implies a connection between Tzili's or Kitty's predicaments and his own, he has referred to his Jewishness as a "sweet secret" cherished during his childhood travails.[14] Being female, like being a Jew, means being susceptible to external, social persecution, but it also allows for an internal or spiritual strength.

Female adolescent growth offers a cogent metaphor for this inward-ness as, in general, a girl experiencing changes in her body must deal more acutely than do boys with that which is internal and hidden. Until menarche the uterus is an unseen, unfelt organ; by the same token, the awakening of sexual urge and sensation is often more gradual and tenta-tive for girls than for boys, more a discovery of something previously hidden, because for the girl it is less dependent on a localized, visible, physical impulse. Tzili's story comments directly on adolescence as an unfolding awareness of inner realms. In her case this emphasis on inner-ness is intensified by initiation into intercourse and pregnancy. And then, given the confinement of her life in the bunker, her bodily experi-ence is peculiarly apt as both an emblem of her situation and a way to cope with it. Seeking shelter in intimacy and taking refuge in an inner, secret world, she finds inspiration and fortitude within herself.

Aspects of this characterization prove troubling for a feminist reading of this novella. Any facile association between femininity and inward-ness recalls vexed questions of biological determinism, and this text sup-poses a narrow equivalence between physical, sexual development and Tizli's developing voice. To be sure, the writer's treatment of his protag-onist's sexuality does not belittle women in common ways that have been vociferously assailed by feminist critiques; any number of studies have chided men writers for viewing pregnancy as a mindless, uncon-trolled act of body.[15] By contrast, *Tzili* is a refreshing change that emphasizes the spiritual and mental growth that accompany, and may spring from, a woman's pregnancy. (A similar movement marks Appelfeld's more recent novella, *Katarina*, published in 1989; there, too, memory, insight, courage, and outspokenness develop along with a pregnancy.) Still, to impute to females a special spirituality because of their physical ability to bear children is as misguided as attributing to women a lack, emptiness, or passivity because of their anatomical struc-ture. Both options ignore the many factors—the complexities of social circumstance, of cognitive processes, and of attitudes each woman takes toward her own body—which may affect relations between female physical experience and its emotional or intellectual consequences.[16]

There is no doubt that Appelfeld's text restricts itself to a schematic construct of female experience. Tzili is more idea than person, and the representations of her consciousness are too slight to sustain in-depth psychological analysis. Instead of portraying a particular female individ-ual during the Holocaust, the novella brings together a singular crystal-lization of abstract notions, and into them it breathes dramatic life. Tzili in this way becomes an effective device for encapsulating many of the author's primary thematic concerns with speech and silence, self and disguise, humiliation and self-respect. This is not to say that the fiction makes of Tzili's abortive motherhood an occasion for masculine self-aggrandizement; male writers have often used images of parturition and brainchildren to speak of their own creativity, even while referring to pregnancy in women as mere procreation.[17] Such is not the case here. Tzili serves as an embodiment of Appelfeld's poetics of loss, but in the process the writer builds on predicaments particular to women and sensitively acknowledges gender and difference in the female experience of the Holocaust.

A comparison with that most famous female adolescent of Holocaust literature, Anne Frank, confirms the power of this symbolism, while also making for instructive contrasts with Appelfeld's fiction. Anne, the diarist, commands a highly articulate voice and speaks directly of her dilemmas as a woman and a Jew. She, therefore, is much more approachable as a psychological or sociological case study than is her fictional counterpart. Tzili's feeble voice is sounded in the most stifled of tones, and her intentionality is quite deliberately subdued in a text written by a man. Yet the diary puts into relief basic patterns of experience shared with Tzili. With its greater psychological depth, Anne's text may indicate why the fictional construct of womanhood in the novella harnesses so much symbolic energy. This contrast also makes clear the understatement of Appelfeld's writing that lends its symbolism a teasing, equivocal effect.

In hiding, Anne—like Tzili—discovers her sexuality. Katherine Dalsimer's reading of the diary traces this process as one of increasing emphasis on metaphors of inner and outer realms (1986, 44-76). That development begins with menstruation, an experience which brings Anne to think about the "wonderful" things that are happening to her ("not only what can be seen on my body, but all that is taking place inside") and which she refers to with the same phrase that took on such resonance for Appelfeld: it is a "sweet secret," that is, an unspoken, highly private source of joy, pride, and longing (January 5, 1944). Dalsimer, a clinical psychologist, notes that menarche is "one of a series of critical experiences that successively articulate for the female the *subjective reality* of her inner sexual and reproductive organs" (57). Menarche, indeed, serves as a pivotal moment for Anne. It is following the onset of menses that the young girl comes to speak of other types of inwardness. Referring, for instance, to incipient sexual stirrings and her feelings toward Peter Van Daan, her companion in the secret annex, Anne remarks that "it is spring within me" (February 12, 1944). Similarly, she comments that a glance from Peter kindles for her "a lovely feeling inside" (February 14, 1944). And, once alert to intimate sensation, she also becomes more introverted. She speaks of herself as two Annes—one a carefree, impudent individual recognized outwardly by others, the second a sensitive individual unknown to the outside world: caring, complex, frightened, and capable of deep loves and loyalties. She moves, too, from adherence to external authority toward attentiveness to an inner voice. As she disengages from her parents' guidance she begins to formulate her own opinions and convictions, declaring finally, "I am a woman of inward strength" (April 9, 1944). All these are experiences that lead her to confide in her diary, i.e., to articulate in her own mind her cognizance of her developments.

Now, the connection between these various modes of innerness—physical, psychic, expressive—is not entirely clear. Certainly, as Dalsimer points out, puberty can bring about clarified body image and important changes in a girl's self-representation or self-esteem. In addition, part of what is going on here is the second individuation process of adolescence, which psychoanalytic consensus has spoken of as "internalization." One of the psychic imperatives of adolescence is a loosening of primary bonds with parents. Ideally, this process should result in the young person's arrival at a new subjective sense of self—that is, an internal inviolability of personhood, accompanied by increased independence.[18] Other factors as well help account for the ins and outs of Anne's diary. This text invites consideration of "the voyage in," a notion promoted by feminist literary criticism.[19] It has been observed that, in many novels featuring adolescent female protagonists, the main romantic freedom—like liberty to achieve success—is in fantasy life. As a result of the girl's powerless status or restrictive rules placed on her, such fiction generally focuses more on the inner life of the young character than on outer adventure, more on her psychological adjustments or her insights into her circumstances than on external accomplishment. Anne conforms to this model to some extent. As a female, certainly, she is aware that it is her role to put brakes on the relationship with Peter. She is the one expected to set limits and demur from too much intimate contact, and so she directs considerable energy to mulling over her feelings rather than acting on them. Surely, too, and more important, her imprisonment and fear of even worse entrapment make it natural to think in terms of inside and outside. The idea of the voyage in, devised to describe narratives of female powerlessness, applies with special severity to Anne's text, which is a response to the powerlessness of being a Jew in Nazi Europe.

It remains indeterminate, then, to what degree Anne's introversion is a specifically female phenomenon. What remains certain is that the diary as a literary text creates enormously moving images of growing up female as inward discovery. As she documents the stages of turning in on her own authority, away from parents, Anne combines the imagery of physical inner revelation with the imagery of confinement and finds inspiration within herself. New interiority gained in this way then leads her to a sense of mission, determination, and capacity for externalized expression. Though the diary begins as a private text, it is writing which can become public, and Anne becomes increasingly attuned to that possibility. She comments on the possibility that her diary might be published, and, as the new critical edition makes clear, she edited it with an eye toward publication.[20] This evolution parallels Tzili's, as it moves from interiority to vocal self-assertion. Anne, however, fleshes out the process with much greater detail. Along the way, consequently, she brings to the fore a host of questions about female development. She spurs the reader to wonder about the relation between introversion and gender; the ways in which psychoanalytic factors and anatomical givens may affect female self-conception (particularly, a sense of inside and outside); the effect of confinement or social restriction on self-image; the impact on a young girl when she is faced with discrepancies between society's recognition (or lack of recognition) of her inner life and her own appreciation of it.

Such issues impinge also on *Tzili*, but are easy to underestimate there due to the novella's schematic characterization. Tzili, through her under-representation in psychological terms, is a reductive or oversimplified fiction of womanhood, yet this same fiction gains resonance as it recalls questions that justify an association between femininity and inwardness. To the extent that it is evocative of issues crucial to female adolescence, the novella makes for a compact, dramatic set of symbols. To the extent that it evades those issues it is elusive, thinner than the diary. It should be kept in mind, though, that this elusiveness is not necessarily a liability, a shortcoming to be measured against the successes of Anne's diary. (The diary, after all, is a different genre altogether, with its own aims and motivations.) On the contrary, this elusiveness is consonant with other aspects of Appelfeld's artistry in the novella. Much as Tzili's words bewilder (her speech is perhaps pregnant with meaning, and perhaps empty and sterile), so the narrative employs a puzzling symbolism that hints at fullness but borders on hollow simplification. Once again, the result is ambivalence that suggests abortive expressive possibility. Once again, Tzili—as a diminished artifice of woman's voice—makes for a rich and compelling projection of Appelfeld's artistic concerns.

As part of Appelfeld's treatment of female experience, it is significantly not menstruation that the author labels a sweet secret. Instead, Tzili's rising sensuality is the focus of that sentiment. Menarche itself is met by the girl with alarm as a sign of death and disease. Referring to menses as a "fresh wound" (26), this account recalls the old dark views promoted by Freudian vocabulary, which associated menstrual blood with castration, fears of punishment, and a girl's presumed feelings of deficiency at not being male. In addition, this imagery calls up folk views of female puberty as something demonic.[21] Tzili has painful sensations and fears that "something alien had taken possession of her body" (26).

This assessment of puberty is far from Anne Frank's joyous acceptance of her physical development. She presents being a woman as a condition of the most positive worth and as a sign of growth and vitality despite the desolation of war. A diabolical interpretation of female adolescence, typical of old-fashioned ignorance, seems doubly objectionable compared with the upbeat outlook of Anne Frank's diary. It should be remembered, though, that this kind of emphasis makes sense dramatically in Appelfeld's novella because of Tzili's own ignorance and deprivations. No one has instructed her in the facts of life, and none believe that she is capable of any mature understanding. More important, the idea of menstruation as a wound, while discredited by feminist revisions of psychoanalytic theory, is effective within Appelfeld's poetics. Womanhood, in the novella, means a simultaneous vulnerability to evil and a deepening spirituality which evolves out of helplessness. In this context it is consistent to present female puberty as part of an originating disaster that finally allows for enriched psychic life. Tzili's moment of entrance into womanhood serves as a kind of equivalent to catastrophe, an experience analogous to, and coextensive in time with, Tzili's loss of her family to the Gestapo.[22] Both these disasters are cast as an unavoidable, accursed fate, but also as a bitterness which is remarkable in its capacity to bear fruit.

This point underscores that Appelfeld's exploration of femininity as powerlessness and resourcefulness is prompted by his interest in collective Jewish powerlessness and resourcefulness. But how extensive is the parallel between femininity and Jewishness, and what valence is finally placed on womanhood as a result? As my reading till now has suggested, any estimation of the text as a positive or negative portrayal of a woman should take into account the versatility of the main character and her multifaceted functions within the text. Tzili is not merely an emblem of Jewish vulnerability and perseverance during a period of catastrophe, nor is she simply a marginal instance of private experience occurring during, but outside of the main events of the Shoah.[23]

Tzili can be understood more profitably by eschewing such polarizations. First, it should be remembered that, because she is a survivor, she is by definition an exception and not the rule. Very few Jews caught in the Holocaust remained alive. In other ways, too, she is neither typical of the Jews nor separable from them. As was mentioned earlier, this girl's stupidity and silence, which challenge the stereotype of Jews, permits her to pass as a non-Jew in a landscape where "cows and speechlessness" (50) predominate. Tzili's dim wits allow her to be overlooked by the Gestapo and abandoned by her family. (At work here, as Gershon Shaked [1985] has noted, is an inverse Darwinism in which the weak survive. Perhaps, too, there is evidence here of survivor guilt; that is, an expression of perplexity that some—in no way especially deserving, meritorious, or representative—people survived, when so many others did not.) Tzili's characterization not only serves Appelfeld's plot, but also furthers an irony he has argued in his essays. If the Jews were really so clever, how is it that in the Europe of the thirties and forties they did not see disaster approaching? Why did they choose to disbelieve signs that the Nazis fully intended to destroy them?

That Tzili is a female raises additional ironies in connection with Jewish identity, and, in particular, with Jewish learning. Readers will remember that Tzili comes from a highly assimilated family that looks on secular education with the reverence once attached to the study of sacred texts. The other children are exhorted to excel in school, and it is only because Tzili cannot handle intellectual challenges that she receives some crumbs of traditional training. Consequently, it falls to the lot of the dull child to keep the spark of Judaism alive. Tzili as feebleminded female is a doubly incongruous candidate for this mission. For many centuries women were forbidden to study the Holy Books, and Hebrew remained closed to their voices. Now, devalued, that knowledge is permitted her and will survive with her, albeit in extremely diminished form .

The irony of her position surfaces in the one passage that directly cites the rudimentary, unvarying formulas her teacher drills into her.

Significantly, this passage flaunts the genderized inflection of Jewish learning:

"מהו האדם".

וצילי היתה משיבה: "עפר ואפר".

"ולפני מי הוא עתיד ליתן דין וחשבון".

"לפני מלך מלכי המלכים הקדוש ברוך הוא" (9).

> "What is man?"
> And Tzili would reply: "Dust and ashes."
> "And before whom is he destined to stand in judgment?"
> "Before the King of Kings, the Holy One blessed be He" (5).

The highly masculinist language of these lessons takes on inverted significance in the mouth of this girl, their traditional impact undermined precisely because these words will soon fulfill themselves. Little do the Jews realize that they are already faced with the fate of "man" and that in a short time Tzili's family will be reduced, literally, to dust and ashes. She, on the other hand, will outlive them and come through the ordeal specifically as a woman and as a symbol of potential rebirth. Implied here is a conviction that the Holocaust challenges the world of faith, even as it refutes the Enlightenment and assimilationist values, which once promised reason and equality for the Jews. The events of the Shoah put into doubt the force of tradition which presents the deity in clearly patriarchal terms and which comes down in this fiction to a weak echo in feminine voice, its last resource.

These remarks indicate that, even in its emblematic use of a female figure, Appelfeld's novella does not rely on a glib homologization equating woman with Jew. More accurately, Tzili is seen as occupying a boundary between two worlds. An outsider even among her own people, she survives as an outsider among Gentiles. Tolerated, but not fully protected by the peasants who give her shelter, Tzili is said to reside on the village borders where lepers, lunatics, prostitutes, and horse thieves congregate. As such she is a signal illustration of the association between madness, threatening sexuality, and femininity which has stubbornly persisted in Western culture.[24] Womanhood is aligned here with repressed values often relegated to the borderline of the social order.

Tzili's marginality has important implications for discussion of her as a positive or negative figure. Torril Moi (1985) advances the claim that women have often been construed as representing the frontier between man and chaos, and so they "share in the disconcerting properties of all frontiers: they will be neither inside nor outside, neither known or unknown."[25] In other words, theirs is a position of ambivalence which has enabled male culture to vilify women or to venerate them as representations of a higher nature. Tzili shares this ambivalence as she stands on the limit between life and death, speech and silence, at a transitional age between girlhood and womanhood. As her experience vacillates between dumbness and self-expression, fresh wound and sweet secret, blankness and rich interiority, she is both admirable and pathetic. In part Appelfeld insists on her defects, as he presses into the service of his artistry the age-old stereotype of woman as enigma, mystery, and blankness. At the same time, the author partially revalorizes these qualities, holding Tzili's lacks in new esteem. As he dwells on her failings and her oppressed conditions, he holds her peculiar blend of ignorance and insight above the supposed wiles of the Jews and above the cruelty of the Nazis.

This revalorizing of lack, negativity, irrationality, and chaos (long associated with the feminine in patriarchal discourse) is much the kind of phenomenon that has gained attention from poststructuralist, European based feminisms,[26] and it makes for a high degree of ambivalence in the novella. Tzili's silences are not without value, not entirely a contemptible sign of weakness. Instead, they represent a partially triumphant weakness, and one with which the author sympathizes. Similarly, even as Tzili's development of voice is celebrated, it remains an equivocal achievement. Neither speech nor silence are of unalloyed, positive worth, for all self-expression and all interpretation in response to the Holocaust are riddled with contradictions. Tzili's adolescence, constructed within that context, itself carries a peculiarly uncertain valence.

NOTES

1. Appelfeld has described his Holocaust childhood and its impact on his art in his essays (1979), and his lectures, such as the ones delivered in 1983.

2. Treatments of female adolescence in literature include Spacks (1972), White (1985), Abel et al. (1983), and Labovitz (1986). For feminist discussions of the Holocaust, see for example Heinemann's *Gender and Destiny* (1986), which bases its findings on memoirs and fiction by women survivors. This study also contains bibliography for this area of inquiry. Notable items include Laska's *Women in the Resistance and in the Holocaust* (1983), and the volume edited by Katz and Ringelheim, *Proceedings of the Conference Women Surviving the Holocaust* (1983).

3. Published in 1983 as *Hakutonet vehapasim*, this work was quickly translated into English as *Tzili: The Story of a Life* by Dalya Bilu (1983). Quotations in English in this essay are taken from the Penguin edition of 1984.

4. I would like to thank Ahron Appelfeld for comments to this effect made in personal conversation.

5. The suppression of female voice, both as literary theme and as political dynamic in matters of canon formation, has been a primary concern of contemporary feminist theory. For an overview of such issues see, for example, Olsen (1978), Rich (1978), and Yaeger (1988), and Showalter's essays in *The New Feminist Criticism* (1987). "Towards a Feminist Poetics," 125-43 and "Feminist Criticism in the Wilderness," 243-70.

6. Fuchs makes this argument in *Israeli Mythogynies* (1987). The wider claim, that men authors frequently impute emptiness to women characters, is the central thesis of Allen's *The Female Blankness* (1976).

7. Shaked 1985, 33-37.

8. On the myth of Echo and its significance for feminist criticism see Greenberg (1980).

9. A prime example can be found in the Appelfeld lectures videotaped at the University of Washington in 1983.

10. For an articulate statement of the issue, see Ezrahi (1987).

11. Shaked (1985, 34) discusses this stylistic change in *Tzili*. In some instances, it should be noted, Appelfeld makes distinct efforts to indicate foreignness. For example, in conversation with a Gentile peasant, the difference in expression from Tzili's own Yiddish background is conveyed through heightened, literary diction. To inquire about the time of day a man asks, "*heikhan ʿomed hayom?*" (13). A farmer, silencing his wife, says "*hasi, ishah*" (27). Offering Tzili some food, another character asks in stilted language, "*hatokhli?*" (13).

12. Appelfeld (1979). For an effective overview of Appelfeld's poetics see Shaked (1970, 149-67); Mintz (1984, 203-238); Fuchs (1982, 223-27); and Ratok (1989). This last monograph provides an exposition of stylistic features throughout Appelfeld's work that ensure a sense of disconnection, lack of transition, and defective causality. Ratok includes extensive bibliography of the Appelfeld criticism surveyed in her book.

13. Much the same dramatic advantage is gained through focus on a child's limited understanding in *Tor hapelaʾot* [The Age of Wonders]. Miron (1979, 49-59) discusses that text in terms of a heightened persuasiveness and realism; in my study *Imagining the Child in Modern Jewish Fiction* there is extended comment on the function

of the child's consciousness in *The Age of Wonders*, including its contribution to the verisimilitude of that novella.

14. Appelfeld has used the phrase in his lectures ("Holocaust Writings: Personal Reflections", 1983, pass.) Compare with *Masot beguf rishon*, 13; there he writes about the "secret" [*hasod*] of his Jewishness but does not include the adjective "sweet" (1974).

15. Ellman (1971) and Gubar (1983) are two prominent commentators on these matters.

16. Psychoanalysis and literary texts have both been guilty of such oversimplification. Erikson's notion of feminine "inner space" is the most well-known example (1978). Erikson assumes that in adolescence alone a girl has a moratorium from inwardness. He does not explain why, at the age when a girl is developing so much physical inwardness, she should suddenly orient herself to outward adventure.

17. See especially Friedman (1989), with reference to Ellman and Gubar.

18. For a definition of internalization see Blos (1979). However, his discussion of differences between males and females would be challenged by feminists such as Belenky et al (1986), who note that self-direction and inner voice often come later for women than for men. I am indebted to Joseph Glickson and Chanita Goodblatt for their discussions with me on pyschological approaches to gender differences among adolescents.

19. See especially the introduction to *The Voyage In*, eds. Elizabeth Abel et al. (1983).

20. For example, Frank changed the names of her characters to protect the privacy of those around her. She also excised portions of the diary dealing with her life before the war and streamlined the text to focus on events in the secret annex. She wrote several entries about her hopes for publication of the diary.

21. White (17) and Dalsimer (1, 11) both provide helpful bibliography on different views of menstruation in medical and psychological literature.

22. Tzili's literal separation from her parents could prompt comparison with another kind of separation: the withdrawal from parents which is an integral part of normal adolescence and which occasions feelings of loss and mourning. Tzili's loss is very concrete. The coincidence between the onset of adolescence and the onset of Tzili's wartime experience amplifies the emphasis on abandonment in the novella.

23. Reviews of the novella which deem Tzili to be an emblem of the Jewish condition (whether that be labeled suffering, uncertainty, or abnormality) include pieces by Lowin (1984), Teicher (1983), and Leclair (1983). Ben Ezer (1984) and Halperin (1989), respectively, view Tzili as a symbol of moral indifference among survivors and as a symbol of the innocence of wandering Jewish youth during the war. In contrast, another review sees this character's indifference as a function of an inherently flawed personality that has little to do with the Shoah (Bar Yosef, 1983). Aschkenasy arrives at an equivocal assessment of Tzili. Hers is private existence, the argument goes, and she is "persecuted as a sex object, not as a Jew" (239). At the same time Aschkenasy writes, "exploited and brutalized, Tzili epitomizes the totality of the Holocaust experience and, as the persecuted outcast she, in fact, reenacts the entire Jewish history" (239).

24. See Gilman (1985).

25. The final chapter of Moi's *Sexual/Textual Politics* (1985) provides a concise overview of this issue.

26. Again, Moi is most helpful in providing an overview, especially in the chapters on Hélène Cixous and Luce Irigaray.

WORKS CITED

Abel, Elizabeth, Marianne Hirsch, and Elizabeth Langland, eds. 1983. *The Voyage In.* Hanover and London: Univ. Press of New England.

Allen, Mary. 1976. *The Female Blankness: Women in Major American Fiction of the Sixties.* Urbana: Univ. of Illinois Press.

Appelfeld, Aharon. 1963. "Kitty," *Bagai haporeh* [In the Fertile Valley]. Jerusalem and Tel Aviv: Schocken Books.

———. 1971. "Kitty." Trans. Tirtza Zandbank. In *Modern Hebrew Stories.* ed. Ezra Spicehandler, 220-46. New York: Bantam Books.

———. 1978. *Tor hapela'ot.* Merhavia and Tel Aviv: Hakibbutz Hameuhad.

———. 1979. *Masot beguf rishon* [Essays in the First Person]. Jerusalem: World Zionist Organization.

———. 1980. *Badenheim 1939.* Trans. Dalya Bilu. Boston: David R. Godine.

———. 1981. *The Age of Wonders.* Trans. Dalya Bilu. New York: Washington Square Press.

———. 1983a. *Hakutonet vehapasim.* Merhavia: Hakibbutz Hameuhad.

———. 1983b. "Holocaust Writings: Personal Reflections." The Samuel and Althea Stroum Lectures in Jewish Studies. Seattle: Univ. of Washington.

———. 1983c. *Tzili: The Story of a Life.* Trans. Dalya Bilu. New York: E.P. Dutton. Reprinted by Penguin, 1984.

———. 1989. *Katarina.* Jerusalem: Keter.

Aschkenasy, Nehama. 1986. *Eve's Journey: Feminine Images in Hebraic Literary Tradition.* Philadelphia: Univ. Pennsylvania Press.

Bar Yosef, Yizhak. 1983. "*Goral akhzar lelo hadar*" [A Cruel, Inglorious Fate]. *Kol Tel Aviv,* 12 September.

Belenky, Mary Field, Blythe McVicker Clichy, Nancy Rule Goldberg, and Jill Mattuck Tarule. 1986. *Women's Ways of Knowing: The Development of Self, Voice and Mind.* New York: Basic Books.

Ben-Ezer, Ehud. 1984. "*Akhzariyut shel nitsolim*" [The Cruelty of Survivors]. *Ha'arets,* 30 March.

Blos, Peter. 1979. *The Adolescent Passage.* New York: International Univ. Press,.

Chatman, Seymour. 1979. *Story and Discourse.* Ithaca, N.Y.: Cornell Univ. Press.

Dalsimer, Kathryn. 1986. *Female Adolescence: Psychoanalytic Reflections on Literature.* New Haven, Conn.: Yale Univ. Press.

Ellman, Mary. 1971. *Thinking About Women.* London: Virago.

Ezrahi, Sidra. 1987. "Ahron Appelfeld: The Search for a Language." *Studies in Contemporary Jewry*, 366-80.

Erikson, Erik. 1978. *Identity, Youth and Crisis*. New York: W.W. Norton and Co.

Frank, Anne. 1989. *The Diary of Anne Frank: The Critical Edition*. Ed. David Barnouw and Gerrold Van der Stroom. New York: Doubleday.

Friedman, Susan Stanford. 1989. "Creativity and the Childbirth Metaphor: Gender Difference in Literary Discourse." In *Speaking of Gender*. Ed. Elaine Showalter, 73-100. New York and London: Routledge.

Fuchs, Esther. 1982. "*Hahasahah hatematit: tashtit mivnit bekitvei Aharon Appelfeld.*" [Thematic Distraction: Structural Underpinnings in the Writing of Ahron Appelfeld.] *Hebrew Studies* 23: 223-27.

———. 1987. *Israeli Mythogynies: Women in Contemporary Hebrew Fiction*. Albany: SUNY Press.

Gilman, Sander. 1985. *Pathology and Difference: Stereotypes of Sexuality, Race and Madness*. Ithaca, N.Y.: Cornell Univ. Press.

Greenberg, Caren. 1980. "Reading Reading: Echo's Abduction of Language." In *Women and Language in Literature and Society*. ed. Sally McConnell-Ginet, Ruth Borker, and Nelly Furman, 300-309. New York: Praeger.

Gubar, Susan. 1983. "The Birth of the Artist as Heroine: (Re)production, the *Künstlerroman* Tradition and the Fiction of Katherine Mansfield." In *The Representation of Women in Fiction*. ed. Carolyn G. Heilbrun and Margaret R. Higonnet, 19-59. Baltimore: Johns Hopkins Univ. Press.

Halperin, Sarah. 1989. Review of "*Hakutonet vehapasim.*" ʿAl hamishmar 11 March.

Heinemann, Marlene E. 1986. *Gender and Destiny: Women Writers and the Holocaust*. Westport, Conn.: Greenwood Press.

Katz, Esther and Joan Miriam Ringelheim. 1983. *Proceedings of the Conference Women Surviving the Holocaust*. New York: The Institute for Research in History.

Labovitz, Esther. 1986. *The Myth of the Heroine: The Female Bildungsroman in the Twentieth Century*. New York: Peter Lang.

Laska, Vera. 1983. *Women in the Resistance and in the Holocaust: The Voices of Eyewitnesses*. Westport, Conn.: Greenwood Press.

Leclair, Thomas. 1983. *The International Herald Tribune*, Paris ed., 13 April.

Lowin, Joseph. 1984. Book Review in *Hadassah*, April, 24.

Mintz, Alan. 1984. *Hurban: Responses to Catastrophe in Hebrew Literature*. New York: Columbia Univ. Press.

Miron, Dan. 1979. *Pinkas patuah: sihot ʿal hasiporet betashlah*. [Current Israeli Prose-Fiction—Views and Reviews]. Tel Aviv: Sifriat Poalim.

Moi, Toril. 1985. *Sexual/Textual Politics: Feminist Literary Theory*. London and New York: Methuen.

Olsen, Tillie. 1979. *Silences*. New York: Delacorte Press.

Ratok, Lilly. 1989. *Bayit ʿal belimah*. [House on a Precipice] . Tel Aviv: Heker.

Rich, Adrienne. 1979. *On Lies, Secrets and Silence: Selected Prose 1966-1978*. New York: W.W. Norton.

Shaked, Gershon. 1970. *Gal ḥadash basiporet haʿivrit* [A New Wave of Hebrew Fiction]. Merhavia and Tel Aviv: Hakibbutz Hameuhad.

————. 1985. *Gal aḥar gal basiporet haʿivrit* [Wave After Wave of Hebrew Narrative Fiction]. Jerusalem: Keter.

Showalter, Elaine, ed. 1985. *The New Feminist Criticism*. New York: Pantheon Books.

Sokoloff, Naomi. B. 1992. *Imagining the Child in Modern Jewish Fiction*. Baltimore: Johns Hopkins Univ. Press.

Spacks, Patricia Meyer. 1972. *The Female Imagination*. New York: Avon.

Teicher, Morton. 1983. "Little Book Will Haunt Memory Forever." *The Jewish Floridian*, 23 September.

White, Barbara. 1985. *Growing Up Female: Adolescent Girlhood in American Fiction*. Westport, Conn.: Greenwood Press.

Yaeger, Patricia. 1988. *Honey-Mad Women: Emancipatory Strategies in Women's Writing*. New York: Columbia Univ. Press.

Oedipal Narrative and Its Discontents:
A. B. Yehoshua's Molkho (Five Seasons)

∽ ANNE GOLOMB HOFFMAN ∽

A.B. Yehoshua's *Molkho* stimulates and frustrates the reader's expectations of gendered plots of male desire.[1] The book takes its protagonist through five seasons, each a section of the novel, that follow the death of Molkho's wife after a long illness. Each season or section initiates expectations of a plot of male desire in which Molkho fails to fulfill the role of the lover that he has fantasized for himself. Instead, the novel prompts an interrogation of gender categories and the consequences of gender distinctions for narrative. It does so through preoccupation with varieties of femininity, a thematics of the body, and the recurrence of body parts in the text, not to mention the feminization of the protagonist, Molkho. Through the play of the text, polarized definitions of gender—male in opposition to female—begin to become undone.

Molkho—the character and the novel—is aware of expectations for certain kinds of appropriative action, preemptory moves towards women, but "he"—character and text—hesitates. *Molkho* the novel is born out of that hesitation. (I prefer to use *Molkho*, rather than the translation title *Five Seasons*, to preserve the suggestion that protagonist and text are interchangeable, or at least, that they cannot be so easily dissociated from one another.) In his stolid, unheroic manner, Molkho opens himself up to the feminine, observes its varieties, and notes it in himself, resisting all the while masculine prototypes of action. *Molkho* the text is self-consciously organized into sections which go nowhere, which take a tour only to end up back where they started. The momentum of the narrative is impeded, if not undone, by the eruption into it of body

- 195 -

parts and by a regressive ambivalence that thwarts the forward thrust of the plot.[2] This double movement both provokes and frustrates the reader's expectations.

The feminization of the protagonist and dismantling of the plot of male desire can be taken as suggestions of a retreat from subjectivity as it is defined through the Oedipus complex. In evidence is a move back to a diffuse relation to the body associated with the pre-Oedipal mother. Feminist critics have observed that "oedipally organized narrative . . . that is based on the determining role of the father and of patriarchal discourse tells a different story from preoedipal narrative, which locates the source of movement and conflict in the figure of the mother" (Garner et al. 1985, 10). To engage modes of experience that are pre-Oedipal, rather than Oedipal, is not in and of itself a feminist move. Nevertheless, there is considerable subversive potential to a text that evokes and then disrupts the triangles of an Oedipal model that is centered on a norm of masculinity.

The Oedipus complex provides us with the elements of which narratives are made. In its triangular configuration, it defines characters structurally, through their relation to each other, producing a story of desire, aggression, and the threat of punishment. Not only does the Oedipus complex offer a model for the study of narrative, it is itself a narrative paradigm through which subjectivity is produced. In the classical narrative sequence of the positive Oedipus complex for a boy, for example, Oedipal rebellion brings on the threat of castration; the crisis is resolved, and the Oedipus complex "normalized" through the boy's acceptance of "symbolic castration," the cost of entry into the social order.

It is through play with gender that *Molkho* initiates its subversion of received values. Therefore, I propose to read the novel in terms of some significant developments in feminist theory. In recent years, feminists have taken on and taken apart the definition of male and female as paired opposites that are interdependent, yet placed in a hierarchy in which the first term is privileged over the second. Not only male versus female, but the opposition of life to death, active to passive, culture to nature, offer examples of gendered oppositions, in which the elevation of the first term, the male, depends on the denigration of the second, the female.

The American theorist Nancy Chodorow draws on and amplifies psychoanalytic insights, when she helps us understand the denigration of the feminine in terms of an "ideology of masculine superiority" that constitutes a reaction to women's mothering (1989, 1). Masculinity is formed out of a negation of femininity, as a defense against attachment to the pre-Oedipal mother. The importance of that pre-Oedipal mother for our reading of narrative can be found in terms of the relationship to the body as it figures in literary texts, including issues of fusion and differentiation, of relationship to an archaic body, that recur and resurface, despite their repression in culture.

On the French side, Luce Irigaray investigates the repressions that underlie the cultural construction of gender (1985). In order to open up and explore gaps and omissions in the psychoanalytic text, Irigaray engages in a line-by-line reading of Freud's writings on femininity. Her work recovers what was effaced or ruled out in order to provide for a scheme of sexual symmetry in which the woman's "castration" affirms the presence of the male genital.[3]

The impact of these psychoanalytic efforts to deconstruct gendered oppositions extends into areas of cultural activity that may have seemed immune to such issues. Thus, Susan Winnett examines the "gender bias of contemporary narratology," in a recent essay in *PMLA*, exploring the notion that our conception of plot is shaped by a scenario of masculine desire. She turns to Peter Brook's construction of a model of plot out of Freud's theory of the pleasure principle (1990, 506). Brooks uses *Beyond the Pleasure Principle* as a model for plot structure that consists of arousal, discharge, and quiescence. As Winnett demonstrates in her analysis, beginnings, middles, and ends correspond to tumescence and detumescence, the visible scenario of male pleasure. It is this "scenario," in effect, that Yehoshua's novel rejects. That "rejection" makes itself felt in the comedy of its protagonist's amorous exploits, but it can be discerned in more subtle movements in the text as well.

A psychoanalytically informed feminism seeks to understand the implication of both men and women in the systems that shape consciousness, in order to elucidate the "unconscious underpinnings of patriarchal culture" (Juliet Mitchell, quoted in Garner et al., 1985, 15-16). So too, if we reflect on our engagement in Yehoshua's *Molkho*, it becomes evident that the very texture of the narrative betrays a discomfort with gendered roles and the assumptions they produce. Literary conventions of character and action reflect the social reproduction of gender. Men and women are *both* caught in the systems of patriarchal culture, the fiction reminds us. The medium of the novel provides a space within which to construct and deconstruct, reflect on and criticize, some of the stereotypical formulations that shape the social world.

Indeed, texts both literary and theoretical offer us ways of reading that are alert to the rough edges and loose threads, through which seemingly dominant structures come undone. I turn to Freud for an exemplary moment in which an assumption of gender comes apart when it is subjected to closer scrutiny in the writing itself. In *Three Essays on a Theory of Sexuality*, Freud observes that the libido is masculine, but he interrupts that assertion with a footnote that proceeds to take apart the opposition between masculine and feminine on which the theory rests. Telling us that "the concepts of 'masculine' and 'feminine,' whose meaning seems so unambiguous to ordinary people, are among the most confused that occur in science," Freud goes on to cite three major uses. The first, which he terms "essential," uses "masculine" and "feminine" to denote "activity and passivity." Next he defines the biological use as indicating "the presence of spermatozoa or ova respectively," a distinction that begins to blur as he notes that greater "muscular development" or "aggressiveness" is not necessarily "linked with biological masculinity." Once he arrives at the third or sociological sense, he concludes, startlingly, that "pure masculinity or femininity is not to be found either in a psychological or a biological sense. Every individual on the contrary displays a mixture of the character-traits belonging to his own and to the opposite sex; and he shows a combination of activity and passivity whether or not these last character-traits tally with his biological ones" (1905: vol. 7: 219). What do we have here? Caught in his own culture, Freud uses available terms, acknowledges his discomforts with them and, in his own annotations, subjects them to interrogation. Freud's footnotes form the locus for his discomfort and the place for an examination which moves towards deconstructing the oppositions that the theory itself continues to utilize. The footnotes are at the margins of the text, constituting a liminal space where the text turns back on itself.

Indeterminacies of the sort that surface in Freud's footnote form part of the narrative substance of Yehoshua's *Molkho*. In effect, the fiction offers the opportunity to explore possibilities that the Freudian text raises. In this respect, Yehoshua joins company with those feminist readers who use Freud's marginalized questions as the starting point for a critique of Freud, one that extends Freud's own reflections on some of the problematic concepts he continues to use. Yehoshua's 1987 novel is a post-Freudian text that plays with redoing gendered subjectivity as we know it in culture—particularly in Israeli culture where the burdens of action are never-abating and are gendered masculine.

Indeed, Yehoshua's novel occupies an intriguing position within modern Hebrew fiction. That literature abounds in male-authored texts that focus on ideological conflicts, demands for action in the public domain, and the dilemmas of sons in relation to paternal inheritances. While Yehoshua's novel acknowledges that agenda of masculine concerns, it also signals its ambivalence, marking out a movement away from the sphere of public action to more private concerns and a concomitant preoccupation with the body.

Insofar as the development of modern Hebrew fiction is closely intertwined with the history of Zionism and the establishment of the State of Israel, this fiction both reflects and challenges national ideologies, exploring tensions between individual and collective identity. The result has been that modern Hebrew literature is marked by an emphasis on collective concerns, a frame of reference that makes itself felt regardless of the degree to which a narrative focuses on the individual.[4]

Significantly, the intergenerational struggles which are a pronounced feature of modern Hebrew fiction lend themselves to interpretation in terms of Oedipal structures. Although the drama of Oedipus unfolds within the family, we must remember that the family is the agency through which the individual achieves entry into the larger social world. Indeed, we can see that part of the power of the novel as a literary form involves its position at the intersection between the individual or the family and culture. Kaja Silverman suggests that family "must be understood as a set of symbolic relations which always transcend the actual persons defined by them"; "mother" and "father" signify cultural positions (1983, 182). That awareness of the role of the family in cultural mediation may be heightened for contemporary Israeli writers. For one thing, the time span of their personal histories is not so very different from the history of the emergence of the nation. So it is not surprising that, for example, the biblical story of the binding of Isaac has been appropriated by a number of modern writers, who put its father-son theme to divergent semantic uses. Recurrences of the ʿakedah as a motif in modern Hebrew literature reflect variations on an Oedipal paradigm, in which emphasis tends to fall on the irrationality of the son's sacrifice.[5] Read into modern Hebrew literature, the ʿakedah story expresses the rage of the sons at the imposition of paternal demands on their lives.

Yehoshua makes a unique contribution to Israeli fiction insofar as his novels move toward closer attention to the individual psyche, while retaining their resonance on the level of the collective. Placing *Molkho* in the context of Yehoshua's fiction, we can remind ourselves of the move from the early, rather allegorical short stories to fictions which attach themselves with greater specificity to everyday life while retaining their mythic suggestiveness. Thus, while the early fiction suggested a Kafkaesque stripping away of particularizing detail, Yehoshua has moved more toward the construction of individualized characters and settings, while retaining suggestive links between individual dilemmas and collective issues. This convergence in Yehoshua's fiction produces a heightened awareness of the interaction between psychodynamics on the level of specific individuals and on the level of the collective. The novel *Molkho* is set at the time of Israel's withdrawal from Lebanon, a collective reversal of direction that receives only incidental notice in the novel. Nevertheless, the reformulation (or reversal) of character and plot that marks this novel resonates with implication in terms of that national crisis of direction. The reader's sympathetic response to the novel may be first engaged by the texture of mundane and bodily experience, but that microcosmic focus never loses its reference to the scale of the political-social macrocosm.

* * *

Molkho narrates a failure of plot, or perhaps more accurately, a regression, through which the preconditions of plot become visible. The text works out a relation to femininity that is not confined to character. We do see a distinct series of females through the five sections—the legal adviser, the Indian girl, and then the two child/women: Ya'ara and the "little Russian." In addition, Molkho has both a mother and a mother-in-law, as well as a daughter. But we have also the dead wife, whose body, at times fragmented and at times inflated, recurs through the text. And we have also to reckon with the woman in Molkho. This array of female signifiers points less to *a woman*, ideal or not, than it does to an archaic relationship to the body, reminiscent of the autoerotic nature of infantile sexuality and the early relationship to the mother. In reading *Molkho*, we find traces in the text of a relationship to the body that exceeds and disrupts neat oppositions between male and female, life and death.

Molkho likewise explores and undoes some of the constraints in the social construction of masculinity. Masculine plots function as narcissistic armor, cultural supports for the denial of castration, and for the power of the phallus. Irigaray (1985) demonstrates the constraints of a phallic economy in which definitions of male and female are produced and reproduced. This economy is "speculative": it uses gender as the basis for a system of value and exchange; it is also "specular," insofar as it assumes the visible presence of the penis in the male and its visible

absence in the female.[6] She puts together the neologism "specularization" to describe this locking of the woman into a constraining system of
value-laden oppositions.[7] *Molkho* engages less in a revision of the position of woman as the object of the male gaze, than it does in a deconstruction of the gaze or the subjectivity of the masculine protagonist
through whom the narrative is focalized.

At the start of the novel, the eerie figure of the early morning bicycle
rider, whose appearance punctuates the wife's death, inaugurates the
play with gender that marks this text. Molkho sees the bicycle rider first
as male, then female, then male (17-18; *11*), and associates the figure with
death, as if it carries "remnants" (*sheyarim*) of his wife (25-26; *21*). (Late in
the novel, when he remembers the bicycle rider, he prefers to think of it
as female [270; *291*]). In its suggestive recurrences, the bicycle rider
constitutes a liminal figure, signaling entry into a magical space where
binary oppositions between life and death, male and female are undone.
These binarisms are culturally constructed oppositions that shape
perception; their confusion in the figure of the bicycle rider draws the
reader's attention to the beginnings of a process of decomposition in the
novel.

"The ego is first and foremost a bodily ego, . . .the projection of a
surface," Freud tells us (1923, vol. 19: 26). A rudimentary sense of self
develops along the outline of the body as interface. In place of a narrative
that takes for granted its characters' size, shape, and gender, Yehoshua's
novel gives us a gentle comedy of their undoing. To take one example,
on the road late on a rainy night, Molkho decides to pick up only a *female*
hitchhiker to set his new amorous agenda into play. In fact, he picks up
not one, but *four* female soldiers. Nevertheless, as he drives, the four
female soldiers appear to form one giant body with four heads: "and he
felt as if he were transporting one gigantic woman, a female pudding,
sleeping, shallowly breathing, and her four-crowned head kept banging
against the windows, opening and shutting pairs of eyes and awakening
at the entrance to Haifa, separating into four thin stems that disappeared
beneath the yellow lights of the damp street" (63; *66*).[8] In the steamy
enclosure of the car, Molkho's expectations of flirtation are displaced by
a more primitive form of experience, as bodies merge to form an engulf-
ing physical presence. Yehoshua's style in this novel conveys this diffuse
sense of merger: clauses, separated yet linked by commas, which insert
pauses into the syntactic flow, creating a rhythmic, lulling effect.

Later in the novel, we find a related decomposition and recomposition
of body parts, as Molkho walks on the beach and imagines assembling a

collage of body parts—here a leg, there a head of hair, a portion of a shoulder or a smile—in order (Pygmalion-like) to assemble a woman whom he might try to love (185; *206*). As if to put the reader through a comparable set of exercises in fragmenting and reassembling bodies, this short sequence ends with a series of reflections on the brutal heat of summer (*"hakayits shel hakayits,"* Halkin's "supersummer"): as Molkho looks at the weather forecaster's diagrams of a high-pressure front, he sees in their place a one-celled creature, a body without shape or smell, the last remnant of his wife, inflated to a cosmic scale (187; *207*). While the novel never quite loses its sense of place, this decomposition and recomposition of the body suggests an alternate geography that recalls an infantile mapping of space on the maternal body.

Another scene dismantling accepted perceptions of the body comes when Molkho sits next to the legal adviser at the opera. Sneaking a look at the outline of his companion's breasts, Molkho worries that his breath is not fresh enough. In the middle of this anxious anticipation of sexual activity, Molkho is reminded suddenly of the aftermath of one of his wife's surgeries, when she commented on the confusion of orifices created by the multiple tubes leading into and out of her body, to the extent that she could no longer tell *in* from *out* (93; *101-102*); and he recalls his own empathic efforts to feel her experience. The image of the body is suggestive; it brings to mind the effect of reading the provocative essays of Georges Bataille (1985), whose writing reverses the humanistic significance of an upright stance and promotes instead a perception of the human being as a tube with holes at both ends.

Molkho's relationship to his own body undergoes changes that suggest gender confusion and a regressive return to infantile sexuality. Throughout the novel Molkho "reads" the signs of a relation to a primitive body as they disrupt the more "active," explicitly "masculine" interactions that are thrust upon him. For instance, his oscillating responses to expectations of amorous activity are marked in his ongoing dialogue with his penis. As he frets over its responses and failures to respond, the narrative reflects his absorption in bodily functions and bathroom activities (see, for examples, 16, *10*; 90-91, *98-99*). He feels like a "fat little boy," as he stands bare-bottomed after urination, looking out the bathroom window of his mother's apartment (138-139; *152*). Examining his penis as he urinates in the bushes on a trip to the Galilee, he perceives it as a "dark little animal" (145; *159*). Tenderly aiming his penis at a toilet bowl in Yodfat, he barely refrains from talking to it (237, *259-260*). The disruption of Molkho's masculinity reaches its most pronounced expression late in the novel as he sits naked in an armchair in a Vienna hotel room, gazing at himself in the mirror. Not only has he gained weight, but he notices breasts sprouting on himself: *"ke'ein shadayim tsamḥu lo 'al ḥazehu"* (282; *301*).⁹

In an Oedipal comedy in which size plays a crucial role, Molkho joins the legal adviser in a Berlin beer hall, where she is surrounded by jovial men. Seated on a low stool, Molkho finds himself a full head shorter than those around him and the apparent butt of jokes he cannot understand. He points to a plate of blood-red sausages and orders one, only to find himself served a sausage that is grotesquely huge. The shifts in size of body and sausage bring a Kafkaesque comedy of adult authority and infantile sexuality to the beer hall scene (123-125; *135-137*).

This mingling of oral and erotic continues into the next section. In an impulse that the Hebrew text identifies as *"kedam minit"* (I would translate "pregenital"), Molkho imagines devouring the buttocks of the young Indian girl who is his guide in the rural settlement of Zeru'ah. The pregenital hunger for the body—a cannibalistic oral drive—finds magical gratification shortly afterward in the village café, where Molkho asks for the special of the day and finds it is a stew made of organs—*"eivarim penimiyim"*—kidneys, lungs, and liver. Molkho shakes with desire— *"ro'ed biteshukah"* (not "hunger," as in the English)—when the steamy bowl of dark, rubbery chunks of meat, each different in consistency, is placed before him (154; *170*).

In the same section, we find the visual image of Molkho gazing at the child-size toilets at the school in Zeru'ah. The scene suggests a further displacement of plot to early levels of instinctual play. Molkho is pleased at the sight of the child-size toilets and tries one out for size without lowering his pants, following which he thinks of the "cannibal stew" that he ate with such relish (170; *188*). The adult becomes confused with the child in the size fluctuation that Molkho experiences, and the mingling of oral-incorporative drives suggests a comedy of regression.

This juxtaposition of infantile gratification of smell and taste with genital sexuality can be seen also when Molkho goes to the movies in Zeru'ah. Anticipating a pornographic film, he sniffs at dirt from the floor that smells of chicken dung flavored with poultry feed and begins to feel hungry, as he watches the screen actors make love and is startled at the experience of an erection (172; *190*).

This erection is especially surprising, because it is the first he has had in a long time. After his wife's death Molkho boldly declares, "Now I am free," evoking the social role of the male as aggressive hunter. And yet, the reader comes upon repeated statements of the problem of desire for Molkho. He has the freedom (*ḥerut*), but lacks the desire (*teshukah*), so that repeated statements of the problem—"how to awaken his desire" (*keitsad leʿorer et teshukato*) (48, 49)—remind the reader of the absence of desire just when it is to be expected.[10] Molkho's failure is all the more striking because, we are told, he has been chaste for seven years. While that magical number, seven, suggests a Sleeping Beauty-like awakening to genital sexuality, the novel turns away from the romantic and sexually polarized plots of Western culture in which male is active, female passive.

In this process Yehoshua notes the imperatives of a stereotypically masculine subjectivity and then marks their reversal. The phrase "to awaken his desire" denotes the plot of male desire in response to woman as the visible object of the male gaze. However, it is not conventional images of femininity that awaken Molkho's desire. He feels "revulsion at perfect, pinkish bodies" in pornographic magazines (48; *48*), or at the brightly lit image of a woman in a bus-stop ad (134; *147*), while he thrills with excitement at the prospect of contiguity to death and the body, in situations that appear to repeat his relation to his wife in illness. Remembering that "scarred body" in the big hospital bed (13; *5*), itself a lost center that cannot be restored, Molkho is drawn back into an archaic relation to the body to which our formation in culture deprives us of access. When he falls ill, shortly after his wife's death, he lies in bed, experiencing a lingering sweetness, smiling to himself as he thinks, "Now I'm dying" (*ʿakhshav ani hagoses*), as he places the earphones on his ears, with the thought that he will die a bit and then come back to life. The prone position in bed and the music in the earphones signal a seductive identification with his wife, who now signifies the lost object. In a related experience of attraction to a body whose borders are indeterminate, Molkho is "seized with desire" (*nitkaf teshukah*) to see again the "big, fat" newspaper boy, the figure of the androgyne (25-26; *21*). Alternative modes of relationship replace the "specularization" of woman (Irigaray's term) with touch, contiguity, and an indeterminacy that derives from shared experiences of the body.

The wife's sickroom with its huge bed at the center takes on, from the start, a sense of magical, regressive place.[11] Molkho's effort to fix the exact time of his wife's death, in the novel's opening paragraph, draws the reader into the enveloping atmosphere of the sickroom, with all its appurtenances, so much so that each time Molkho encounters disease, sickness, medication, or death, it is with deep familiarity and even nostalgia. He thrills repeatedly in anticipation of visits to the terminally ill patients (*"hagosesim"*) on the fifth floor of the old age home (179; *198*).

This diffuse attraction to the body extends to the perception of physical space. After his wife's death, Molkho sees the mysterious wadi in back of his house as her place, the place of death (39; *37*), an association that is repeated and amplified in the bones that Molkho later finds at the bottom of the wadi (178; *197*). Similarly, he experiences the legal adviser's hotel room turned sickroom in Berlin as a mysterious "subterranean cave" (*"me'arah 'amukah"*) (115; *126*). Ramras-Rauch notes that when Molkho buys a new car, he chooses a Citroen for what he cites as specifically feminine qualities; while agreeing that Molkho's perception of the car can be taken as an indication of his feminization, I would extend that reading to suggest that the perception of the car as female supplies a graphic image of enclosure within the body.

What emerges from the novel's sequence of sections is the female figure in bed, or the male protagonist's wish, fetus-like, to take her place in bed. As the flip side of a comedy of foiled expectations, the five sections of the novel trace a journey back into the female body, a journey whose movement is signaled at the start and moves more explicitly into the foreground. In the third section, Molkho sinks into the bed of the Indian girl, whispering to his dead wife, "Look at where I've ended up for you" (158; *174*). In the fourth section, Molkho wonders if Ya'ara, who has suffered repeated miscarriages, is penetrable or blocked (210; *232*), as if it is he who wants to get back in. He thinks of Ya'ara's uterus and imagines the last of her dead babies in her slightly bulging belly (214; *236*, and 224; *246*).

In the fifth section, on his second trip to Berlin, Molkho lies in bed next to the "little Russian" in fetal position, thinking that there is something quite animalistic in sleeping together without a common language (311; *328*). When she touches him, however, he feels no longer like a live fetus, but a "dead one in the grip of a fateful womb" (*"ukhevar lo hayah 'ubar-shat elah 'ubar-meit, davuk lerehem hazak vegorali shelahats 'alav mikol 'eiver"*) (313; *330*). Completing the reader's sense that Molkho has been tracking a lost female object, he follows a girl with whom he identifies his dead wife as a child down an East Berlin street. Molkho talks to himself, in a curious statement that simultaneously denies and affirms the significance of the place at which he has arrived: "After all," he says, "I never lived here, . . . nor did I lie here for long months in order to give birth to dead babies" (331; *345*). Nevertheless, he is unable to tear himself away from the street that he experiences "as if it had been destroyed in his heart and badly rebuilt" (345; *331*).

It is in the last section of the novel, on the East Berlin street that he imagines to have been his wife's, that Molkho enters what the text describes as the cancerous red cell of the old elevator in East Berlin, imaginatively reliving his wife's girlhood. The increasingly explicit imagery of cells, organisms, and enclosures reaches its fullest expression here in references to "the small red cage" ("*kluv ʿets adamdam*") and "the malignant cell" (*[ha]ta hasartani*") of the elevator cab (331-332; *345-346*).[12] This entry into the elevator cab repeats numerous enclosures in the novel, including elevator rides in the housing project where Yaʿara and Uri live, and the sword-decorated elevator cab of the pension. But this last East Berlin elevator cab is additionally encrusted with the imagery of a demonic cancer, the cancer that is here understood as the return to the body with a vengeance.

When Molkho rings the bell of a randomly selected East Berlin apartment to ask about Dr. Starkmann, his wife's father, who killed himself fifty years earlier, we understand the moment to amount to enclosure in a deathly circle (332; *346*). Unfortunately, the English translation omits the following description of Molkho on the doorstep, at the threshold of return: "this was the moment that he would be able to slip back into his home ("*lahamok hazarah leveito*"). The "home" here, Yehoshua's wording suggests, is the original home or *Heim* of which Freud writes in his essay on the uncanny. Interpreting the sensation of the *Unheimlich* or the "uncanny" in terms of its apparent opposite, the *Heimlich* or "familiar," Freud refers to the womb as the original *Heim*, from which we all emerge. (With this psychoanalytic bit of deconstructive play, Freud goes on to note that the feeling of the *Unheimlich* or the uncanny may be evoked by reminders of the original *Heim*, the womb.)[13]

For Molkho, the movement back into an enclosure that he experiences as "his home" remains incomplete. Instead, he leaves rapidly, seeking the underground to ascend, finally, to the Alexanderplatz. Nevertheless, it is curious that, despite Molkho's flight from the chance to slip "back into his home," he is described as returning now to the above-ground Alexanderplatz, "like one who arrives at a familiar and known place" ("*kemi shemagiʿa el makom mukar veyaduʿa*") (332; *346*), a wording that echoes, even more precisely, Freud's description of dreams that signify a return to the mother's body. The reiterated notation of "familiarity" confirms the direction of Molkho's journey back towards an archaic body. At the same time, the narrative resists assignment of that body to a particular address.

These events point beyond psychological realism to the realm of myth and magic. Music plays a suggestive role in this process, as a form of cultural reference.[14] For example, Molkho tries to recreate the moment of his wife's death by playing back the tape and listening to the music that marked the moment of her demise, but the boundaries have blurred. Thinking about his role in relation to her illness, he portrays his Orpheus-like devotion in pulling her back from the underworld, so that, later in the novel, when he hears a surprise performance of *Orfeo ed Euridice*, the reader's sense of a mythic frame for his efforts is confirmed. References to Haydn's *Creation* and Vivaldi's *Four Seasons* (54, 56; 55, 57) point to a cosmic and cyclic frame. Molkho sees himself as if he were in an opera (102-103; 112). He thinks he is going to hear *Don Giovanni* in Berlin, but the program is changed unexpectedly (and quite magically) to *Orfeo ed Euridice* (118; 130). That program change underscores the shift in Molkho's relationship to the legal adviser from a nascent Don Juanism to a deathly attachment to an underworld of the body. Furthermore, at that surprise performance of *Orfeo ed Euridice*, Molkho is stunned to see that Orpheus is played by a woman (120; 131), an operatic switch that antici- pates his own feminization. Playing his own Orpheus in turn, Molkho descends into the body/womb and returns. Musical cues signal a seduc- tion back into pre-Oedipal pleasures of the body, in a direction that opposes or resists the demands for action of Oedipal plot structures.[15]

The novel's mythical dimensions invite interpretation on the level of the collective. As early as his 1981 essay on the *Golah* (Diaspora), Yehoshua makes reference to the unconscious influence of Oedipal dynamics in order to examine conflicts on the level of the collective. Within that Oedipal frame, Yehoshua describes the creation of a monotheistic people in terms of the intervention of God, the father, who appropriates the land, eliminating its maternal associations. As he puts it, paternity is a powerful abstraction that is used to evade the mother who is identified with the land. That appropriation and repression of the maternal body set up the neurotic conflicts of the *Golah* (1980, 27-44). *Molkho* the novel is a narrative exploration of a "return" to the place of the female body and survival of that return, with accompanying modifications and adjustments, ever so slight, in protagonist and text.

That the point of deepest return for the Sephardi protagonist should be his wife's birthplace in East Berlin raises questions about the function of place in narrative geography. Place has significance in a geography of the body, as well as on the map of world politics, and both of these are at work in the shape of Molkho's journey. On the level of political-cultural allegory, Molkho's journey to Berlin brings the Sephardi protagonist to the birthplace of his Yekke wife, using her personal history, as well as the city's divided status to remind the reader of Germany's Nazi past. This play of culturally loaded signifiers evokes the violent contradictions of modern European history, in a manner that is attuned to the ambivalence of Jewish participation in European culture.[16] Through Molkho the character, the novel introduces a new perspective on that cultural complex: it positions its Sephardi protagonist as the naive explorer whose journey highlights those contradictions by contrast to his very innocence of them.

This question of the place of the Sephardi brings a welcome complication to the Israel-Diaspora issue. In effect, the novel works against cultural binarisms, from the male-female split so generally pervasive, to oppositions that reflect modern stereotypes that have structured the history of modern Israel. Similarly, although one can easily make the thematic connection between Yehoshua's fiction and his more polemical essays, it is to the credit of the fiction that it cannot be reduced to the theses of his essays. Yehoshua may set up dichotomies that resonate with political and cultural values, but the elements of the fiction resist simple identification in terms of those values. Despite the novel's use of the political geography of East and West Berlin, not to mention the landscape of Israel to which Molkho returns, the narrative resists generalization to the level of national politics, although it derives some of its power from that collective frame of reference. Thus, Molkho's *Heimweh*, or homesickness, reads more as the culmination of regressive trends on the level of the individual, rather than in terms of a generalization to the collective.

Molkho's feminization can be read as something of a counterpart to Yehoshua's choice of a protagonist who is of Sephardic origin, a reflection of Yehoshua's own cultural heritage to which he had not before devoted major focus.[17] Feminization extends the exploration of otherness that the choice of ethnicity begins. Issues of ethnicity and gender coincide in this novel to produce a text that challenges some Israeli stereotypes, concerning the role of the Ashkenazic population in the development of the State and the dominance of that group in its political structure, along with the more general association of masculine with active and feminine with passive.[18]

* * *

In a provocative work of feminist criticism, Alice Jardine finds in modernist writing indications of a breakdown of the paternal metaphor and a concomitant exploration of that which is different, maternal, and female. She argues that "woman" and "the feminine" "have come to signify those processes that disrupt symbolic structures in the West" and coins the term "gynesis" to suggest "a new kind of writing on the woman's body, a map of new spaces yet to be explored" (1985, 33-34; 42; 53).[19] Jardine points us to an important dimension of signification. Indeed, her study implies a process in the modernist text akin to the psychoanalytic undoing of a repression. It is necessary to note, however, that despite the move to map the body that her work discloses, there is *no body* to be recovered. We have access only to constructions of the body in culture, and those constructions of the body are, inevitably, gendered. In our reading of the text, we are responding to the formative imprint of early, preverbal experiences that are prior to signification but that have an impact on it. Yehoshua's novel heightens our awareness of the inscription in the text (and in ourselves as readers) of strata of experience that precede the gendered configurations of an Oedipally defined subjectivity.[20]

There is a further danger here of going too far and embracing or valorizing the pre-Oedipal, rather than using it as a means towards a critique of Oedipally organized patriarchal culture. The pre-Oedipal, let it be said, is not a goal. "You killed your wife" (*"ve'atah pashut heimatetah otah le'at le'at"*), the legal adviser says to Molkho. Is her comment a reaction to the deathly and regressive pull she feels in his tender care of her injured ankle? If so, she offers an important cue to the reader, insofar as her response suggests a vigorous rejection of the "erotic infantilization of death," a phrase David Gurvits applies to some Israeli novels of the 1980s.[21] If the magical or mythical realm of this novel involves death and the body, then Molkho too moves in and out of it (a peculiarly modern Orpheus), flirting with its dangers and attractions, but never completely succumbing to them. On his way back from his last foray into East Berlin, Molkho enters the "original" Berlin opera house, observes a rehearsal with great interest, but runs from a "musical commissar," afraid he will be accused of stealing musical notes. Is he Orpheus or is he Siegfried, the name by which they call him back (334-335; *348*)?[22] Or is he resisting the burdens of those mythic identifications in his stolid return to the point from which he set out?

The conclusion of the novel returns to language of "active" and "passive," but with a difference. Molkho indicts himself for passivity and repeats the necessity "to love" (*lehit'ahev*)—"*mukhraḥim mamash lehit'ahev*," but his sentence is suspended (346; *358-359*). Syntactically, it has nowhere to go. While he acknowledges a new feeling of "freedom" (*ḥerut*), there is no indication of the direction it will take. The conclusion echoes ironically with the language of gender, but the nouns and verbs, subjects and objects of the gendered plots of amorous activity, have lost their moorings.

In terms of linear narrative outcomes, the novel offers some indications of resolution. Molkho has buried the little Russian's trunk with its four seasons of women's clothing and sanitary napkins labeled with Hebrew lettering. He sits in the room with death and his mother-in-law, but leaves it, apparently shedding the attachment to death and his wife, relinquishing the role of Orpheus by giving up his insistence that his mother-in-law have music to accompany her dying. Yehoshua returns Molkho to his doorstep, back to the threshold, allowing for the five seasons of his experiences, allowing for some alteration, but stopping short of any transformation of his protagonist. Molkho's yearlong journey may follow the morphology of the hero's journey, but the change is there more for the *reader* than for the character.[23]

While the book's five seasons may each offer a new female object to Molkho's male desire, each discloses instead the seemingly regressive journey back into the bed and the body of the woman. Nevertheless, if Molkho is Orpheus, his Eurydice is ultimately nowhere to be found. Nor does Molkho the character dissolve into Eurydice. We may better appreciate this tension between the loss of identity and the retention of identifiable details that hold "character" together, if we turn for a moment to a more radical example of the sort of reversal that Yehoshua's novel plays with. In the novels of Samuel Beckett, the reader witnesses the dissolution not only of character, but of the world of the fiction. Indeed, in contrast to Yehoshua's fiction, the trend of Beckett's fiction is, if anything, antinational. We have only to remind ourselves that one of Beckett's motives in turning from English to French was to deprive himself of familiarity with the nuances and local color with which his native language supplied him. Narrative changes direction in Beckett's trilogy, in a move that can be seen in the opening of the first novel, *Molloy*: "I am in my mother's room. It's I who live there now. . . . Was she already dead when I came? Or did she only die later? I mean enough to bury. . . . In any case I have her room. I sleep in her bed. I piss and shit in her pot. I have taken her place. I must resemble her more and more" (1965, 7). The constitutive elements of narrative dissolve, in an unbearable process that continues through the first two novels to the final one, *The Unnameable*. In that last piece of the trilogy, the voice that speaks to us is no more than a membrane separating inner from outer, a membrane, moreover, whose impermeability is by no means assured.

In reading *Molkho*, we do not meet Beckett's Unnameable. Molkho repossesses himself in the last moment of the narrative, nor has he been all that dispossessed. In fact, the narrative sustains its terms and differentiations, including gender, in part with the help of its mythic references. Those mythic cues may communicate to us some of the larger movements in the text, but they also defend against them with the assertion of form. Fiction gives Yehoshua a medium through which to interrogate constructs of gender and national identity, but the fiction does not dispense with formal distinctions, even as it calls them into question. Nevertheless, as *Molkho* pushes to the limits its decomposition of received values, it makes possible an exploration of the unconscious dichotomies that underlie so much of our thinking.

Molkho plays out a comedy of the diffuse body—the lost, archaic body which seems to surface in bits and pieces, here and there. Not quite the delegitimation of one kind of narrative—the Oedipal, nor yet the affirmation of another—the pre-Oedipal—Yehoshua's novel testifies to an alteration of the text that it cannot quite assimilate. It raises the possibility of finding the feminine within the process of signification, while avoiding the trap of essentializing the woman. It alters a specular narrative economy in which woman is the object of the male gaze, by admitting to the text signs of a relation to the body that transgress, exceed, and call into question gendered dichotomies. Nevertheless, far from envisioning a space free of such dichotomies, *Molkho* retains its links to an identifiable social world in which masculine and feminine continue to name a hierarchized set of oppositions. In effect, the novel both reflects and challenges cultural assumptions concerning gender and body. A symptomatic text, *Molkho* allows us as readers to read ourselves in culture.

NOTES

1. A.B. Yehoshua (1987); translated by Hillel Halkin (1989), as *Five Seasons* . For quotations, page reference is made first to the Hebrew, then, in italics, to the translation. In some instances, translations have been modified. I would like to thank Yael Feldman and the editors of this volume for helpful comments on an earlier version of this essay.

2. Contrast Yehoshua's success in *Molkho* with Oz's efforts in *Lada^cat isha* (*To Know a Woman;* 1989), a novel that fails to move past or even jostle gender categories, despite narrative support for its male protagonist's effort to alter his John le Carré-type spy life and to espouse domesticity after the death of the wife.

3. See Hélène Cixous and Catherine Clément (1986) for a collection of essays that examine gendered oppositions and their deconstruction.

4. Alan Mintz (1989) offers literary historical insight into this tension in his study of the brief period in the development of Hebrew literature during which the form of fictional autobiography offered writers the literary shape within which to probe individual experience. Even in the form of fictional autobiography, as Mintz demonstrates, the exploration of individual experience served to express the dilemma of a generation of young men.

5. Stanley Nash (1986) traces variations of the ^cakedah and considers its uses as a vehicle for expressing some of the tensions between "fathers" and "sons" in Hebrew literature of the last forty years. See also the discussion of uses of the ^cakedah story in modern Hebrew literature in David Jacobson (1987). Yael Feldman (1989) offers valuable insights into the literary use of the ^cakedah to express conflicts between individual and collective.

6. In *The Newly Born Woman*, Cixous and Clément also find in Freud a specular or voyeuristic sexual economy in which genital exteriority forms the primary criterion of value.

7. Irigaray (1985, 103) enables woman to speak in a multiplicity that exceeds the binarism through which culture defines her: "The multiplicity of woman's erogenous zones, the plural nature of her sex, is a differentiating factor that is too rarely considered in the male/female polarity, especially as far as its implications for 'signifying' practices are concerned." I suggest that a comparable subversion of gender categories is at least potential in *Molkho* through the play of body parts in the text.

8. This is one instance in which Halkin's translation falls short of the effect of the grotesque simplicity of the original: *"vehu ḥash shehu movil ishah aḥat ^canakit, ^cisah nikevit redumah noshemet ḥalushot, veroshah ba^cal arba^cat hakodkodim neḥbat beḥalonot hamekhonit"*; Halkin reaches instead for verbal cuteness in his reference to a "tetracephalous female pudding."

9. We can keep in mind here Freud's formulations as to the inherent bisexuality of the human being, as well as Chodorow's analysis of the boy's formation of masculine identity out of the negation of an identification with the pre-Oedipal mother.

10. To take another example, Molkho anticipates a situation that will call for intimacy with the legal adviser, but feels no desire at all (85; *93*). (The English misses the repetition, translating the phrase as "he didn't feel at all sexy.")

11. Gila Ramras-Rauch (1987) points out that during the wife's illness, Molkho slept in a narrow bed, next to or almost under his wife's hospital bed. She finds irony in its designation as an officer's field cot, since Molkho is so passive: his relation to his wife is more that of a nurse than a commanding officer.

12. Halkin works up the metaphor a bit, when he refers to a small room in the West Berlin pension as the "original cell" from which the hotel had grown (336). The Hebrew has simply "*haheder harishon hakadmon*" (321).

13. "It often happens that neurotic men declare that they feel there is something uncanny about the female genital organs. This *unheimlich* place, however, is the entrance to the former *Heim* [home] of all human beings, to the place where each one of us lived once upon a time and in the beginning. There is a joking saying that 'Love is home-sickness'; and whenever a man dreams of a place or a country and says to himself, while he is still dreaming: 'this place is familiar to me, I've been here before,' we may interpret the place as being his mother's genitals or her body. In this case too, then, the *Unheimlich* is what was once *heimisch*, familiar; the prefix *'un'* ['un-'] is the token of repression" (1919, vol. 17: 245).

14. As a nonverbal medium, music is well suited for this function. Julia Kristeva (1986, 93-95) argues that the musical aspects of language, such as rhythm, convey traces of prelinguistic aspects of experience. Kristeva offers insight into the manifestations of the pre-Oedipal in language when she differentiates the semiotic (equivalent to the Lacanian imaginary) from the symbolic order and posits a semiotic *chora*: "the *chora* precedes and underlies figuration, and is analogous only to vocal or kinetic rhythm" (94); "Drives involve pre-Oedipal semiotic functions and energy discharges that connect and orient the body to the mother" (95).

15. Similarly, Molkho's involvement with the heap of boxes of the expensive painkiller, Talwin, takes on a fairy-tale air, as the medicines become talismans, signifying an involvement with his wife's illness that he is loath to relinquish. He takes pleasure in arranging and gazing at the stack of boxes (29; 25), so much so that when he is able to sell them, he immediately misses their presence (64; 67). And then, of course, we have his magical experience in the Berlin drugstore: in the dead of night, those hard-to-obtain boxes of Talwin appear, over the counter, only to have vanished the next day in true fairy-tale fashion. Their magical appearance, like a treasure in a cave, marks the repetition that is involved in the positioning of the legal adviser as invalid in a recreation of the dead wife's sickroom.

16. S.Y. Agnon's *Shira* (1978; Eng. trans. 1989) is noteworthy here, for its exploration of the cultural contradictions that inform the relationship of German Jews to German culture. (See the chapter on *Shira* and German-Jewish culture in my 1991 book on Agnon.)

17. In an interview with Avraham Balaban, Yehoshua acknowledges the impact of his father's death, in 1982, in determining his own artistic turn to a more personal past (*Hado'ar*, 14 December 1990, 90). Nevertheless, he also makes note, in an interview with Yakov Besser, of the ultimate absurdity of the demand that a writer represent his ethnicity (Besser, 1990, 28).

18. It remains to Yehoshua's latest novel, *Mar Mani*, to explore more fully the Sephardi "alternative" and to bring the historical frame into greater prominence. With its indirect and fragmented account of the members of the Mani family over the generations, *Mar Mani* gives even more play to the encounter of the Eastern with the European. See, for example, the prominent references to Greece as the "womb" of

civilization in the monologue of the young German officer that forms the second section of the novel, set in Crete during the Second World War. Yehoshua describes the interweaving of the two novels, *Molkho* and *Mar Mani*, in terms of his own writing: he began working on *Mar Mani*, left it to write *Molkho*, and then returned to complete *Mar Mani*. Describing the "softening" effect of *Molkho* on *Mar Mani*, he goes on nevertheless to differentiate between the two novels by pointing to the political obsessions that characterize the members of the Mani family (Besser 1990).

19. She points out, furthermore, that "Gynesis . . . is either static or dynamic, depending upon the narrative in which it is embedded" (69). As a standard of evaluation, she is more interested in writers who affirm and internalize loss of the "master narratives" and use gynesis as a means of exploring alternatives; she is less interested in writers who use gynesis as part of a nostalgic move to retrieve past modes of signification.

20. Irigaray analyzes *The Republic* and, in particular, the image of the cave as a representation of the "original matrix/womb which these men cannot represent" (244). Her reading of Plato uses the female body to subvert the order of representation, suggesting that it is that which cannot be represented, that which defeats the order of representation.

21. Gurvits (1990, 5) applies the phrase to Yakov Shabtai's fiction in the context of a critical survey of Israeli literature of the 1980s.

22. Jardine notes that Orpheus has proved an attractive mythical figure for modern philosophy. She offers the example of Lyotard's use of Orpheus to set up an opposition betwen "face" (masculine) and "figure" (feminine).

23. As an alternative to this linear reading, the novel's structure can be looked at as a set of enclosures. Esther Yiftah-El (1987) points out the frame-within-a-frame structure of the novel. In the outermost frame we have the death of the wife that begins the novel, and at the end, the death of the mother-in-law that closes it. That frame encloses an inner frame, consisting of Molkho's two trips from Haifa to Berlin, each time with a different woman and a renewed set of romantic expectations. This double frame encloses the two sections in the center of the novel, "Spring" and "Summer," each involving a different female and a different location: spring and the Indian girl at Zeruʿah, summer and Yaʿara in Jerusalem and Yodfat. The double-frame structure points the reader's direction inward, to the center of the text. There at dead center, in those two middle sections, we find Molkho immobilized in the situation of desire. In each of these sections, as Yiftah-El observes, Molkho is particularly passive and is overshadowed by another male presence, the charlatan Yaʾir ben Yaʾish and the *luftmensch* Uri Adler; each of their names signifies, ironically, "light." Yedidyah Yitshaki also comments on the circular structure of the novel in the context of a comparison to Kafka (1989, 26).

WORKS CITED

Agnon, S.Y. 1978. *Shira*. Jerusalem and Tel-Aviv; Schocken Books.

_____. 1989. *Shira*. Trans. Zeva Shapiro. New York: Schocken Books.

Balaban, Avraham. 1990. *"Hakivun hanegdi"* [The Opposite Direction]. *Hadoʾar* 14 December, 14-19.

Bataille, Georges. 1985. *Visions of Excess: Selected Writings 1927-1939*. Ed. Allan Stoekl. Trans. Allan Stoekl, with Carl Lovitt, Donald Leslie Jr. Minneapolis: Univ. of Minnesota Press.

Beckett, Samuel. 1965. *Three Novels: Molloy, Malone Dies, The Unnameable*. New York: Grove.

Besser, Yakov. 1990. *"'Mani'—mah ani bavikuah hagadol?"* ['Mani'—Who Am I in the Big Debate?]. *ʿIton 77*, 14 (May-June), nos. 124-25.

Brooks, Peter. 1984. *Reading for the Plot: Design and Intention in Narrative*. New York: A.A. Knopf.

Chodorow, Nancy J. 1989. *Feminism and Psychoanalytic Theory*. New Haven, Conn.: Yale Univ. Press.

Cixous, Hélène and Catherine Clément. 1986. *The Newly Born Woman*. Trans. Betsy Wing. Minneapolis: Univ. of Minnesota Press.

Feldman, Yael. 1989. "Back to Vienna: Zionism on the Literary Couch." In *Vision Confronts Reality: Historical Perspectives on the Contemporary Jewish Agenda*. eds. Ruth Kozodoy, David Sidorsky, Kalman Sultanic, 310-335. New York: Herzl Press; Cranbury, N.J.: Associated Univ. Press.

Freud, Sigmund. 1974. *The Standard Edition of the Complete Psychological Works*. Trans. and ed. James Strachey, with A. Freud, A. Strachey, and A. Tyson. 24 vols. London: Hogarth.

_____. 1905. Vol. 7, "Three Essays on a Theory of Sexuality."

_____. 1919. Vol. 17, "The Uncanny."

_____. 1920. Vol. 18, "Beyond the Pleasure Principle."

_____. 1923. Vol. 19, "The Ego and the Id."

Garner, Shirley Nelson, Claire Kahane and Madelon Sprengnether, eds. 1985. *The (M)other Tongue: Essays in Feminist Psychoanalytic Interpretation*. Ithaca, N.Y.: Cornell Univ. Press.

Gurvits, David. 1990. *"Tsematim basiporet haYisraʾelit baʿasor shehalaf"* [Crossroads in Israeli Fiction in the Past Decade]. *Moznayim* 64 (Feb.-March): 3-9.

Hoffman, Anne Golomb. 1991. *Between Exile and Return: S.Y. Agnon and the Drama of Writing*. Albany: State Univ. of New York Press.

Irigaray, Luce. 1985. *Speculum of the Other Woman*. Trans. Gillian C. Gill. Ithaca, N.Y.: Cornell Univ. Press.

Jacobson, David C. 1987. *Modern Midrash: The Retelling of Traditional Jewish Narratives by Twentieth Century Hebrew Writers*. Albany: SUNY Press.

Jardine, Alice. 1985. *Gynesis: Configurations of Woman and Modernity*. Ithaca: Cornell Univ. Press.

Kristeva, Julia. 1986. *The Kristeva Reader*. Ed. Toril Moi. New York: Columbia Univ. Press.

Mintz, Alan. 1989. *"Banished from Their Father's Table": Loss of Faith and Hebrew Autobiography*. Bloomington: Indiana Univ. Press.

Nash, Stanley. 1986. "Israeli Fathers and Sons Revisited." *Conservative Judaism* 38, 4: 28-37.

Oz, Amos. 1989. *Lada‘at ishah*. Jerusalem: Keter.

Ramras-Rauch, Gila. 1987. *"Mesirut nefesh o hona’ah ‘atsmit?"* [Devotion or Self-Deception?]. *Hado’ar* 23 (Sept): 42-45.

Silverman, Kaja. 1983. *The Subject of Semiotics*. New York: Oxford Univ. Press.

Winnett, Susan. 1990. "Coming Unstrung: Women, Men, Narrative, and the Principles of Pleasure." *PMLA* 105: 505-18.

Yehoshua, A.B. 1980. *Bizkhut hanormaliyut: ḥamesh masot beshe’elot hatsiyonut*. Tel Aviv: Schocken Books.

_____. 1981. *Between Right and Right*. Trans. Arnold Schwartz. Garden City, N.Y.: Doubleday.

_____. 1982. *Gerushim me’uḥarim*. Tel Aviv: Hakibbutz Hameuhad.

_____. 1984. *Late Divorce*. Trans. Hillel Halkin. New York: Doubleday.

_____. 1987. *Molkho*. Tel Aviv: Hakibbutz Hameuhad.

_____. 1989. *Five Seasons*. Trans. Hillel Halkin. New York: Doubleday.

_____. 1990. *Mar Mani*. Tel Aviv: Hakibbutz Hameuhad/Siman Kri’ah.

Yiftah-El, Esther. 1987. *"Lei’ut veḥerut: hirhurim le’aḥar kri’at Molkho le’A.B. Yehoshua"* [Weariness and Freedom: Some Thoughts on Reading A.B. Yehoshua's *Molkho*] *Bitsaron* 9: 82-85.

Yitshaki, Yedidyah. 1989. *"Misimliyut mufshetet lere’alizm samlani: ḥomrei tashtit bitsirat A.B. Yehoshua"* [From Abstract Symbolism to Symbolic Realism in the Work of A.B. Yehoshua]. *‘Iton 77* (13; 111-112): 24-26.

Feminism and Yiddish Literature: A Personal Approach

∾ CHAVA ROSENFARB ∾

It was a wintry Montreal spring day when I decided to prepare my remarks for this symposium. The weather served as an appropriate backdrop for me to make clear to myself my approach to the subject of feminism—an approach, which in its ambivalence is akin to just such a contradictory day. I am not a card-carrying feminist. But the intellectual luggage which I carry on my literary road is nonetheless colored by my awareness of being a woman. Feminist literary criticism arouses my curiosity and even fascinates me. And yet, feminist thinking has not managed to penetrate to the core of my basic literary interests. I asked myself whether my wavering attitude towards feminism was not rooted in the specificity of my being a Yiddish woman writer. And so I have decided to explore this specificity from a personal point of view.

It appears on the surface that *"vi es kristlt zikh azoi yidisht zikh"*—that there is little difference between Yiddish literature and any other literature. But this is not so. If a people's literature is a mirror in which it finds its own reflection, then modern Yiddish literature is just such a mirror of Jewish life. But just as our history has for the last two thousand years meandered through a path very different from that of any other people, so has our literature also followed a distinctive route. Consequently, the attitude of Jewish male and female writers toward life and toward their craft also differs from that of non-Jewish writers. How then does it differ in my particular case, as a Yiddish woman writer and a survivor of the Holocaust? The first answer that enters my mind is that there have always been so many more important issues to worry about in Jewish history, that the problem of women's liberation and womens rights has always seemed a trivial and irrelevant matter.

I think back to the perished Eastern European Jewish world from which I spring, from which every Yiddish writer springs, and from which he extracts the inspirational nourishment for his Yiddish-speaking muse. It was a world marked by poverty and want and by deep religious spirituality. It was a world often shaken to its foundations by anti-Jewish decrees, by persecutions and pogroms. I would say that in such a world the Jewish people, in their relationship to their God, assumed a feminine role which differed from the one expressed in the symbolic interpretation of the Song of Songs. In the Eastern European context, God was no longer the lover of a free-spirited, vibrant Shulamite, i.e., the people of Israel. Rather, God's people acquired the attributes of femininity by virtue of their passivity and helplessness. Here God was the father of an effeminate son. The Jewish male, so exalted and praised in the scriptures as the son of God's chosen people, suffered terrible blows to his manhood at the hands of his hostile non-Jewish neighbors. Although heroic in his perseverence and determination to protect his existence and his way of life, he was, for the most part, deprived of any effective possibility for doing so. In order to save his soul and often his life, he was forced to surrender, to submit in a way usually associated with women.

Thus the Jewish male assumed the role of master in his home, not merely because he was a male but also because of his need to compensate for his loss of pride when facing the outside world. In order to sustain his self-esteem he had only one means at his disposal—that of the spirit, the intellect. Learning was the only form of masculine action left to a Jew in the *Galut,* in exile. Therefore he sat day and night *el Torah* and *el ʿavodah,* studying the Scriptures, while his wife served him and eked out a living for the family. He took care of the *ʿOlam habʾa* (the next world) while she took care of the *ʿOlam hazeh* (this world) and bore and raised *di kleine yidelekh.* He thanked God every day for not having been created a woman, while she looked forward to the Friday evening when he would serenade her with *"Eshes khayil mi yimtsa"* (who shall find a woman of valor).

Excluded from the brotherhood of those who studied God's word, the woman was reduced to being a kind of benign resourceful *golem*—a workhorse with a tender ever-loving heart, a never-resting womb, and never-resting hands. In the sphere of Jewish social life, it was she who assumed the role of the oppressed Jew vis-à-vis the Jewish male, and was thus burdened with a double load of suffering.

The Jewish woman's life was like a tight shoe; it hurt to walk in it, yet she had no choice but to wear it. What sense would it have made for her to complain about her debasement and enslavement both as a Jewess and a woman, if the life of a Jew was fraught with such danger and the general oppression of the people was so great? And then, God willed it so. She and her mate had no choice but to accept their lot and to wait for the coming of the Messiah. In the meantime, she consoled herself that in the afterworld, in Paradise, she would serve as her husband's footstool and have no worries on her head.

So, despite the disparity in their roles, there existed an exceptionally powerful bond in the relationship between the Jewish man and woman—the bond of their Jewishness. Facing the hostile world together and trembling over the safety of their homes and their children created a particular understanding between them and introduced an emotional link into their marital union. True, they were unequal partners in the struggle for survival; nevertheless they were comrades-in-arms.

It was this oppressed, and yet powerful Jewish woman who throughout the centuries prepared the fertile ground for the emergence of Yiddish literature. She was the creator of Yiddish prayers and the anonymous author of countless folktales, folk-songs, and lullabies. A Yiddish proverb says that a *"Yidene hot nayn mos reyd,"* a woman has nine measures of talk. Talking was the only means of self-expression available to her. By means of her spoken words she produced a Yiddish literature *"bal peh"*, an oral literature. With her intimate knowledge of the *Tsenerene* and midrashic tales, she remained attuned to the people's collective unconscious, repeating and embellishing the biblical legends or creating new ones. She created the rhythms, the cadences of the language, and ceaselessly enriched the Yiddish vocabulary, modifying and molding it into a pliant, expressive tongue.

The sons of these Jewish women, whose souls were nurtured by their mothers' "nine measures of talk,"created modern Yiddish literature as we know it today. Their mothers' imagination and linguistic inventiveness put wind into the sails of the Yiddish writers' creativity. They in turn transformed the mother into the primary figure among their female heroines.

Modern Yiddish literature attained its maturity with the advent of the three classic masters: Mendele Moykhr Sforim, Sholom Aleichem, and Y.L. Peretz. These three masters were the literary forebears whom future generations of Yiddish writers both emulated and rebelled against. Under the influence of the liberating movements of socialism and

Zionism, the Jewish male, surer of himself, had begun to consider the woman as his equal. However the Yiddish writers' inner attitude towards women, gleaned from their *kheder* and yeshiva years took a longer time to change and has not yet changed completely.

On the other hand, the Yiddish women writers had no modern literary forebears of their own sex. Their creative ancestors remained their story-telling mothers and grandmothers, whose lot they were determined to escape. By the mere activity of writing, of encroaching on a male preserve, they proclaimed their break with the past. But in the process of doing so, they unconsciously assimilated their male colleagues' attitude toward themselves and toward women in general.

Celia Dropkin's is that rare angry voice that stands out from the chorus of female literary voices by giving free rein to her pent-up hostility. She may be considered the Yiddish Sylvia Plath. In one of her poems, she says to her lover, "I've not yet seen you asleep. I wish I could see you asleep, when you lose power over yourself and over me. I want to see you helpless, weak, mute. I want to see how you look with your eyes closed, with no breath. I want to see you dead."

I have hardly ever seen such words repeated in the writing of other Yiddish women. I think that the bitterness and resentment which accumulated in the Jewish woman writer's heart was stifled by her Jewish consciousness. The common fate shared by Jewish men and women has remained as powerful a bond between them as ever. Even when they rejected traditional religiosity, they held on to the moral precepts of Judaism. To give free rein to anger and hostility, especially against fellow Jews, was not the Jewish way, and certainly not the Jewish woman's way. So the Yiddish woman writer tried to sublimate her bitterness and to transcend it, by expressing instead her deeply felt humanity, her tenderness, sensuality, and love.

The Yiddish writer, with a few exceptions, could never make a living from his writing, and most of his days were spent working at all kinds of odd jobs. Even when he came to America, this did not change. Leivik was a housepainter, Mani Leyb was a shoemaker. The Yiddish woman writer was likewise either busy earning her living, or acting as housekeeper, mother, and cook.

Yet, there was a difference in the daily lives of the Yiddish male and female writers. The male writer usually had a wife, who revered him in much the same way as the religious Jewish woman revered her husband, the talmudic scholar. She acted as his pillar of support, his guardian angel, his kindly critic, his faithful servant who walked around on tiptoe whenever he was at work writing and admonished the children to be quiet. Thus Oscar Wilde's maxim, that women inspire men to create great works but prevent them from accomplishing them, is not valid in the case of the Yiddish writer's wife. Such a godsend, such a wife, the Yiddish woman writer never had and badly needed.

The greater part of Yiddish literature after the Holocaust consists of poetry. By contrast, in the times between the two world wars, when Yiddish literature flourished, there was a healthier balance between poetry and prose writing. The women writers, however, have been overwhelmingly poets and only rarely prose writers. And their prose usually takes the form of short stories; seldom do they write novels. This may be so, because of the woman writer's inherent sensitivity, her lyricism, and drive to express her emotions, or, she may have accepted the male opinion of her as incapable of executing the complex structure of a novel. But mostly, I think, women wrote poetry for practical reasons. A working woman or housewife could not sustain such a long-term project as a novel. A man, once his work day is finished, had time to himself. A woman's work was never done. A poem has the advantage that it can be conceived from beginning to end while scrubbing floors, or ironing laundry, and then written down in the blink of an eye. Whatever the reason, it is a fact that in contrast to other literatures, in particular English literature, there are very few women novelists in Yiddish literature. Consequently, the female heroine in Yiddish literature is exclusively a product of the male imagination.

The male Yiddish writer commiserates with the Jewish woman and in most cases he idealizes her, but he tends to avoid speculating on the complexities of her personality. He seems to be saying along with Goethe, *Das ewige Weibliche zieht uns hinan* (the eternal Feminine exerts its pull on us). And yet he shies away from approaching head-on the essential "eternal Feminine" in his works of fiction, and does so with even greater caution in his poetry, as if in fear that he might unleash dangerous passions within himself.

In her poetic self-portraits, the Yiddish woman writer also seems to shy away from examining her own femininity, as if she too were afraid of unleashing dangerous passions within herself—passions which, both the male and female writers fear, might lead them beyond the accepted constricting boundaries of Jewish sexual morality. In Yiddish literature, the subject of sexuality is approached in a roundabout way—cautiously, suggestively, or metaphorically. Nevertheless, it is the woman writer who comes closer to transgressing the accepted boundaries of morality by being more explicit and direct. Her marginality gives her a greater sense of freedom. The veiled eroticism in her poems is a form of defiance and rebellion.

Between the two world wars, the male writer became a respected and admired personality. As for the woman writer, although she too was respected and honored—after all, these were times of camaraderie between the sexes—her treatment, both by the general public and the literary establishment, was mixed with a dash of amazement, with a kind of condescending admiration.

Of course these attitudes have changed in recent years. Yet if one looks through the anthologies of Yiddish literature published in our times, one still sees how poorly women writers are represented. Yiddish literary criticism itself has always been recognized as a male domain, and there have never been any prominent Yiddish women critics. This means that Yiddish literature has always been influenced by the male point of view, and the male critic's judgements have acquired the status of *Toras Moshe miSinai*, The Law from Sinai.

Up to now I have been speaking in generalities. Now, if you will permit, a few words about myself. How do I fit into this general picture?

Although the time I have devoted to writing has always been limited, writing has never been just a pastime for me. Sometimes it was a substitute for living, an escape; at other times it was an encounter with myself, or a form of confession. Always, it has been a necessity, which made me feel that my life had an accompanying motif, an accompanying music.

I started to write poems when I was about eight years old, and continued doing so through my early youth, until, along with my parents and sister, I found myself incarcerated for four years in the Lodz Ghetto. There, despite the hunger, the cold, and the fear, I wrote poems more ardently than ever before—or since.

On a dark day in August 1944, a cattle-train unloaded me and my family, along with a transport of three thousand Jews from the liquidated ghetto, onto the ramp of the train station at Auschwitz. There I stood, knapsack on back, one arm embracing my father, who was ordered to join the column of men. I held the small bundle of my ghetto poems under the other arm. A kapo tore the bundle out from under my arm and threw it onto a heap of discarded prayer books, letters, and photographs. Then came the selection. My mother, my sister, and I were sent off through the gate with the inscription *Arbeit macht frei*. Soon I stood naked, with my head shaved, but my life spared. It was then that the thought of one day writing a book about the Lodz ghetto flickered for a split second across my mind.

From Auschwitz we were transported to the camp Sasel, near Hamburg. I occupied the upper bunk in my barrack. I had wheedled out a pencil stump from a friendly German supervisor at work. In the evenings, before falling asleep, I inscribed from memory some of my lost ghetto poems on the ceiling above my head: those poems which I could remember. I memorized them and later published them in my first book of poems right after the war.

When the battlefront approached Hamburg, we were transported to Bergen-Belsen. I fell ill with typhus and only returned to consciousness and to freedom in a *lazaret* on the other side of the concentration camp's barbed-wire fence. While convalescing, I allowed the past to live on within me. One moment I relished the joy of rebirth. Every blade of grass, every tree and shrub seemed to me to be retelling the story of Genesis. I was drunk with the happiness of being, of breathing, of sensing, of seeing how the flesh began to cover my skeletal body. The next moment I hugged my sorrows so, that they poisoned the previous moments of joyful oblivion.

From time to time, the thought of writing a book again entered my mind. The need to write and make order in the chaos raging within me was great, yet the fear of writing, of again plunging into the abyss of terror, was greater still. More than once, I was ready to take pencil in hand, and more than once, I decided never to touch upon the subject of the ghetto and the camps. I doubted whether it was at all possible to impose a form, a discipline on the painful phantasmagoria whirling within me. The more strongly I felt the urge to write, the weaker I felt in face of the enormity of the subject. I feared it, and this fear accompanies me to this day, whenever I try to write on the subject of the Holocaust.

For the last two years in the Lodz ghetto, my friend and mentor, the poet Simcha Bunim Shayevitch, had been working on a long epic poem about the ghetto, which, had it survived, would have doubtless been acclaimed as a work of high artistic achievement. I used to criticize him, saying that in order to write such an epic, it was necessary to have perspective, distance of time, whereas he did not even know whether he would have the good fortune to finish his work. But he would tell me: "We have no choice. Since we are not given the luxury of time or perspective, we must take the moments as they come, and let them drip onto the page with the ink of our pen."

He was right. After the liberation, we were finally given the luxury of time and perspective. But could we remember precisely the air of the ghetto and those camp days? Hadn't we changed merely by virtue of our survival? How many times did we ask ourselves: Did it all really happen—to us? Consequently, I was convinced that the nightmarish past could never be captured in words.

In such a state of mind I left Germany at the end of 1945, and along with my mother and sister crossed illegally into Belgium. In Brussels, the stanzas of a ballad, which I named "The Ballad of Yesterday's Forest," began to pour out from my pen almost involuntarily. I stopped analyzing and rationalizing about art, about form and style. Everything was clear as day and came to me as easily as if I were a medium and some other voice were dictating the lines.

And so I wrote poetry. But the ghetto world, which lived on within me, never ceased calling me. I had to free myself by recreating it, as it filtered through the prism of my awareness. I wanted to write about day-to-day life in the ghetto, about trivial matters, and about interpersonal relationships. I wanted to write about holidays in the ghetto, about love and spring.

And so the work started to germinate within me. But I did not dare to begin. I was about to become a mother and to emigrate to Canada. A new chapter in my life was soon to begin. And then it happened, that on my arrival in Montreal I found myself in my new abode, pregnant, both physically and mentally, sitting at a table with pen in hand and a blank sheet of paper in front of me. I put the pen down thirteen years and almost two thousand pages later.

That is how I began to write prose. It was not that I agreed with Adorno that there is no place for poetry after the Holocaust. Poems have been created in the ghettos and even at the threshold of the crematoria. As long as there is life, the human heart will never cease singing of its joys and sorrows. But in telling my tale, I began to feel confined and restricted by the poetic form. That I might be committing an act of rebellion by breaking with the female tradition of writing exclusively poetry or short prose hardly occurred to me. The subject matter imposed the form on me. What I wanted to say was impossible to sing. The brutal reality of the ghetto demanded the dry precision of words. Not that I wanted to ban the poet within me; on the contrary, I wanted her to stand by me, but I wanted her to creep with me through the maze of ghetto streets as low to the ground as possible.

And so for thirteen years I led a divided existence. I lived with my family in the Canadian immigrant reality. I was a greenhorn, a mother of two, the daughter of a sick mother. I worked in factories and did all kinds of odd jobs in order to help my husband finish his studies—and I lived in the Lodz ghetto. My characters more than once interfered with my actions and behavior in real life; and, even when I did not hold the pen in my hand, in my mind, their fates intermingled with mine. At the same time, my day-to-day life was always threatening, if not actually to cut the thread of my narrative, then at least to postpone its end. I had to get up at four o'clock in the morning to do my writing. Those dawn hours were the only ones that belonged solely to me.

In the meantime, I paid for my absentmindedness with burned pots and overcooked meals, and paid a much dearer price with attacks of tremendous guilt-feelings for neglecting my dear ones and my friends. I felt guilty for neglecting my own life. I often asked myself whether the end product would be worth the sacrifice.

The years passed. The more entangled I became in the story I was telling, the less and less satisfied I was with it, and the more worries it caused me. A question began to nag at me: whether what I had already written should remain as I originally wrote it. Because through the long span of time that my work required, my own life was not at a standstill. I grew older. Shattering events occured in my life and in the world at large. My outlook on life underwent various transformations; even my writing style underwent changes. Whenever I reread the pages that I had started to write as a younger woman, I grew bitter and angry at myself, and had to correct and set things straight. So that no part of my work was ever in a finished condition, but was always in the process of becoming. And so it went until the manuscript of my first novel, *The Tree of Life*, was out of my hands.

From this short account of the birth of my novel, I think it is clear that the fact of my being a woman has had significance only in the sphere of my daily life. Although my being a woman, no doubt, shines through in my work, I am not consciously aware of being one when I write; rather, I am conscious of being some kind of extrasexual, or bisexual creature. What mystifies me in human nature is precisely that which defies gender, heredity, or upbringing. But if my hero is male, I must try to immerse myself in his masculinity, in order to inhabit his soul.

If it is true that Adam was androgynous until Eve was separated from his body, the process of separation of their inner beings probably never took place—which is why Flaubert could say, "*Madame Bovary c'est moi.*" I believe that in a successful work the writer transcends the confines of his or her own gender; that in such a work it makes little difference whether the female characters are described by a male or a female writer. In such a work, the author—man or woman—is a feminist. In it the woman writer is truer to her own self, while the male writer sees the woman as an autonomous human being, much like himself and yet different. Such a work makes us realize that we all have an equal share in our common humanity.

In conclusion I would like to say that the present-day attitude toward women, the fact that the old cultural influences are still so strong, is one of the great disappointments of my life after the Holocaust. However, my concern about the Yiddish woman writer's specific condition tends to fade into insignificance in light of the situation facing Yiddish post-Holocaust literature in general. What affects me the most is the continual sense of isolation that I feel as a survivor—an isolation enhanced by my being a Yiddish writer. I feel myself to be like an anachronism wandering about a page of history on which I don't belong. If writing is a lonely profession, the Yiddish writer's loneliness has an additional dimension. His readership has perished. His language has gone up with the smoke of the crematoria. He or she creates in a vacuum, almost without a readership, out of fidelity to a vanished language—as if to prove that Nazism did not succeed in extinguishing that language's last breath, and that it is still alive. Creativity is a life-affirming activity. The lack of response to creativity and being condemned to write for the desk-drawer are stifling, destructive experiences. Sandwiched between these two states of mind, struggles the spirit of the contemporary Yiddish writer, male or female.

Fortunately, there are signs on the horizon that we are not yet the last Mohicans. Strange as it may seem, a new breed of young Yiddish writers is coming into its own, here in New York, and in Israel and Eastern Europe. They are like trees miraculously growing without soil for their roots, as if they too were defying annihilation, by proving the power of the Yiddish language and its spirit. The proverb says that hope is the mother of fools. But who knows? Perhaps the fate of the Yiddish language is like the fate of the Jewish people, and Yiddish might still rise from the ashes like a phoenix. I also hope that by that time the problems raised by the feminist movements concerning the unequal treatment of women will be things of the past.

On Being a Writer

৶ RUTH ALMOG ৶

Being a writer—that is to say, a storyteller—allows me to open with a story, a somewhat strange story which I would like to *use* later in two ways: as an example and as a metaphor.

Well, this is what happened:

Every Sunday I go from Tel Aviv to Petah Tikvah, my birthplace, to visit my mother. Going there I take Bus No. 82, which comes every half hour. Usually I take the bus on King George Street from a stop that faces some shops. On one particular Sunday I missed the bus. I saw it passing as I was going toward the stop. It was four in the afternoon of a very hot day, and I had to wait half an hour for the next bus. So I sat down on a bench nearby, took out a book from my bag and started reading. I was sitting beside an old couple. I noticed the man first, as he was sitting next to me. I would guess he was about eighty years of age. He looked a bit repulsive, for he had a sore covered with iodine on his upper lip, and his skin was tinted by stains of old age. He wore a French beret, and his eyes were very blue—diluted almost to the color of water. His wife looked neglected. She, too, wore a French beret on her white hair, and she whispered the smell of old age. I started reading. It was a novel by an Irish woman writer, Deidre Madden. Beautifully written, but depressing—filled with shadows of decay and death.

And then, all of a sudden, there came into my ears strange, foreign words. For a moment I was bewildered, but immediately afterward I understood that it was the old man speaking. He was talking in a low voice. Strange words. It took me a second to realize he was speaking Latin. I was amazed. Latin in the midst of Tel Aviv! I looked at the woman and saw that she was listening attentively. Then I noticed that a certain name was recurring in the old man's words. The name was Catilina. Furthermore, I noticed that it was not just a recurring name but a whole sentence, like a refrain, and I understood that someone was accusing Catilina again and again of having abused the patience of the Roman Senate. So it came about that I understood at last that the old man was reciting a speech. I guessed it was Cicero. I relaxed and lost interest.

I went back to my book, but only for a minute or two. For the old woman who had kept silent up to now suddenly started talking, very excitedly, in German. She pointed to the shops across the street, saying: "Look, you see? There he is. Catilina! Look, look, over there!" The old man said nothing. She turned to him and said: "Do you think he came here from Rome?" But the old man remained silent. So she said: "No, he couldn't have come from Rome. He must have come from Romania." The old man was finally aroused, it seemed, for, now speaking in German, he said to his wife: "Well, you know, of course, that the Roman legions settled down in Dacia, and Dacia is today's Romania. So that is where Catilina must have come from."

For a while they were silent, separately lost in thought. I looked at the shops on the opposite pavement, and, there I saw it—large and clear—the sign above the shoe store: "Katalina Shoes," it said.

After a while the old man said: "So many years have passed. More than sixty years, and I still remember, I can still recite the speech by heart." I took out a piece of paper and a pen from my purse and wrote down all that had passed, knowing that one day I would use it.

This story is an example of the way I work. I pluck material met on my way as food for thought. I look upon everything that happens around me, life itself, as first and foremost material for stories. I think being a writer means the splitting of the ego into two egos. While the one ego lives and experiences, the other ego remains an alienated onlooker who weighs whatever happens as working material, worthy or unworthy of being used.

But more than being an example of the way I write, there is in that bizarre story a metaphor. There sat next to me an old couple. The man was rooted in reality. He saw in front of him a sign. The sign reminded him of the ancient Roman politician. He put his memory to the test and triumphed. Remembering Cicero by heart after all those long years made him very proud indeed, for it proved him to be, in spite of his age, capable and even powerful. There he was, old, but still a man with a hold on his life, on his mind, on reality. Whereas the old woman, in sharp contrast to the man, was detached from reality, and her mind wove a fantasy in which there were no boundaries between the past and the present, between living reality and distant history.

What seems to me to be the most interesting aspect of the whole situation is the way the old man cooperated with her. He did not protest, he did not correct her. He never even tried to connect her to real life. He accepted what she said without comment, and just asked and wondered: "Why from Romania?"

Maybe he asked that question because he was curious about the way her thoughts were entangled. Perhaps it made him feel superior to her—his having a hold on reality and even understanding what was happening to her, and her being unconscious of living in a world of her own, a world of semidarkness. These two people seem to embody a metaphor of male writers and female writers in modern Hebrew literature.

Before going on, I have to stress that I am referring to a context very different from the American one. In Israel, the problems of the collective, of the nation, are the problems that matter, and not those of the individual. In Judaism, writers and poets have always been regarded as assuming the task of the ancient prophets, persons working in the service of the nation. Bialik did not become a national poet because of his beautiful love poems. Israeli society, being ideologically oriented, demands that a writer be its voice. All this must be kept in mind when I use my old couple as a metaphor.

This is what I mean:

While male Israeli writers cope with living reality in its entirety, the female writer deals with only a portion of it. Male writers like Yehoshua Kenaz write about the army; others like Yizhak Ben-Ner and David Grossman and Amos Oz write about the Arab-Israeli conflict and the *Intifada* and try to cope with political issues; and still others like Ahron Appelfeld and Yoram Kaniuk write about the Holocaust. On the other hand, women writers relate mostly to their private and personal lives. They write stories about love, marriage, birth, childhood, and so on. They don't write as representatives of the collective. They write about themselves. This is why they prefer short stories, because the novel demands a wider scope.

I became aware of this situation the moment I started to publish on the eve of the Six Day War. Although I had fought so hard for that very moment, having aspired to be a writer from the age of ten, I somehow felt how insignificant my writing seemed in the light of Israel's fight for survival. My goal was not to be easily accomplished. My youthful aspiration to be a writer is connected with painful memories. I remember clearly that when adults asked what I'd be when I grew up and I answered "A writer," they would laugh. I soon learned not to divulge this truth. Later at high school, a religious one, the boys would laugh at the poems I had published in the class newspaper, maybe because they were about love and loneliness or, more likely, because as a girl I was not entitled to such a spiritual-creative life. I must confess that the old insult still hurts. Later, when I decided to give up the academic career expected of me in order to dedicate myself to writing, my mother and my husband, both teachers, almost went into mourning.

Later, when I became a mother, I had to fight for every moment I stole for myself, and I always felt guilty.

All this reminds me of the story of Beruryah, a story every woman should keep in mind. Although you may be familiar with it, I must tell it here—the way we Jews must read the *Hagadah* every Passover so that we don't ever forget the Exodus from Egypt. I think that the story of Beruryah should have the same status among women.

It is told in the Talmud that Rabbi Meir fled to Babylonia. Rashi explains that he fled because of what had happened to Beruryah, his wife.

Beruryah was known to be a learned woman. It is said that she learned three hundred laws from three hundred rabbis. She argued with many of them and is said to have formulated new laws. And once she even opposed her father, Rabbi Hananiyah ben Teradyon, with such success that the rabbi's response was to say: "Well said, Beruryah."

But one day she must have gone too far. She dared challenge the authority of the rabbis. She laughed at her husband, Rabbi Meir, because of what the rabbis said about women—that women are frivolous. In response, Rabbi Meir said: "I swear that in the end you'll have to agree that they were right." And so he went and ordered one of his pupils to seduce her. For many days the pupil courted her and entreated her until finally she surrendered. When all was made known to her, she strangled herself.

What is there to say but that Beruryah dared trespass onto men's territory—that of wisdom, that of spiritual-intellectual activity—and was punished by her very own husband, the father of her children. And we have to bear in mind that Beruryah was very pious. It is said that at the time of the plague, when two of her children died on the Sabbath, she covered them with a blanket so that they would seem to be sleeping. And she refrained from telling even her husband about their death until the Sabbath was over, for it is forbidden to mourn on the Sabbath.

Has the situation really changed since then? Maybe it has. My own deepest inner feeling is that the change is only superficial and that deep-down, at the roots of the human psyche, very little has changed. All this relates to the fact that I started writing late. It is also connected to the fact that creativity is very often identified with madness. A close male friend in whom I confided my decision to dedicate myself to writing reacted by saying: "Don't do it. Don't get near the realm of madness."

I published my first story in April 1967, two months before the Six Day War. I wrote quite a lot at that time. After many years of silence, a period of abstinence, everything burst out, and my writing flowed. The story was "Rachel Stern Looking for Fellini." It was about a woman who tries to find solace in daydreams, yet even there she finds herself unable to create for herself the kind of life she would like to have. She can never finish that web her fantasy weaves. She starts again and again and every time there is a point beyond which she can't go, even in fantasy.

I wrote stories about Rachel Stern, about other women, and about my childhood. And then the war broke out, and I was hurled into a conflict which has tormented me for many years. In the perspective of the war (and we have been living in a war ever since), what I was writing about seemed to be of little importance. It was almost immoral to deal with private issues at such a time. My inner need and the moral obligation I felt to address the war did not coincide. In a story entitled "It Was Possible to Buy Guns," Rachel Stern detaches herself from reality as she had done before and goes to Rome again in her search for Fellini, only this time she takes a young soldier with her as a companion in her day-dreams. This time it is not only longing that leads her to Rome. It is terror, too. However, I must confess that this story was my one and only attempt to appease my conscience. Having written it, I went on writing in my former vein.

I wrote a novel about a woman going into exile which alluded to the Holocaust, and a novella, *The Stranger and the Enemy*, about suicide and against psychiatry, and *Death in the Rain* about the impossibility of romantic love.

However, with my volume of short stories, *Women*, I reached a turning point, because here, at last, I left the above-mentioned conflict and dedicated myself to researching the lives of seven women who had something in common. They were, all but one, sick women. One had asthma, the second suffered from psoriasis. Two others had cancer, and so forth.

Only one of them was not sick. Only one of them speaks in the first person. That is why the reader does not know her name, for she is the narrator. She is called Phyllis by the man she loves; but it is a name she does not want. She refuses to accept the name her lover has chosen for her. Thus she deprives him of his power, of his hold on her.

It is really strange for me now to discover that this act, her refusal, makes it possible for the story to become political. Renouncing the name he gives her makes her understand that the difference and difficulty of communication between them lies in the fact that she lives in one country, while he lives in another—a foreigner and therefore always a stranger.

Why were the other women sick? I used to think that their different illnesses were only a metaphor. Thus, Rachel Stern has become sick with cancer in the latest version of that first story of mine, because cancer reflected her inner inability to realize her wishes even in fantasy. Whereas Martha, who was unable to face the truth, covered her face with sores.

But now I ask myself whether these women did not express, without my then knowing it, how I unconsciously understood what it meant to be a woman. Meaning that, for me, to be a woman meant to be sick in some way.

Why so?

Virginia Woolf wrote about the need of the woman writer to have a room of her own. I ask myself if a room is not just a metaphor, and, if it is, what does it stand for?

Having no walls around you, no door you can close behind you, seems to me to signify the basic female condition. Is not the female perceived as an entity open to penetration? Is she not looked upon as having no defined boundaries; a "thing" whose territory can be legitimately trespassed, for is it not her nature to be trespassed upon? And I think now that there is a fundamental gap between a woman's deep need to create for herself a private, impenetrable space, and the desire of those surrounding her to steal it from her. This gap creates a frustration so painful that I had to call it a sickness.

After *Women* I found myself capable of writing what I would ironically call a male novel—that is, a political novel, *Roots of Air.*

Before going on to elaborate on a problem I had with this novel, I need to make clear that writing is not a conscious process. There are conscious decisions made by a writer relating to structure, style, plot, protagonists, and so on. But these make up only about 40 percent of the text.

The literary text is like a sea. Water comes from different sources. There are the rivers that nourish it, there are the hidden springs, deep underground, and there are the primordial waters, some of which turn into clouds and fall back as rain.

The rivers comprise the conscious material. The primordial waters metamorphosed as rain are the material absorbed from the collective unconscious; and the hidden underground springs supply material from the individual unconscious of the writer.

Roots of Air is comprised of two books. Most readers like the first book better. It took me time to understand why, and the reason is what I want to understand now.

The first book concentrates on a mother-daughter relationship, almost a symbiosis. The story is set within a beautiful paradisiacal landscape. Ruhama, the mother, and Mira, the daughter, are the inseparable pair Demeter-Persephone, as I have come to see in retrospect.

In the second book, Persephone, having been abducted by her father, is turned into Artemis. There, in the exile of urban Hades, she becomes an active and independent person. Finally, but not before visiting the land of the dead, she turns into the third daughter of Demeter, Athena, the wise one.

Many an ancient myth has this pattern. The young girl (Kore) is attached to her mother, or both her parents. Later she goes into exile, or starts wandering, looking for Amor, or is taken prisoner by Hades, like Snow White in the forest. Then she either loses Amor or comes back from the kingdom of the dead to a life of suffering, often loneliness.

In looking back, I can see that this pattern recurs in many of my stories, also in the novels. As a matter of fact, one of the heroines of an earlier story of mine is called Anasthasia—meaning, one who comes back to life.

It is surprising to find the same pattern in Amalia Kahana-Carmon's short novel *Up in Montifer*, in Shulamith Lapid's novel *G'ei 'oni*, and even in *Where Am I?*, a novel by one of our youngest writers, Orli Castel-Bloom.

In the short novel *Up in Montifer* by Kahana-Carmon, we find the protagonist in the realm of legend. The protagonist is a young girl abducted by a black rider and held prisoner in Montifer. Somewhere in the story the protagonist asks: what is the difference between rape and captivity? And she answers: the only difference is the time it lasts. In time she regains her freedom and becomes a merchant—that is, an active woman aspiring to independence.

Lapid preferred history to legend. There she explores the fate of her protagonist, a young girl who has been raped and who flees into exile—which, ironically, is Palestine. After many hardships she, too, gains independence and becomes a merchant.

Castel-Bloom's protagonist escapes reality by means of fantasy. Her answer to the question hidden in the title of her book—*Where Am I?*—is hell. Reality threatens her so much that her skin grows a thin, soft fur. She is still a captive in Hades.

Now I come back to the question I stated earlier: why did most of the readers like the first book of *Roots of Air* better?

I used to think that the first book was like a womb; the story taking place in a small, closed, protected world. A kind of Eden. It even had its keeper and its snakes. Whereas in the second book we find, as I said, the protagonist in an open, alien world. There, like Eve expelled from Eden, she has to fend for herself. And, of course, Eden is more seductive. But now I have come to think that the objection to the second book signals something else. I think it reflects a non-acceptance, even a dislike, of Mira as the active and independent person she has become. I now think that Mira, the politically committed person, antagonizes readers and that they would rather have her back in the protected womb.

I have no consciously formulated poetics, but I have what I call a leading principle that says: never repeat yourself; always aspire to do something new, something that is the opposite of what is expected of you. If ever I thought that I have succeeded at this, I understand now that, although I have found new forms, I am still working within the same pattern. Now that I am conscious of it, I may be able to free myself and to embark on a new kind of journey—or so I would like to hope.

The Song of the Bats in Flight

ᘓᕲ　AMALIA KAHANA-CARMON　ᕲᘓ

I.

Instinctively, thinking about women's writing means thinking about decorative writing, about good taste, sensitivity, delicacy, an eye for minutiae, and, naturally, writing that is artless and charming.* And, instinctively, from the reader's point of view, these should be the criteria that guide an assessment of a story's value. From the point of view of a woman author, however, all the attributes mentioned above are in themselves no more than tools, the means by which she transmits what she wishes to say.

Where does this gap in attitude originate—namely, that in his eyes, and only in her case, her tools are the main thing, and her contents no more than secondary; while in her eyes, the order of priorities is just the opposite?

It seems to me that the answer—while standing on one leg—is as follows: in each and every field, every activity responds to the real need that stimulated it. *Ex post facto,* every tool a person prepares so as to make this work possible proves to be an idiosyncratic solution to the problems which face that individual and which are bound up with the activity itself. In this regard I hope no one disagrees with me.

The difficulty arises when any existential reality that produces a specific need for a specific act comprises a system lying beyond the experiential range of others who attempt to relate to it. When the issue is literary expression, and when the system in question lies beyond the range of the reader's personal spectrum of understanding, or beyond his capacity for first-hand identification—in this case the reader will not have the insight to grasp what the writing is about.

As for women's literature, concerning this lack of insight, one can apply the proverb: "there is none so deaf as he who will not hear." In what follows I shall attempt to explore why.

For the moment I shall point out that the only thing such a reader's eye will perceive is the author's tools. Just as he might react to the sight of archaeological artifacts, ritual tools whose purposes are nowadays unknown, so this reader will react to the tools of the woman writer as if they were objects ("every sentence of hers is a pearl"); he will not respond to the substance, contained in her words, that created the need for these tools in the first place and and then shaped their form.

Indeed, this content is hidden from his eyes, much as the eyes of a person wearing black sunglasses are hidden. Speaking to him we do not speak to his eyes, but to his mouth. Or, for example, much as you and I, unfortunately, cannot enjoy the highly perfected song of the bats in flight. Because they are nocturnal creatures, bats have developed their hearing and their ability to emit sounds as a substitute for sight. Their song takes place in a range of frequency beyond the limited perceptual capabilities of our ears.

If so, the problem for the woman writer, apparently, inheres in the subject matter about which she attempts to speak. In the world of Hebrew fiction, such material still has low visibility.

II.

But how does it come about that the woman writer's subject lies beyond the reach of the discerning reader: one who has been nurtured, from the dawn of childhood, on the central traditions of Hebrew fiction? Is it reasonable to think that Hebrew fiction did not equip him, did not prepare him for every possible subject?

It prepared him, and how.

While standing on one leg, I shall answer the question this way:

The central traditions of Hebrew fiction make up a signifying system. Like every other system of thought (for this is the nature of signifying practices), it organizes the world for us in a such a way that it predetermines our attitudes. Without it, we would be unable to make any distinctions whatsoever.

And, historically, according to the signifying patterns of Hebrew fiction, it is naturally accepted that the way a woman experiences herself in the world is limited, and less important than the way a man experiences himself in the world. It is conventionally assumed that, essentially, the way a woman experiences herself in the world—in one manner or another—depends on and is determined by a man's experience, to which she is merely an adjunct. His experience is the last upon which her experience is meant to be stitched like a shoe.

Why has this state of affairs prevailed in Hebrew fiction throughout the generations?

The answer is not simple.

And here I think that it is not possible to answer while standing on one leg. For my part, I have tried to undertake this task to the best of my ability in a series of articles that have appeared in recent years. Each one, in turn, met with opposition, and I am glad to see that with the passage of time many of the ideas I expressed have become common currency. To return very briefly to a thesis of mine regarding but one aspect of the phenomenon, I will say only the following:

To be a Jew means to relate to the collective, as part of a community. Personal spiritual reckoning is only for Yom Kippur. The other days of the year, to stand in public prayer for Israel means to act on behalf of all. Whereas to pray privately, by oneself, in the name of the self for the self, means to act in the name of a partiality—that is, subordinate to the whole.

Which is to say: the supplications of the individual are preordained as trivial or inferior, compared to the central act, collective prayer. And this central activity—where does it take place? In the synagogue, a forum out of bounds for women.

By being a woman, her one place in this arena is in the ʿezrat nashim (the women's gallery). As a passive observer, she does not contribute anything. Someone else, acting in the name of all Israel, speaks also on her behalf. And so, anything that is likely to happen to the woman seated in the women's gallery will be defined ahead of time as peripheral, a hindrance, and a deviant incident. Likewise, it will not be a regular part of the shared course of events; it will be subordinate to the main events conducted in the central arena. That is to say, if suddenly, God forbid, something should occur in the women's section, or on the steps to it, this happening will in all cases be prejudged as a mishap. Since this is an event which cannot be of interest to all, it is of interest to women only, and in the domain of the synagogue, it would be better were it not to happen at all.

Fiction-writing in many regards may be compared to prayer. I will not belabor the point here, but the two activities stem from and address the same needs of the self. It was almost inevitable that in Hebrew fiction there would be imitation of models. Ever since there has been a modern Hebrew fiction, the Hebrew writer has seen himself as someone sanctified, in the highest form, to pass before the ark, there to carry the word of the congregation and to place communal matters on the spiritual agenda. In the entire history of Hebrew fiction, the less the writer speaks through his work in his own name and in the name of his personal acquaintances—and, by contrast, the more he documents the values, the encounters, and the aims of the average Israeli in light of a given era by means of an ideologically representative character or series of characters—the more he is deemed praiseworthy. This is true because Hebrew literature, even if it is secular, has been seen by both the writer and the reading public as a kind of national synagogue of the mind. In fact, for the secular man, maybe there is no other synagogue today.

In this regard—at odds with all other forms of artistic expression (each and every one, including poetry), for better or worse—Hebrew fiction remains a startling kind of nature preserve.

The existing thought-structure of Hebrew fiction has almost certainly come to the end of its road, along with the clumsy apparatus of teaching and criticism that it fostered. At least I would like to believe so. And perhaps the following fact is one of the outstanding signs that these are the last days of this anachronistic school of thought: in comparison to the eager public that is animated and engaged, that arrives with a gleam in its eye to attend lectures about other branches of the Israeli arts—painting, sculpture, architecture, cinema, and so on—anyone who comes to an evening lecture on any aspect of Hebrew literature in Beit Hasofer (including those lectures considered most successful), will get the impression that he has landed in a cemetery. The action is somewhere else.

III.

Nevertheless, this synagogue of the mind known as Hebrew fiction is a fixed and abiding structure, and its word is law. Consider, for instance (and the example that I shall give is purely hypothetical) an adventure story. The tale, either real or imaginary, may be about a young Israeli soldier just out of the army, with his rucksack on his shoulder, setting out for the jungle in South America or Nepal. This story will be perceived as an allegory or as a literary expression, loaded with implications, either of the spiritual state of contemporary Israel, shaped by its past tradition, or of the new face of the secular pilgrim, a staple figure of Hebrew literature throughout the generations. By way of contrast, let us take as an example the adventure story, either real or imaginary, of a young Israeli woman just out of the army, with her rucksack on her shoulder, going to the self-same destinations. To the extent that this young woman does not serve as a companion to her counterpart, the secular pilgrim, this story will be seen in every case as the chronicle of an eccentric or peculiar adventuress and nothing more. Her story then will stand or fall, and its value will be measured, in terms of the naiveté of the writing, its sensitivity, its good taste, its eye for fine detail, and all the rest. The content will be less significant.

Whosoever thinks otherwise, may he stand up and be counted.

Because the central traditions of Hebrew fiction comprise a conceptual system that educates us in light of its own basic perceptions, it prepares us to acquire insights accordingly and trains us for what it considers our expectations of a text should be. This conceptual framework stands firm and abiding.

Whosoever does not believe this would do well to look within himself and note the following facts: through his reading, not even consciously, it is as if an inner switch is flipped every time he reads a Hebrew story. That is, by contrast with a story in translation, it is as if the reader dons another pair of ears. For better or for worse, such a person extracts from the text before him a different set of values or framework of expectations.

The hierarchical form of the myths mentioned above is already internalized by the sensitive reader (whether male or female). This reader is trained from earliest childhood according to these conceptual frameworks as if they were the Law given at Sinai. Second nature, they are accepted without protest and taken for granted as timeless, so that to break away from this outlook is tantamount to a minor intellectual revolution. But who, in these crazy times, is Hebrew fiction likely to interest so keenly?

The conceptual system which dominates Hebrew fiction still defines, organizes, and categorizes for us the spiritual and concrete experiences treated in this literature: his social experiences and her social experiences, his experiences of her, and her experiences of him. And in this way the literature tells us what reality is, and what a correct understanding and judgment of it should be. And according to the way that we understand life and the world through literature, our reading also determines our horizons as it establishes the kind of questions that we are likely to ask. Indirectly, the aforementioned conceptual system guides us, as conceptual systems do, to discern those areas we should disregard, where it is an injunction to be "so deaf as one who will not hear."

However, it is in the nature of signifying systems that they begin to crumble, if and when there opens up some minor fault line which cannot be reconciled with the theory. When the methodology is not structured to deal with such a fissure, it must make way for new explanations. And these, of necessity, will bring about a general change in outlook. When a general change in outlook occurs, there will be, among other things, a change in emphasis on what is central and what is peripheral.

IV.

Instead of the newly discharged soldier with his rucksack on his shoulder, it is possible to construe a hypothetical example of: a *yored* (an Israeli who leaves Israel) / a man who abandons the kibbutz / a settler / a soldier in the territories / a protester / the Israeli who keeps a low profile / a *ba'al teshuvah* (one who returns to the faith) / a young man in love with an Arab girl / a child of a mixed marriage searching for his roots / the ugly Israeli / the beautiful Israeli / the macho Israeli / the Israeli who has been shafted / a drug addict / a successful Israeli / an unemployed Israeli / a loner in the Negev / a lapsed yeshiva student / a career officer who retires in middle age / a student / an academic / a second-generation child of Holocaust survivors / a young artist / an aging artist / any of the above a thousand years ago / in Mesopotamia / in the time of the First Temple / in the time of the Second Temple / in the ghetto.

The whole gallery. As always, the same Israeli strain: male. His story will be an expression of the collective situation, of the average Israeli in light of past tradition, and so of general interest. As for the female, if she does not act the role of his partner but is a character in her own right, her tale will always be the "true life story" of a woman and her destiny, and the attitude of readers will be: come let us see if she knows how to write a story.

This does not happen by chance. In this establishment, the imaginary synagogue known as Hebrew literature, it is problematic to record the events of her "self" who is seated in the women's gallery. It is difficult to write about the different stages of her development (if, indeed, that's what she is determined to recount, instead of telling about the normative experience: being a helpmate to one whose activity is regarded as focal, a central phenomenon, in any given period).

Recording her independent experience (and all literary writing, even the most poetic, is a record of experience) is considered in advance as merely a record of woman's activity. That is, not a legitimate subject for public consideration, not worthy to pass before the ark, bearing the word which represents the collective "I" of Israeli Man, when he and only he is the focal point in communal activity. The average Israeli cannot identify with the collective "I" she records. It is not seen as something that can represent him. The principle of equality does not apply here.

Therefore, every attestation by her is considered, in advance, anomalous. She tells about events in a realm where every activity is seen as disturbing the social order—disturbing, in that it deflects attention away from what is considered central. And then a strange positive-negative polarity creeps into the game: to the degree that this account of hers is blessed with vision, the more likely it is to be perceived as substandard. To the degree that it is blessed with energy, the more it is deemed alienated or unstable. To the degree that it is blessed with imagination, it is considered a less serious work, lacking in intellectual ballast, the fruit of weak, if not wild reasoning. The more creative it is, the more it is considered a mere experimental exercise, and so less weighty, less the Eastern Wall of respected fiction. To the extent that it is original, it is gratuitously capricious, self-centered, hysterical, an expression of a tempestuous spirit. The literary agenda should be rid of it, for it is an event which stands outside the chronicles of Hebrew literature.

In contrast, the more her work is characterized by a familiar, well-liked, conservative approach, and by characteristic feminine lack of daring (expressed as uncertainty about how to justify each and every decision, including stylistic ones), and the more her work is marked by clear signs of the attitude that "I am nothing more than a hesitant young girl writing a diary"—then the more her work will be perceived as genuine, sincere, and truthful, and so it will elicit a warm response. She will be a good little girl.

Furthermore: if and when, in their next works, more than one of the writers considered the Eastern Wall of respected literature integrate into their writing many of her innovations (those of the other girl, the misunderstood one, the one about whom they say that they don't know what she wants, or that it's hard to fit her into existing models of fiction); if and when not a few of them adopt for their own purposes her tone and the areas of inquiry which her spotlights alone had singled out and illuminated—only then, wonder of wonders, those same elements which in her work were considered negative and odd will be copied, through her detractors, into the normative arena of events. There they will be seen as positive, apt, right on target, timely, original, refreshing. They will be thought of as path-breaking: a turning point in Hebrew literature.

The dividing line will remain clear.

In her writing, which is obliged to be a view from the women's gallery, the lady—with all her inventiveness, her innovations, and her spotlights—will be seen as forever wasting herself on peripheral matters.

Her writings will be seen as peripheral, because the self sitting in the women's gallery cannot represent the general collective I, Israeli Man, who is the official representative of that which is primary in our lives. But if you try to check and place this collective self of the average Israeli man under the microscope, you will see that today he no longer reflects anything but the shrunken macrovision and the detailed, wearisome microvision of the relationship this ego bears to his own demand to be ever so manly.

V.

Why, then, does she persist in speaking on behalf of the woman confined to the women's gallery? Why should she persist in speaking about a topic that has no direct connection with the demand facing the average Israeli man—to be a man?

Surely this is not worth her while. From the point of view of communication, won't the position of this writer in the world of Hebrew fiction resemble another phenomenon: the plight of the author who composes in the exotic language of a remote nation where few know how to read and write? Such a writer's position contrasts unfavorably with that of authors who compose in languages widely disseminated throughout the world. Why doesn't the woman writer of Hebrew fiction abandon her exotic language and train herself to write in the more prevalent one?

This is the answer:

Every author longs to embed in his words objective and finely minted universal truths, truths that extend beyond individual beliefs. Otherwise he would not bother to utter these ideas. Unfortunately, there is no escaping the fact that this reflection of the universe (whose truths the writer wishes to portray) are imprinted in the writer's consciousness. They depend to a large degree on the openness and on the biography with which he is endowed. Accordingly, if the writer is no mere imitator following in the footsteps of others, in the well-trodden paths already paved by predecessors, then the point of departure authentic to him, his scale of values and priorities, will of necessity transmit a view of the universe as he knows it. This view is based on the vision that appears to him as he stands in the special corner his life has marked out for him. Of necessity it will express the manner in which this writer absorbs, transforms, and understands the world.

And so, if perforce, given your natural circumstances, there is no alternative, and you are a person who has landed in the women's gallery of the imaginary synagogue known as Hebrew fiction, then from the outset you are condemned to being a person whose writing will be thought of as reflecting only the women's gallery. In other words, from the outset you are robbed of the feeling—necessary for the act of writing—that a great privilege has been bestowed upon you and that you are a relay station for something larger than yourself—i.e., that you are totally dedicated to a message meant for all, a universal truth which is yours to utter.

Or, to put it another way, in the fossilized definitions of Hebrew fiction: from the outset you are a person whose work will not reflect what is central in our lives. You are the person whose work does not reflect the collective ego of the average Israeli. And in most cases you are condemned in Hebrew fiction to speak of contents invisible to the eye.

This means that in the marriage between women's writing and Hebrew fiction, the condition of the author who is a "good girl" can be seen roughly as parallel to marital rape—to use the language of the social worker. The other writer, the girl who is uncompromising in her subject matter, no matter what, can be seen as a parallel to "the rebellious wife"—to use the language of Halakhah (Rabbinic Law). In the pilpulistic, hairsplitting language of the sages it works like this: the rebel "is not declared [a rebel] except in synagogues and Houses of Study" (*Ketubot* 63b) and "one who rebels against her husband is awarded less than the sum stated in the Marriage Contract" (ibid.). In the marriage between Hebrew fiction and the writing of this author, the punishment of the aforementioned lesser sum is this:

Instinctively, certain criteria will guide assessment of the story she writes. Is it decorative, in good taste, sensitive, and refined? Does it show an eye for minute detail, a clean and charming style ("every one of her sentences is a pearl")? That is to say, all that in your view is no more than secondary to the main thing.

What is of cardinal importance for *you*, in their ears, remains a kind of bat song.

* * *

ADDENDUM, JULY 1990

Of late I sense a new era dawning in Israeli literature. A surprising new wave of women writers (most of them in their thirties and forties) has recently emerged on the literary scene. (Four of them, I'm happy to note, were students at my workshops on creative writing.) The fiction produced by this younger generation has met with far greater openness than was once accorded women's writing in Hebrew.

To what can this openness be attributed?

There is a feeling in Israel that the times are changing, and that the nation stands on the threshold of a new, as yet unnamed reality. On the one hand, the flood of new immigrants promises an end to deadlock and heralds growth in all aspects of life here. On the other hand, the present is a time of growing unease and a sense of waiting out a crisis: due to polarization amongst Israelis, a growing rift between the people and the corridors of power, the impact of the Intifada and all the issues, external and internal, related to it. People are aware that we are in the midst of a fluid situation, witnessing events that will change the face of the country. The books we write now may very well be historical novels when they come out. Accordingly, a new consciousness has begun to take shape; namely, that in every area, old ways and means have become outmoded. This consciousness must have been latent for some time now, and perhaps it is this phenomenon that accounts for the growing stature of women writers.

In eras of change, literature enjoys open-mindedness and a spirit of adventure. Such was the case for women poets in Hebrew during the 1920s. Much the same circumstance may obtain again now. In today's social climate women writers benefit, for they travel light. That is to say, they are less burdened by the cumbersome structure of the old mission and codes of mainstream Israeli fiction. Since, for many years, their sensibilities and reflections remained outside the pale, they were never part and parcel of what was considered the glory of the old literary school of thought. That school of thought is now collapsing. Today even male writers—the young ones, in particular—shy away from giving utterance in their books to the so-called issues of national-collective consciousness, responsibility, and destiny. All in all, it is mostly women writers who begin to have, at least at present, the pronounced impact on the new course of events in Israeli fiction.

This is a trend I predicted a number of years ago, in my essay "To Be Wasted on the Peripheral" (1985). I raised the matter again in discussion at a symposium celebrating the centennial of Devorah Baron's birth (Tel Aviv University, January 1988). On that occasion, though, little did I, or anyone else present, realize that this predicted transformation of Hebrew literature would become a striking fact so soon.

Then again, could it be that my tentative interpretations of the present are tinged with wishful thinking? Only time will tell.

NOTES

* This essay originally appeared in Hebrew in 1989, as *"Shirat Ha'atalefim beme'ofam"* in *Moznayim*, (Nov.-Dec.): 3-7. Translated by Naomi Sokoloff and Sonia Grober.

WORKS CITED

Kahana-Carmon, Amalia. 1985. *"Lehitbazbez 'al hatsedadi"* [To Be Wasted on the Peripheral]. *Yedi'ot aharonot*, 15 September, 25.

ᔕ SELECT ANNOTATED ᔕ BIBLIOGRAPHIES

The items in these bibliographies deal with feminist approaches to modern Hebrew and Yiddish literature. The lists do not cover the considerable amount of scholarship that has been done in related fields such as (1) feminist issues in biblical and rabbinic literature or other Jewish sources; (2) women in Jewish history; (3) modern Jewish writing in languages other than Hebrew and Yiddish; (4) commentary on women writers that does not directly enter into dialogue with feminist criticism or take into consideration issues addressed by feminist approaches. The Yiddish section does include several titles concerning premodern, devotional literature, where those titles are of special interest for feminist study of modern Yiddish literature.

Gender Studies and Yiddish Literature

⌣ꝏ KATHRYN HELLERSTEIN ꝏ⌣

Adler, Ruth. 1980. *Women of the Shtetl—Through the Eyes of Y. L. Peretz.* Cranbury, N. J.: Associated Univ. Presses.

Examines the fiction of Y. L. Peretz in terms of the writer's empathy with the difficulties Eastern European Jewish women encountered in their lives. Links Peretz's depictions of women's inner lives with his personal quest for identity and his self-assumed role as an "outsider." Shows how opposing types of women in Peretz's fiction—the passive wife and the shrew; nurturing and denying mothers; submissive, promiscuous, renegade, duplicitous, and martyred daughters—comprise a multifaceted portrait of the collective Jewish female.

Beck, Evelyn T. 1981. "The Many Faces of Eve: Women, Yiddish and I. B. Singer." *Studies in American Jewish Literature* 1: 112-123.

Examines negative depictions of female characters—in terms of a sexual double standard and of types (witches, shrews, willing victims)—in the "male-centered world" of Bashevis Singer's fiction. Argues for an acknowledgment of parallels between the positions of women in society and Judaism, of Yiddish within the Jewish community, and of Jews within the Gentile world.

Bilik, Dorothy. 1975. "Love in Sholem Aleichem's Early Novels." *Working Papers in Yiddish and East European Studies.* YIVO. 10 (April).

Studies, in part, the development of Sholem Aleichem's heroine through an analysis of his 1884 novel, *Taybele.* Argues that Sholem Aleichem soon after rejected this "liberated woman" heroine because, despite the actual existence of such women among urbane, enlightened Jews, the type would not comport well with his fiction's "realistic" shtetl settings.

———. 1989. "Jewish Women and Yiddish Literature." *Transactions of the Seventh International Congress on the Enlightenment*. Vol. 3. Oxford: The Voltaire Foundation.

———. 1989. "Glückel von Hameln" In *Women Writers in Germany, Austria, and Switzerland*, ed. Elke Frederiksen, 83. New York: Greenwood Press.

A brief biographical and critical essay on the seventeenth-century Yiddish memoirist.

———. 1992. "The Memoirs of Glikl of Hameln: The Archeology of the Text." *Yiddish* 8,2: 1-18.

A lively recasting of this seventeenth-century woman's Yiddish memoirs. Examines the most available yet distorting abridged translations—the often reprinted 1913 German by Alfred Feilchenfeld and 1932 English by Marvin Lowenthal. Compares their attempts to "improve" upon Glikl with the more accurate but less known 1896 Old Yiddish edition by David Kaufmann, 1910 German translation by Bertha Pappenheim, 1929 English translation by Beth-Zion Abrahams, and 1967 modern Yiddish translation by Joseph Bernfeld. Makes a case that the two famous versions were malformed by patriarchal assumptions about Jewish learnedness as centered in the Talmud. Reveals Glikl's models to be the Yiddish *muser* or morality literature, *Tsenerene, tkhines*. Concludes with a theory of women's ethical wills written in Yiddish.

Cohen, Sarah Blacher. 1982. "Hens to Roosters: Isaac Bashevis Singer's Female Species." *Studies in American Fiction* 10, 2: 173-184.

Examines the female characters in Bashevis Singer's novels *Enemies* and *Shosha* to support Singer's own defense of his fiction against "feminist" attacks of misogyny. Claims both that Singer's female characters, representing actual types of women, give the fiction verisimilitude and stabilize the male protagonists, and that the female characters serve the symbolic end of disorienting and thus forcing self-discovery upon the male protagonists.

Cooper, Adrienne. 1989. "About Anna Margolin." In *The Tribe of Dina: A Jewish Women's Anthology*. ed. Melanie Kaye/Kantrowitz and Irena Klepfisz, 154-159. Boston: Beacon Press.

A brief biographical essay about this unconventional Yiddish poet, accompanying translations of six poems (two printed with Yiddish en face).

Drucker, Sally Ann. 1987. "Yiddish, Yidgin, and Yezierska: Dialect in Jewish-American Writing." *Yiddish* 6, 4: 99-113.

Analyzes Yiddish dialect in fiction by Anzia Yezierska, in favorable contrast with similar usage in fiction by earlier and contemporary American Jewish or American writers (Abraham Cahan, Montague Glass, Myra Kelly, Samuel Ornitz). Contends that Yezierska's language presents a positive image of "ghetto life" and a sympathetic portrait of immigrant women characters. Concludes that the effectiveness of Yezierska's dialect comes in part from her accurate reflection of Yiddish-speaking women's speech patterns (as distinct from those of men), which echo the female orientation of Yiddish devotional literature and oral folk traditions.

Falk, Marcia. 1987. "Mother Nature and Human Nature: The Poetry of Malka Heifetz Tussman." *Lilith* 17 (Fall): 20.

An appreciation of Tussman's life and work.

―――. 1991. "With Teeth in the Earth: The Life and Art of Malka Heifetz Tussman: A Remembrance and Reading." *Shofar* 9, 4: 24-46.

Surveys the life and poems of Malka Heifetz Tussman, enumerating major themes in the poems in terms of gender and highlighting the relationship between translator and poet.

Hadda, Janet. 1988. *Passionate Women, Passive Men: Suicide in Jewish Literature.* Albany, N.Y.: State University of New York Press.

Uses psychoanalytic methods to illuminate the surprisingly recurrent theme of suicide in Yiddish fiction. Focuses on how pre-World War II authors—from the classic Sholem Aleichem and Y. L. Peretz to the virtually unknown Rokhl Faygnberg—sympathetically portray their suicidal characters, contrary to traditional Jewish attitudes. Organizes the analysis according to the gender of the suicidal characters and raises issues of sexuality, social circumstances, and family dynamics as factors in the suicides. Contrasts post-World War II works—by Chaim Grade and Isaac Bashevis Singer—with earlier ones to explicate the Holocaust's disruption of human values, whereby, with the ideal of the family no longer at the center of Jewish experience, suicide becomes honorable.

Hellerstein, Kathryn. 1988a. "A Question of Tradition: Women Poets in Yiddish." In *Handbook of Jewish-American Literature: An Analytical Guide to Themes and Sources,* ed. Lewis Fried,195-237. New York: Greenwood Press.

Shows that a women's literary tradition (linking devotional and secular poetry) existed within and preceded the invention of tradition by modernist Yiddish poets and anthologizers; reads the double vision of nature and culture with which male Yiddish critics defined women as readers and poets. Places within this context an assessment of Ezra Korman's anthology of women poets, *Yidishe dikhterins: antologye* (1928), and offers readings of individual poems by Anna Margolin and Malka Heifetz Tussman that exemplify the conflicts of culture and gender shaping the literary tradition and creativity of women.

―――. 1988b. "'A Word for My Blood': A Reading of Kadya Molodowsky's 'Froyen-lider'(Vilna 1927)." *AJS Review* 13, 1-2: 47-79.

A close reading of the eight-poem sequence by this major Yiddish poet in light of current feminist theory. Demonstrates how the woman poet's conflict between culturally—or biologically—defined gender roles and the writer's imagination works itself out in figurative language and poetic forms that signal a Jewish intertextual struggle between secular and sacred, Yiddish and Hebrew texts.

————. 1989. "Fear of Faith: The Subordination of Prayer to Narrative in Modern Yiddish Poems." In *Parable and Story as Sources of Jewish and Christian Theology,* ed. Clemens Thoma and Michael Wyschogrod, 205-236. New York: Paulist Press.

Contrasts the modern Yiddish prayer-poem, in which narrative structure subordinates the device of prayer, to the Hebrew *piyut,* in which prayer dominates narrative content. Considers how the subordination of prayer evolves from figurative devotion in modernist poems (by Moyshe-Leyb Halpern, Yankev Glatshteyn, Celia Dropkin, Anna Margolin) to literal devotion (in poems by Kadya Molodowsky and Miriam Ulinover) to narratives of prayer (in poems by Malka Heifetz Tussman).

————. 1990a. "Hebraisms as Metaphor in Kadya Molodowsky's *Froyen-Lider* I." In *The Uses of Adversity: Failure and Accommodation in Reader Response,* ed. Ellen Spolsky, 143-152. Cranbury, N.J.: Bucknell Univ. Press.

Argues that Hebraic words disrupt the linguistic pattern of Germanic words in the Yiddish poem to create a metaphor for the dilemma—between woman and text, secular poetry and Jewish law—that the poem attempts (and fails) to resolve.

————. 1990b. "Songs of Herself: A Lineage of Women Yiddish Poets." *Studies in Jewish-American Literature* 10: 138-150.

Examines poems by Royzl Fishls (1586), Miriam Ulinover (1922), Kadya Molodowsky (1927), and Malka Heifetz Tussman (1949) to show how the depiction of literary lineage evolves from the patriarchal, Hebraic tradition to secular, culturally Jewish, feminist models for women writing in Yiddish.

————. 1991. "Canon and Gender: Women Poets in Two Modern Yiddish Anthologies." *Shofar* 9,4: 9-23.

Considers the role of gender in the canon formation for modern Yiddish poetry. Contrasts the representation of women poets in two early twentieth-century anthologies—M. Bassin's *Finf hundert yor yidishe poezye* (1917) and Ezra Korman's *Yidishe dikhterins: antologye* (1928). The former gives fewer poets, fewer poems per poet, and a more limited selection based on the editor's sense of "women's poetry"; the latter presents many more poets, with more poems, and a wider range aesthetically and thematically. Focuses analysis on four poets—Zelda Knizshik, Yehudis, Rokhl Yakubovitsh, and Fradl Shtok—all virtually unknown today.

Kay, Devra. 1988. "Words for God in Seventeenth Century Women's Poetry in Yiddish." *Papers from Second Annual Oxford Winter Symposium in Yiddish Language and Literature, 14-16 December 1986.* In *Dialects of the Yiddish Language,* ed. Dovid Katz, 57-67. Oxford and New York: Pergamon.

Compares seventeenth-century *tkhines* by named women authors, often entitled *"lid"* (song or poem) and in metrical and rhymed form, with other contemporaneous Yiddish literature (standard *tkhines,* *tkhines* by named men authors, Hebrew *teḥinot,* Yiddish translations of canonical Hebrew prayer, Yiddish epic poems, seventeenth century German Bibles, and the 1526 Prague *hagode*). Demonstrates that, because the women's *tkhines* contain a more numerous, richer, and more varied set of names for God, they constitute a new genre, the "poetic *tkhine,*" which is a precursor to later Yiddish poetry.

Klepfisz, Irena. 1989. "Secular Jewish Identity: *Yidishkayt* in America." In *The Tribe of Dina: A Jewish Women's Anthology,* ed. Melanie Kaye/Kantrowitz and Irena Klepfisz, 32-50. Boston: Beacon Press.

A personal essay that traces the evolution of the author's secular Jewish identity through her innate and acquired knowledge of Yiddish culture, language, and literature. Makes an impassioned case for the opening of communications between the diminishing Yiddish world and aspects of American culture, especially the feminist/lesbian movement.

Lyons, Bonnie. 1981. "Sexual Love in I. B. Singer's Work." *Studies in American Jewish Literature* 1: 61-74.

Examines fiction by Bashevis Singer for the theme of sexual love as the ultimate fulfillment of human happiness (joining male to female and individuals to the community), in contrast to lust and failed sexual love. Contends that Singer depicts women characters realistically and positively and that his work has more Jewish resonance and spiritual depth than most American Jewish literature.

Norich, Anita. 1990. "The Family Singer and the Autobiographical Imagination." *Prooftexts* 10, 1: 91-107.

Compares and contrasts the autobiographical narratives of the siblings Esther Singer Kreitman, Israel Joshua Singer, and Isaac Bashevis Singer, in the context of feminist and other recent theories of autobiography and self. Shows that while each writer depicts the desire of his/her rebellious spirit to transcend the restrictive religious environment of their family, the two brothers' memoirs serve primarily to authenticate their well-established reputations as fiction writers. The sister's riskier autobiographical novel portrays a subtler account of the failure of a female self to evolve within this Jewish familial and cultural milieu.

Novershtern, Avram. 1990. "'Who Would Have Believed That a Bronze Statue Can Weep: The Poetry of Anna Margolin." Trans. Robert Wolf. *Prooftexts* 10, 3: 435-467.

A comprehensive study that places Margolin's poetry in the context of her fellow modernists—the *Yunge* (especially Mani Leyb) and the *Inzikhistn*—as well as of 1920s Yiddish "women's poetry" (especially by Kadya Molodowsky). Shows through close readings of poems that her work's distinctive characteristics—sculputural "hardness," repeated mask motif—distinguish it from the norms and conventions of her contemporaries.

Peczenik, F. 1988. "Encountering the Matriarchy: Kadye Molodowsky's *Women Songs.*" *Yiddish* 7, 2-3:170-173.

Attests that Molodowsky's "*Froyen-lider*" traces the search of "a young married woman" who—caught between traditional Jewish and modern secular worlds—rebels, commits adultery, and comes to understand the limitations of rebellion and "the inevitability of a woman's fate."

Pratt, Norma Fain. 1982. "Culture and Radical Politics: Yiddish Women Writers, 1880-1940." 1987. Anthologized in *Decades of Discontent*. New York: Greenwood Press and Northeastern Univ. Press. First published 1980, in *American Jewish History* 70 (September): 68-90.

Introduces fifty-three Yiddish women writers and poets. Surveys their literary works as reflections of their lives in the context of the historical moment and the political movements in which many of them were involved.

———. 1983. "Anna Margolin's *Lider*: A Study in Women's History, Autobiography and Poetry." *Studies in American Jewish Literature* 3: 11-25.

Presents a reading of Margolin's 1929 collection of poems as a "document of her private despair." Considers the texts in light of the psychobiographical narrative written by her third husband, Reuven Iceland. Argues that two factors resulted in the intense personal and intellectual isolation of Eastern European Jewish women, who were of the first generation to receive a secular education: (1) the rupture of relation to the mother's traditional Jewish role; and (2) the impossibility of identifying with the father's "intellectuality."

Schulman, Sarah. 1989. "When We Were Very Young: A Walking Tour through Radical Jewish Women's History on the Lower East Side, 1879-1919." In *The Tribe of Dina: A Jewish Women's Anthology*, ed. Melanie Kaye/Kantrowitz and Irena Klepfisz, 262-283. Boston: Beacon Press.

A guide with historical commentary that explains what significance twenty sites on the Lower East Side of Manhattan had for Yiddish-speaking immigrant women—locations of strikes, residences of radical women activists such as Emma Goldman or tragic figures such as Lena Meyers, cafés, theaters, factories, community centers, schools, union buildings, settlement houses, literary clubs, markets, newspapers, and areas of prostitution.

Seller, Maxine S. 1988. "World of Our Mothers: The Women's Page of the *Jewish Daily Forward.*" *The Journal of Ethnic Studies* 18, 2: 85-118.

A thorough summary and analysis of the *Forvert's* "Women's Page" in the year 1919 (chosen for its proximity to the Bolshevik Revolution and the passage of the Nineteenth Amendment). Contends that the columns were a means of educating and advising immigrant women readers about the often contradictory themes of socialism, feminism, and Americanization, in terms of both private and public life.

Weissler, Chava. 1987. "The Traditional Piety of Ashkenazic Women." In *Jewish Spirituality: From the Sixteenth-Century Revival to the Present,* ed. Arthur Green, 245-275. New York: Crossroad.

A path-breaking study of the religious life of Eastern European Jewish women that surveys and analyzes *tkhines*—Yiddish supplicatory prayers composed by women as well as by men, and published in collections from the sixteenth through the nineteenth centuries, for a popular (and primarily female) readership. Highlights the different emphases in *halakhic* practice among women and men. Reveals how women comprehended their religious acts. Examines folk religious practices that were exclusively female and shows how the *tkhines* themselves (through representations of biblical heroines) present images of women and women's religious lives.

Zucker, Charlotte (Sheva). 1987. "The Emergence of the Modern Woman in Yiddish and Western Literature." *Dissertation Abstracts International* 48, 3 (September).

Compares the themes of marriage and adultery among female protagonists in late nineteenth- and early twentieth-century Yiddish fiction by Y. L. Peretz, Sholem Aleichem, Joseph Opatoshu, Dovid Bergelson, and in poetry by Kadya Molodowsky, with those in "Western" works by Fontane, Ibsen, and Flaubert. Argues that the Yiddish authors portray the heroines' distancing from traditional religious values with greater ambivalence than the mainstream European writers because of the actual precarious position held by Jews in Western society.

———. 1992. "Yente Serdatzky, Lonely Lady of Yiddish Literature." *Yiddish* 8,2.

Reads the short fiction of the Yiddish writer Yente Serdatzky in the context of her biographical and historical circumstances in New York City in the early decades of the twentieth century.

———. 1992. "Kadya Molodowsky's '*Froyen-lider.*'" *Yiddish* 9,1 (in press).

Gender Studies and
Modern Hebrew Literature

‿ NAOMI SOKOLOFF ‿

Alkalay-Gut, Karen. 1989. "Poetry by Women in Israel and the War in Lebanon." *World Literature Today*, (Winter): 19-25.

Argues that before 1982 Hebrew poetry had few examples of poems about war by women; that the war in Lebanon led to a dissolution of political consensus and so spurred protest movements and protest poetry by women. Covers both Hebrew and English texts by Dalia Rabikovich, Maya Bejerano, Alkalay-Gut, and others.

———, ed. 1989. *Woman in Israeli and American Literature and the Arts.* Tel Aviv: Tel Aviv University and the Open University of Israel.

Abstracts from a conference held in Tel Aviv in March 1989. Includes items dealing with modern literature, as well as with biblical texts, rabbinic texts, folklore, and other areas of research.

Aschkenasy, Nehama. 1986. *Eve's Journey: Feminine Images in Hebraic Literary Tradition.* Philadelphia: Jewish Publication Society.

Studies images of the Jewish woman in an array of Hebrew writings, including biblical passages, rabbinic and kabalistic texts, hasidic tales and modern Hebrew fiction. Illustrates the persistence of archetypal and prototypical feminine figures across generations and cultures, distilling four major categories of imagery: woman as demonic Lilith figure, woman as mother, women as individuals oppressed by patriarchal social systems, women striving to work around oppression (as tricksters, artists, and others).

———. 1988. "Women and the Double in Modern Hebrew Literature: Berdichevsky/Agnon, Oz/Yehoshua." *Prooftexts* 8,1 (January).

Examines female protagonists who create their own doubles and project themselves into multiple images in reaction to social pressures.

Bar Yosef, Hamutal. 1988. ʿAl shirat Zelda [On Zelda's Poetry]. Tel Aviv: Hakibbutz hameuhad.

A monograph which includes a biographical chapter and discussion of the special pressures on a woman who is at once pious and a poet.

Berlowitz, Yaffa. 1984. Sifrut nashim benot haʿaliyah harishonah [Literature of the Early Pioneer Women]. Tel Aviv: Tarmoil.

An anthology of writing by women from the period of the First Aliyah, accompanied by an introduction.

Cohen, Tova. 1991. Yesharim utsevuʿim, elilot veliliot - ʿiyunim bitsirot Mapu [Honesty and Hypocrisy, Idols and Liliths: Studies on Mapu]. Tel Aviv: Papyrus.

Explores the conventions of the romantic heroine, the Lilith archetype, and psychological realism in Mapu's fiction.

Elinav, Rivka. 1990. "The World of the Intellectual Heroine: A Comparative Study of the Prose Writings of Elisheva Bikhovsky and Leah Goldberg." (Diss., Jewish Theological Seminary of America.)

Considers characterization of the intellectual heroine in narratives by Bikhovsky and Goldberg. Discusses relations between this fiction and the writers' biographical background. Explores affiliations between the prose and poetry of each writer.

Feldman, Yael. 1985a. "Roman histori o otobiografiaʾ bemasekhah—ʿal Gʾei ʿoni uvenei mino besiporet ʿakhshavit" [Historical Novels or Masked Autobiographies?]. Siman Kriʾah 19: 208-213.

Observes that contemporary women novelists evade self-disclosure by creating a vicarious self, located in an anachronistic setting.

———. 1985b. "Inadvertent Feminism: The Image of Frontier Women in Contemporary Israeli Literature." Modern Hebrew Literature 10, 3-4: 34-37.

Examines Shulamit Lapid's Gʾei ʿoni as feminist protest projected onto an earlier era.

———. 1988. "Gender/Indifference in Contemporary Hebrew Fictional Autobiography." Biography: An Interdisciplinary Quarterly 11, 3: 189-209. Reprinted in Sex and Signs: European Journal for Semiotic Studies 1(1989): 435-56.

Building on the idea of the masked autobiography, notes that the struggle to define collective identity in Israel precludes liberation of women as individuals and leads to protrayals of a communal self in fiction.

———. 1990. "Feminism Under Siege: The Vicarious Self of Israeli Women Writers," *Prooftexts* 10, 3: 493-514.

Expanded analysis of gender and autobiography in connection with Shulamit Hareven's *City of Many Days,* Shulamit Lapid's *Gʔei ʿoni,* and fiction by Amalia Kahana-Carmon and Ruth Almog.

———. 1991a. "Ideology and Self-Representation of Women in Israeli Literature." In *Redefining Autobiography in Twentieth Century Women's Fiction,* eds. Colette Hall and Janice Morgan, 281-301. New York: Garland Publishing.

———. 1991b. *"Androginiyut bamatsor: hafeminizm haselektivi shel Shulamit Harʔeven"* [Androgyny Under Seige: The Selective Feminism of Shulamit Hareven]. *Siman Kriʔah* 23.

A Hebrew version of the first part of "Feminism Under Seige" (Feldman 1990).

Fuchs, Esther. 1984a. "Casualties of Patriarchal Double Standards: Old Women in the Fiction of A.B. Yehoshua" *South Central Bulletin* 43, 4: 107-109.

Focuses on elderly female characters, who serve as allegorical embodiments of social ills while male figures receive fuller characterization and more positive attributes.

———. 1984b. "The Beast Within: Women in Amos Oz's Early Fiction." *Modern Judaism* 4, 3: 311-321.

Argues that Oz perpetuates negative stereotypes of women as purely sexual beings without moral concerns or intellectual depth.

———. 1984c. "The Sleepy Wife: A Feminist Consideration of A.B. Yehoshua's Fiction." *Hebrew Annual Review* 8: 71-81.

Maintains that women characters are generally asleep, silent or otherwise blank, vacant figures in Yehoshua's fiction.

———. 1986a. "The Representation of Biblical Women in Israeli Narrative Fiction: Some Transformations and Continuities." In *Identity and Ethos: a Festschrift for Sol Liptzin,* ed. Mark H. Gelber, 361-374. New York: P. Lang.

Claims that modern retellings of biblical tales have often deepened the characterization of male figures, but not of females, who are represented as demeaned, auxiliary characters more pernicious than their original counterparts.

———. 1986b. "Images of Love and War in Contemporary Israeli Fiction: Toward a Feminist Re-vision." *Modern Judaism* 6, 2: 190-196. A revised, expanded version of this article, entitled "Love and War in Israeli Fiction" appears in *Arms and the Woman,* ed. Adrienne Munich et al., 1990, North Carolina Press.

Citing works by Yoram Kaniuk, Amos Oz, and Yizhak Ben-Ner, argues that Israeli fiction of the seventies and eighties turned women to icons of death. Presentations of woman as conjugal and national enemy reveal resentment of women's alleged nonparticipation in the country's war efforts.

———. 1987. *Israeli Mythogynies: Women in Contemporary Hebrew Fiction.* Albany: State University of New York Press.

Examines representations of women in writing by men, and considers women's voices speaking back against male preconceptions. Begins with a critique of mythogynies—misogynistic patriarchal myths in Israeli culture—by concentrating on fiction by A.B. Yehoshua and Amos Oz. Also analyzes narrative by Amalia Kahana-Carmon, whose women characters often maintain rich inner lives but remain misunderstood and unappreciated by the males around them. Provides, along with these readings, a prefatory overview of women depicted in fiction of the Statehood Generation. Argues that this literature projects onto women values that the authors condemn in society and that Hebrew fiction uses women to expose gaps between the idealistic dreams of Israel's founders and the disappointing compromises which have characterized actual statehood.

———. 1988a. "Amalia Kahana-Carmon and Contemporary Hebrew Women's Fiction." *Signs: A Journal of Women in Culture and Society.* 13, 2: 299-310.

Examines passive, victimized protagonists who escape from a hostile social world into their own inner creative life and capacity to think and feel. Argues that celebrating this act as a special kind of valor romanticizes women's imprisonment in patriarchal settings, but lauds this fiction's attention to female conscience and consciousness.

———. 1988b. "Amalia Kahana-Carmon's *And Moon in the Valley of Ajalon. Prooftexts* 8, 1: 129-141.

Finds that male critics have misread and underestimated the importance of this fiction, because they see the protagonist as an eccentric. Sees Noah Talmor's unhappy marriage as paradigmatic of female predicaments, for she is denied options, "denigrated as a 'mere' mother/wife and suspect as a divorcée."

Ginsburg, Ruth. 1992. "*Bidmi yamehah metah Tirzah: o, yafah at reʿayati keTirzah, navah kirushalayim, ayumah kenidgalot*" [And Tirzah Died *In The Prime of Her Life*: or Thou art beautiful, o my love, as Tirzah, comely as Jerusalem, terrible as an army with banners]. *Dapim lemeḥkar besifrut* 7.

Concentrates on the female narrator of Agnon's story and discusses her relation to her mother. Explores biblical allusions that serve Tirzah's subversive language and deals with "maternal" vs. "paternal" language acquisition.

Glazer, Myra. 1979. Introduction to *Burning Air and A Clear Mind: Contemporary Israeli Woman Poets.* Athens, Ohio: Ohio Univ. Press.

Comments briefly on the treatment of collective and personal issues in the poetry of eighteen women represented in the anthology.

Golan, Efrat. 1990. *"Kriᵓah feministit shel 'Bidmi yamehah'"* [A Feminist Reading of *In the Prime of Her Life.* ꜥAlei siaḥ 27/28: 81-92.

A reading of Agnon's novella that emphasizes the failed rebellions of the female characters.

Govrin, Nurith. 1988. *Hamaḥatsit harishonah: Devorah Baron, ḥayehah vitsiratah* [The First Half: Devorah Baron, Her Life and Work]. Jerusalem: Mossad Bialik.

Documents changes between Baron's early stories and her late ones, charting the author's movement away from passionate, bitter, individual protest to more universal, restrained, antipathetic style; discussion of narratives not anthologized during her life and so left out of the Baron canon.

———. 1989. *Devash miselꜥa: meḥkarim besifrut Erets Yisraᵓel* [Honey from the Rock: Studies in Eretz Israel Literature]. Tel Aviv: The Ministry of Defense.

Includes essays on the contributions of women to literature and the arts in the early days of the Yishuv, with special attention to Hemdah Ben-Yehuda, Nehama Puchachewsky, and Ira Jahn.

Grober, Sonia. 1988. "First Axioms: A Writer's Attempt at Self-Definition." *Modern Hebrew Literature* 13, 3-4: 10-14.

Examines Amalia Kahana-Carmon's poetics in short fiction that adopts a male narrator.

Hazelton, Lesley. 1977. *Israeli Women: The Reality Behind the Myths.* New York: Touchstone (Simon and Schuster).

A historical, sociological survey of woman in Israeli society, written for a popular audience. Draws on literary texts as illustrations for its main arguments.

Hoffman, Anne Golomb. 1991a. "Gender, Writing, and Culture: *Shira,*" *Between Exile and Return: S.Y. Agnon and the Drama of Writing.* Albany, N.Y.: SUNY Press.

A poststructuralist/psychoanalytic reading of Agnon's novel, which shows how this fiction associates the female body with subversions of culture and instabilities of meaning in language.

———. 1991b. "Constructing Masculinity in Yakov Shabtai's *Past Continuous.*" *Prooftexts* 11, 3: 279-295.

Kahana-Carmon, Amalia. 1984. *"Lihyot ishah soferet"* [To Be a Woman Writer]. *Yediꜥot aharonot*, 4 April, 20-21.

The first in a series of path-breaking feminist essays by one of Israel's major writers. Argues that women's experience is considered subordinate to men's, and so when women write about their own lives their work is dismissed as trivial.

——. 1985a. *"Lehitbazbez ʿal hatsedadi"* [To Be Wasted on the Peripheral]. *Yediʿot aharonot*, 15 September, 22-23.

Notes that women writers in Hebrew are greeted first with admiration, as an oddity, but deemed trivial. Later, especially as they develop strong, independent work, they are resisted by the critical establishment.

——. 1985b. *"Ishto shel Brenner rokhevet shuv"* [Brenner's Wife Rides Again]. *Moznayim* 59, 4: 13.

An elaboration on her earlier essays, written on the occasion of receiving the Brenner prize for literature. Fondly recalls Chaya Brenner, the wife of the famous author, who was Kahana-Carmon's kindergarten teacher and early on helped foster her aesthetic sensibilities.

1988. *"Hi kotevet dei nehmad aval ʿal shebiyarkhatayim"* [She Writes Rather Well, but . . .] *Yediʿot aharonot*, 2 May, 20; 25.

States that there is not yet a firm female tradition in Hebrew fiction, and finds that the existing norms and expectations are a procrustean bed for women writers.

Lerner, Anne Lapidus. 1990. "Lost Childhood in Eastern European Hebrew Literature," In *The Jewish Family: Metaphor and Memory*, ed. David Kraemer. New York: Oxford Univ. Press.

Compares traditional Jewish girlhood and boyhood, as depicted in the fiction of Devorah Baron and Isaac Dov Berkowitz.

Miron, Dan. 1979. *Bein hazon leʾemet: nitsanei haroman haʿivri vehayidi bameʾah hateshaʿesreh* [From Romance to the Novel: Studies in the Emergence of the Hebrew and Yiddish Novel in the Nineteenth Century]. Jerusalem: Mossad Bialik.

Within larger discussion of the nineteenth-century Yiddish and Hebrew novel, devotes several pages (395-403) to ways in which Sh.Y. Abramovitch broke away from the conventions governing the portrayal of women and love in Enlightenment literature.

——. 1991. *Imahot meyasdot, ahayot horgot* [Founding Mothers, Stepsisters]. Jerusalem: Hakibbutz Hameuhad.

A volume that includes several studies, one a book-length examination of the emergence of women's poetry in Hebrew; work that evolved out of a two-part essay, carrying the same title, published in *Alpayim* (1989: 29-58, and 1990: 120-770). Poses the question: why did poetry in Hebrew by women establish itself so forcefully in the 1920s and not earlier? Posits that this writing emerged in the Soviet Union and in Eretz Yisrael, and not in other Hebrew literary centers, because of the revolutionary social milieu in those two places. Focuses on how the loosening of Bialikean standards and conventions allowed the entry of women poets into Hebrew. Argues that even as Hebrew literature welcomed poets such as Rahel, Esther Raab, Elisheva, and

Yocheved Bat-Miriam, it placed certain limitations and expectations of modesty on them. Also includes a long essay on the poetry of Tel Aviv (and women's contributions to that poetry) along with an article on Rahel Katznelson-Shazar and a personal appreciation of Yocheved Bat-Miriam.

Ratok, Lilly. 1988. "*Deyokan ha'ishah kimshoreret Yisra'elit*" [Portrait of a Woman as an Israeli Poet]. *Moznayim* (May): 56-62.

Postulates a female literary tradition in Israel which emphasizes intimacy as opposed to national concerns, favors smallness over grand themes, and brings ambivalence to the self-revelation poetry entails.

Sokoloff, Naomi B. 1988. "Feminist Criticism and Modern Hebrew Literature." *Prooftexts* 8, 1 : 143-56.

A review essay. Rehearses some of the major issues of importance for the Hebrew literary circumstance and critiques Aschkenasy's *Eve's Journey* and Fuchs's *Israeli Mythogynies.*

————. 1989. "Narrative Ventriloquism and Muted Feminine Voice: Agnon's *In the Prime of Her Life.*" *Prooftexts* 9, 3: 115-137.

Approaches silence and vocal self-assertion in Agnon's novella through the framework of feminist sociolinguistic studies. Argues that speech as plot action regulates matters of will, power, and social relations. The author's adoption of a female narrator brings to the surface conflicts submerged in her subconscious that complicate the notion of voice.

————. Forthcoming 1992. "The Impact of Feminist Research in Modern Hebrew Literature." In *Feminist Perspectives on Jewish Studies,* ed. Lynn Davidman and Shelly Tenenbaum. New Haven, Conn.: Yale University Press.

A survey that defines clusters of materials which have received attention from critics. Proposes directions for future research.

◑ CONTRIBUTORS ◐

RUTH ALMOG is an Israeli fiction writer and journalist. Her books include a collection of short stories called *Nashim* (Women; Keter, 1986) and the novels *Et hazar veha'oyev* (The Stranger and the Enemy; Sifriat Poalim, 1981), *Mavet bageshem* (Death in the Rain; Keter, 1983), and *Shorshei avir* (Dangling Roots; Hakibbutz Hameuhad, 1987).

HAMUTAL BAR YOSEF is a Senior Lecturer in the Department of Hebrew Language and Literature at Ben-Gurion University of the Negev. Her many publications include *'Al shirat Zelda* (On Zelda's Poetry; Hakibbutz Hameuhad, 1988), and several books of poems—most recently, *Batsefifut* (In the Crush; Hakibbutz Hameuhad, 1990).

JANET HADDA is Professor of Yiddish at UCLA and a member of the Southern California Psychoanalytic Institute and the Institute for Contemporary Psychoanalysis. She is the author of two books, *Yankev Glatshteyn* (G.K. Hall, 1980) and *Passionate Women, Passive Men: Suicide in Yiddish Literature* (SUNY Press, 1988), as well as numerous articles and reviews.

KATHRYN HELLERSTEIN currently teaches Yiddish language and literature at Gratz College and the University of Pennsylvania. She is translator and editor of Moshe-Leyb Halpern's early poems, *In New York: A Selection* (Jewish Publication Society, 1982). Her own poems have been published in *Poetry* and *Without a Single Answer* (Judah Magneson Museum, 1990). She is completing a critical book on and an anthology of women Yiddish poets.

ANNE GOLOMB HOFFMAN teaches comparative literature at Fordham University, College at Lincoln Center. She is the author of *Between Exile and Return: S.Y. Agnon and the Drama of Writing* (SUNY Press, 1991). Her essay on A.B. Yehoshua forms part of a study of the construction of gender in the Hebrew novel.

AMALIA KAHANA-CARMON, Israeli novelist, short-story writer, and essayist, was the recipient of the Brenner Prize for literature in 1985. Her books include *Bikhfifah aḥat* (Under One Roof; Hakibbutz Hameuhad, 1966); *Viyareiah beᶜmek ᶜayalon* (And Moon in the Valley of Ayalon; Hakibbutz Hameuhad, 1971); *Sadot Magnetiyim* (Magnetic Fields; Hakibbutz Hameuhad, 1977); *Lemaᶜalah beMontifer* (Up in Montifer; Hakibbutz Hameuhad, 1984) and *Liviti otah baderekh leveitah* (With Her On Her Way Home; Hakibbutz Hameuhad).

ANNE LAPIDUS LERNER is Dean of Albert A. List College of Jewish Studies and a member of the Department of Jewish Literature at The Jewish Theological Seminary of America. Her publications include "Who Has Not Made Me a Man: A Study of the Movement for Equal Rights for Women in American Jewry" and *Passing the Love of Women: Gide's Saul and Its Biblical Roots* (University Press of America, 1980). She is currently writing a book on the Israeli poet Esther Raab.

DAN MIRON is a member of the faculty of Columbia University and of Hebrew University of Jerusalem. He is the author of numerous books on Hebrew and Yiddish literature, including *Bodedim bemoᶜadam* (When Loners Come Together: A Portrait of Hebrew Literature at the Turn of the Twentieth Century; Am Oved,1987); and *Haperidah min haʾani heᶜani* (Taking Leave of the Impoverished Self: H. N. Bialik's Early Poetry, 1891-1901; The Open University of Israel, 1986).

ANITA NORICH is an Associate Professor in the English Department and the Program in Judaic Studies at the University of Michigan. She is the author of *The Homeless Imagination in the Fiction of Israel Joshua Singer* (Indiana Univ. Press, 1991). Her research and teaching concentrate on modern Yiddish literature, Jewish American Fiction, and literature of the Holocaust.

ILANA PARDES, Lecturer in the Departments of Comparative Literature and English at the Hebrew University of Jerusalem, has also taught at Princeton University. She is the author of *Countertraditions in the Bible: A Feminist Approach* (Harvard Univ. Press, 1992).

CHAVA ROSENFARB, Yiddish novelist, poet, and playwright, has been a winner of Yiddish literature's prestigious award, the Manger Prize. Among her works are a play, *Der foygl fun geto* (The Bird of the Ghetto; H. Morgentaler) performed by the Israeli National Theater (Habima) in 1965, and a 2,000-page trilogy, *Boym fun lebn* (The Tree of Life; Farlag Hamenorah, 1972).

NAOMI B. SOKOLOFF teaches Hebrew and modern Jewish literature at the University of Washington in Seattle. Her book *Imagining the Child in Modern Jewish Fiction* will be published by Johns Hopkins Univ. Press in 1992. Her current research focuses on representations of female voice in modern Hebrew fiction.

∽ INDEX ∽

- 269 -